Trying Your First Case

A PRACTITIONER'S GUIDE

Trying Your First Case

A PRACTITIONER'S GUIDE

NASH LONG, EDITOR

FIRST
CHAIR
·PRESS·

Cover design by Jill Tedhams/ABA Publishing.

Printed in the United States of America.

18 17 16 15 14 5 4 3 2 1

Library of Congress Cataloging-in-Publication Data

Trying your first case : a practitioner's guide / Nash Long, editor First-Chair Press.
    pages cm
Includes bibliographical references and index.
  ISBN 978-1-62722-733-9 (softcover : alk. paper) -- ISBN 978-1-62722-734-6 (e-book) 1. Trial practice--United States. I. Long, Nash E.
  KF8915.T79 2014
  347.73'75--dc23   2014022104

Discounts are available for books ordered in bulk. Special consideration is given to state bars, CLE programs, and other bar-related organizations. Inquire at Book Publishing, ABA Publishing, American Bar Association, 321 N. Clark Street, Chicago, Illinois 60654-7598.

www.ShopABA.org

Contents

Chapter 4
Assembling the Trial Record, Pre-Trial Objections, and Motions in Limine

Jason P. Eckerly and Elaine M. Stoll

Chapter 5

Chapter 6

Chapter 13
It's Not Over Until It's Over: *Post*-Trial Proceedings

Preface

This book represents the collaborative effort of the Trial Practice Committee of the American Bar Association's Section of Litigation. The Trial Practice Committee, open to all Section of Litigation members, seeks to promote fairness and justice in the American legal system by enhancing the lives and careers of trial lawyers. The Committee does so by providing (1) innovative, entertaining, and thought-provoking continuing legal education programming across the country; (2) publications on trial skills; and (3) leadership opportunities for new and experienced trial lawyers alike.[1]

The Trial Practice Committee conceived of this book as a practical, "how-to" guide to the nuts and bolts involved in presenting a case at trial, for use by younger lawyers. With opportunities to "learn by doing" how to try cases growing fewer and farther between, other forms of education must play a larger part in lawyer development. Otherwise, the retirement of the baby boom generation of litigators will produce a skills gap—with negative implications for the justice system as a whole. Indeed, the rationale for our adversarial system of justice—that truth is more reliably determined by the clash of opposing viewpoints—presupposes a basic level of competency in its advocates. Otherwise, the contest can devolve into a mere exercise of power that judges may not be able to correct. As Justice Holmes cautioned in 1897,

> [t]he language of judicial decision is mainly the language of logic. And the logical method and form flatter that longing for certainty and for repose which is in every human mind. But certainty generally is an illusion, and repose is not the destiny of man. Behind the logical form

---

1. For more information about the Trial Practice Committee, please visit its website: http://apps .americanbar.org/litigation/committees/trialpractice/home.html.

lies a judgment as to the relative worth and importance of competing legislative grounds, often an inarticulate and unconscious judgment, it is true, and yet the very root and nerve of the whole proceeding. You can give any conclusion a logical form.[2]

The trial lawyer plays a critical role in our adversarial system of justice: presenting the arguments that tap into the "inarticulate and unconscious judgment" of the audience. For the system to produce its best results, its players must play their roles well.

By broadening and raising the skill level of trial lawyers, the ABA Section of Litigation plays an increasingly vital role in the legal industry.

To that end, the Trial Practice Committee has produced this book.

To that end, the Section of Litigation has published it.

To that end, may you read it and benefit from it. To quote Justice Holmes again, "[y]our education begins when what is called your education is over."[3]

---

2. From "The Path of the Law," reprinted in THE ESSENTIAL HOLMES: SELECTIONS FROM THE LETTERS, SPEECHES, JUDICIAL OPINIONS, AND OTHER WRITINGS OF OLIVER WENDELL HOLMES, JR. 167 (Richard A. Posner ed., 1992).

3. From "The Profession of the Law," the conclusion of a lecture delivered to undergraduates at Harvard University on February 17, 1886. Reprinted in THE ESSENTIAL HOLMES, *supra* note 2, at 219.

Editor's Acknowledgments

The editor wishes to thank Alana Bassin, who conceived of the idea for this book as a Trial Practice Committee project, and Lawrence D. Rosenberg, for reviewing and commenting on its chapters.

The editor dedicates this book to his parents, for instilling in their children a love of learning and an appreciation for good teachers, and to his wife, Maria, and daughters Rebecca, Hannah, and Sarah, for their inspiration and enthusiastic support of this book.

About the Authors

Nash E. Long, editor, is a partner with Hunton & Williams LLP in Charlotte, North Carolina. He focuses his practice on complex litigation, including jury trials, bench trials, class actions, and arbitrations related to environmental, business torts, commercial contract, intellectual property, construction, consumer law, and product liability disputes. He has tried cases in Alabama, Pennsylvania, Tennessee, and New York in addition to his home state of North Carolina. Mr. Long did his undergraduate work at Southern Methodist University and Oxford University, and received his law degree, magna cum laude, from Harvard Law School, where he worked as a research assistant for noted constitutional scholar Laurence H. Tribe. Between law school and joining Hunton & Williams LLP, he clerked for Chief Judge Frank W. Bullock on the United States District Court for the Middle District of North Carolina.

For the last four years, Mr. Long has served as a co-chair of the Trial Practice Committee in the ABA Section of Litigation. He is a frequent speaker at ABA and industry conferences and has been recognized in Best Lawyers in America and Chambers USA and by Law360 as a "Rising Star."

Brian Antweil is a trial partner with Katten Muchin Rosenman LLP in Houston, Texas. Licensed in both Texas and New York, Mr. Antweil represents clients in a full range of business, commercial, and tort cases in state and federal courts and in domestic and international arbitrations. He has significant experience in energy, oil and gas, bankruptcy and insolvency, insurance coverage, and technology disputes.

Mr. Antweil is a frequent speaker and writes for bar and other trade and professional organizations on trial practice issues. For several years, he has been in a leadership role for the Trial Practice Committee of the ABA. In addition, Brian is an adjunct professor, teaching trial advocacy at the University of Houston Law School.

Joice Bass is a litigation partner and business trial lawyer with Lewis Roca Rothgerber LLP in Las Vegas, Nevada. Ms. Bass is a Certified Information Privacy Professional with the International Association of Privacy Professionals and has an AV/Preeminent Attorney rating with Martindale-Hubbell. She is a Fellow of the American Bar Foundation, an honorary organization of lawyers, judges, and legal scholars whose careers have demonstrated outstanding dedication to the welfare of their communities and to the highest principles of the legal profession. She is also a Fellow of the Litigation Counsel of America, a trial lawyer honorary society. Ms. Bass has been named in Nevada Business' 2013 Legal Elite in the "Southern Nevada Best" category, their 2012 "Top 150" list, and their 2009–2011 "Top 100" lists. She is also featured in the 2013 edition of *Mountain States Super Lawyers* and the 2009–2010 editions of Super Lawyers' *Mountain States Rising Stars*. Ms. Bass is listed as a "Top Lawyer" in the 2013 and 2012 editions of *Vegas Inc.*

Alana K. Bassin is a partner with Bowman and Brooke, LLP in Minneapolis, Minnesota. She practices in the areas of product liability litigation and personal injury defense. Ms. Bassin has defended cases in more than 25 different states around the country involving medical device and pharmaceutical manufacturers, nursing homes and hospitals, construction, and building products, as well as toxic tort claims. She is a Vice-Chair of the ABA Trial Practice Committee, a member of the Defense Research Institute, and a member of the North Dakota State Board of Law Examiners.

Cynthia Cohen, Ph.D., contributes to the world of psychology and law as a jury consultant and a survey expert. Her education includes psychology degrees at the University of California, Los Angeles (B.A.) and the University of Southern California (M.S., Ph.D.). In 1986, she founded Verdict Success LLC, which specializes in jury research and trial strategies. Dr. Cohen qualifies as an expert in trademark confusion studies. As a Vice Chair of the Trial Practice Committee, she has been a frequent speaker and planner for CLE programs across the country. As a member of the ABA Section of Litigation's Task Force on the Image of the Profession, she designed programs at the USC Annenberg School and the University of Texas Law and Journalism Schools. Dr. Cohen critiques the trial skills of beginning trial lawyers for the LA County Bar Association's Trial Advocacy Program. In her spare time, she started a golf league with a Southern California Golf Association Golf Handicap and Information Network license for the Women Lawyers Association of Los Angeles.

Neal Dickert is a partner with Hull, Barrett in Augusta, Georgia. Mr. Dickert began practice with this firm in 1974. He is admitted to practice in Georgia and South Carolina and has tried numerous jury trials in the state and federal courts of these states. Mr. Dickert also served as a Superior Court Judge for the Augusta circuit from 1997 through 2007 and returned to private practice on January 1, 2008. While on the bench, he was Chairman of the Board of Trustees of the Institute of Continuing Judicial Education for the State of Georgia. He is a frequent lecturer at Continuing Legal Education programs throughout the Southeast. Mr. Dickert is the author of the *Georgia Handbook of Foundations and Objections*, published annually by Thomson Reuters since 2003, and has published articles in numerous legal publications.

Jason Eckerly is a shareholder at Segal McCambridge Singer & Mahoney in Chicago, Illinois. He is an experienced litigator and trial counsel whose practice focuses on the defense of toxic tort, asbestos, and general liability litigation. He serves on many of the firm's national coordinating counsel teams, developing and coordinating the defense of large corporations across the country. Mr. Eckerly is licensed in Michigan, Illinois, and Pennsylvania and has been admitted to practice pro hac vice in numerous other states. He has acted as trial counsel in Michigan, Illinois, Iowa, California, Pennsylvania, and New York. He received his B.A. from Michigan State University and his J.D. from DePaul University College of Law.

Philip N. Elbert, a 1981 graduate of Vanderbilt University Law School, is a partner with Neal & Harwell, PLC, in Nashville, Tennessee. He has experience in a broad range of litigation cases in both state and federal court, including catastrophic personal injury, civil rights, commercial, and white-collar criminal defense cases. He recently served as lead counsel for the plaintiffs winning a personal privacy rights case before the United States Supreme Court in *Maracich, et al. v. Spears, et al.,* 133 S. Ct. 2191 (2013).

Doreen Spears Hartwell is a shareholder at Lionel Sawyer & Collins, a full-service firm in Las Vegas, Nevada. Ms. Hartwell joined the firm in 2000 following her graduation, with honors, from the McGeorge School of

Law, University of the Pacific. She is a civil litigator who defends employers in federal and state courts against statutory and common law claims. Ms. Hartwell has successfully litigated many trade secret violation, non-compete, and other business-related disputes. She has also built a strong reputation for her commitment to the community and has received awards from multiple organizations honoring her dedication to providing pro bono services. She currently serves on the Pro Bono Advisory Council and the Nevada Access to Justice Commission. Ms. Hartwell recently completed a two-year term as President of the Las Vegas Chapter of the National Bar Association, is a Fellow of Litigation Counsel of America, and has been selected as a Nevada Legal Elite.

Aaron Krauss is a commercial litigator who practices in Cozen O'Connor's Philadelphia office. For nearly 25 years, he has tried cases on behalf of companies, their officers, and directors who used to like each other, but now don't. Prior to entering private practice, Mr. Krauss clerked for Judge Edward N. Cahn, of the United States District Court for the Eastern District of Pennsylvania. He received his law degree, magna cum laude, from the University of Pennsylvania Law School, where he served on the law review and as a member of the Order of the Coif. Mr. Krauss received his undergraduate degree, magna cum laude, from the University of Michigan, where he was a member of Phi Beta Kappa. When not practicing law, he serves on non-profit boards (three of them at the moment) and tries not to embarrass his teenage children unduly.

Wayne Morse is a partner and trial and appellate lawyer handling high-profile cases at Waldrep Stewart & Kendrick. A fellow of numerous legal honor societies, Morse—as he is known to colleagues—has tried lawsuits in the Southeast and litigated appeals in the Supreme Courts of the United States, Alabama, and Tennessee and in the Eleventh Circuit. He assists death-row inmates with habeas proceedings pro bono and is a guest lecturer in trial advocacy at Samford University's Cumberland School of Law. An active member of the Cathedral Church of the Advent (Episcopal), Morse attended West End High School, Birmingham-Southern College, Samford University, and the University of Alabama. He was licensed to practice law in 1976. In reverse order of importance, he has summited Mt. Rainier, enjoys jazz and long walks, and has been married to Amy Morse for 28 years.

Sandra B. Wick Mulvany is a partner with McKenna Long & Aldridge LLP in Denver, Colorado. She focuses her practice on complex commercial and government contracts litigation, including breach of contract actions, business torts, and defense of False Claims Act cases. She has litigated cases in various jurisdictions throughout the country and has extensive experience in all aspects of managing and litigating complex business disputes. Originally from the East Coast, Ms. Wick Mulvany received her undergraduate degree from the University of Rhode Island and her law degree from the University of Connecticut School of Law, graduating with honors. She clerked for Justice Alex J. Martinez on the Colorado Supreme Court prior to joining McKenna Long & Aldridge LLP. When not practicing law, Ms. Wick Mulvany can be found exploring the Rocky Mountains with her family.

Eli Rosenbluh is a litigation associate at Boies, Schiller & Flexner LLP's Armonk, New York, office, where he began practicing following his graduation from the Benjamin N. Cardozo School of Law in 2010. Since joining Boies, Schiller & Flexner LLP, he has represented several global financial institutions in a variety of matters in state and federal courts, including residential mortgage-backed securities and tax litigation. Mr. Rosenbluh has also represented pharmaceutical companies in various breach-of-contract matters, both in court as well as in arbitration proceedings. During law school, he served as a junior law clerk in the chambers of Hon. Jose L. Linares, United States District Court for the District of New Jersey and completed a year-long internship at the Innocence Project, where he assisted with the representation of the wrongfully convicted in their quest for exoneration through DNA evidence.

J. Todd Spurgeon is a litigator with significant trial experience. He routinely appears in state and federal courts, handling a wide range of insurance defense matters. Since 2010, Mr. Spurgeon has been selected for inclusion on the Rising Stars list published in *Indiana Super Lawyers Magazine*. He is active in the Indiana State Bar Association and American Bar Association, holding positions on various sections and committees over the last several years, including the Trial Practice Committee of the Section of Litigation of the ABA. He is also a member of DRI and the Defense Trial Counsel of Indiana.

Elaine M. Stoll leads a team of attorneys dedicated to critical motion practice at the Cincinnati, Ohio, litigation firm Montgomery, Rennie & Jonson. She works with attorneys handling cases across the firm's practice areas and specializes in dispositive motions in large-exposure cases, contesting punitive damages claims, and challenging and defending expert evidence of all kinds. Ms. Stoll's recent *Daubert* and *Frye* motions have targeted imaging evidence and neuropsychologist testimony in brain injury cases, engineering testimony and other occurrence evidence in products liability cases, and the testimony of accident reconstruction, biomechanical, medical, and human factors experts in injury and wrongful death cases. Translating complex factual scenarios and scientific and technical concepts into lay terms is a skill she developed in her prior career as a newspaper reporter. Ms. Stoll is licensed to practice in Ohio and Kentucky and has authored motions filed in state and federal courts in 13 states. She earned her B.A. from Smith College and her J.D. from the University of Cincinnati College of Law.

Robert Sumner is a member of Moore & Van Allen in Charleston, South Carolina. Mr. Sumner's practice focuses on complex civil litigation for a variety of clients, including Fortune 500 companies, banks, manufacturers, builders, small businesses, property owners, vessel owners, institutional trustees, and private trustees. He is licensed to practice in North and South Carolina and has tried jury and non-jury cases in state and federal courts in both states. Additionally, he has handled appeals before the Court of Appeals and Supreme Courts of North and South Carolina, as well as the Fourth Circuit. Mr. Sumner received his B.A. from the University of North Carolina at Chapel Hill and his J.D. from the University of South Carolina. He is a regular presenter at industry conferences and continuing legal education seminars, focusing on the development of trial skills and motions practice. He is an active member of the Trial Practice Committee of the ABA Section of Litigation and the South Carolina Defense Trial Attorneys' Association. Mr. Sumner also serves on the Board of Directors for South Carolina Legal Services.

Chapter 1

Introduction: The Keys to Trying Your Case Well

Nash E. Long

It has finally come: the chance to try a case on your own (or lead the trial team) for the first time. With this opportunity may come some pangs of self-doubt. If "there is no substitute for experience," does that mean that you will start the trial behind? Not necessarily. If you do not have experience trying cases, you can borrow from those who do. This book offers you the benefit of several authors' experience in trying cases. This introductory chapter contains tips and practical advice for you to consider in navigating your case to and through trial. The remaining chapters that follow discuss the nuts and bolts of each discrete task you will likely encounter along the way. From these pages emerges a consistent theme: the importance of persuasion, perception, and preparation. These three concepts (the "Three Ps") represent the keys to a good performance at trial your first time out.

Persuasion

As noted trial lawyer and former Chair of the ABA Section of Litigation Michael Tigar wrote 15 years ago, persuasion—that is, how to convince judges and juries to find for our clients—is the litigator's art.[1] Not a modern invention, the study of rhetoric runs back to ancient times.[2] One early student of the art, Aristotle, described a speaker's persuasiveness as depending upon three things: *ethos, pathos,* and *logos. Ethos* is "the speaker's power of evincing a personal character that will make his speech credible."[3] *Pathos* is the speaker's "power of stirring the emotions" of the audience.[4] *Logos* is the speaker's "power of proving a truth, or an apparent truth, by means of persuasive arguments."[5] The elements of persuasive oral advocacy are well known, even to those of us that are not students of classical rhetoric.[6]

In building a persuasive case, you will need to draw upon these same elements. Because a trial is more complicated than a speech, however, it should not surprise you to learn that there are more elements—five, not three—that make up a persuasive case presentation. They are:

- Narrative
- Arrangement
- Style
- Memory
- Delivery

In order to make a persuasive case, you need to pay attention to all five elements.[7]

Narrative

The first element of a persuasive case is a strong story, or narrative. One prominent element of human nature is our tendency to think in terms of stories. Tigar calls this "the primacy of story"—that is, the power of a narrative

---

1. MICHAEL E. TIGAR, PERSUASION: THE LITIGATOR'S ART (1999).
2. *See* Aristotle's RHETORIC (W. Rhys Roberts trans. 1954).
3. *Id.*
4. *Id.*
5. *Id.*
6. *See* Lawrence D. Rosenberg, Using the Lessons of Aristotle to Present Outstanding Oral Arguments, http://www.americanbar.org/tools/digitalassetabstract.html/content/dam/aba/publications/litigation_committees/trialpractice/rosenberg_lessons_of_aristotle.pdf.
7. TIGAR, *supra* note 1, at 6.

to make sense of a jumble of facts.[8] Because the narrative is our preferred mode of processing information, you will need to supply a good narrative in your trial presentation in order to have any hope of giving your case the hearing it deserves. If you do not, the jury will adopt your opponent's narrative or—absent that—develop a narrative all on their own.[9]

Why does this matter? Because the pull of a good narrative is so strong that it will lead jurors to accept or reject facts depending on the extent they fit within the adopted narrative. A trial represents the clash of opposing narratives. This places jurors, at the beginning of trial, in the uncomfortable position of having to decide which narrative is true. As television personality (and jury consultant) Dr. Phil McGraw noted at a lecture delivered at the ABA Section of Litigation Annual Conference in Los Angeles in 2006, the jury at the beginning of a trial will feel as if they have been dropped barefoot into the middle of an asphalt road on a hot Texas day. The parties to the case stand on opposite sides of the road and beckon them to join a side. The jurors stand there in agony on the hot asphalt, until they feel they have enough information to pick a side (that is, a narrative) and dash over. Having done so, the last thing in the world they want to do is cross the hot asphalt road again. From that point forward, the jurors will reject the facts that do not fit within the adopted narrative. A strong narrative therefore constitutes the first—and most critical—element of a persuasive case.[10]

Arrangement

The second element of a persuasive case presentation consists of the arrangement of the presentation. Which facts (or arguments) do you include, and which do you leave out? You cannot include everything. For one reason, the judge will impose some time constraints on you.[11] Even if that does not occur, you must still narrow down the focus of your case. Complexity

---

8. *Id.*
9. *Id.*
10. The same is true for bench trials as well as jury trials. Trial judges will typically decide cases by adopting one party's narrative—or developing their own—in order to provide context for a decision. *Id.* For more on the importance of story and theme, see Chapter 2.
11. More and more these days, judges will impose a time limit and ration it between (or among) the parties in a trial. I find this often leads to better, more crisp trial presentations, because it forces you to focus on the key points and the big picture. The rationing of time also favors the organized and prepared advocate.

is the enemy of a good narrative: the more facts you throw at your audience (and the more exhibits and witnesses you use to introduce those facts), the more difficult it will be to present a clear and coherent picture. In putting together your narrative, remember to keep it simple and eliminate all unnecessary detail.

For some reason, we tend to remember things in threes. You will likely have used this rule in your brief writing, by including the three best arguments for your proposition (and cutting out the rest).[12] You should apply the same rule at trial: arrange your opening, your examinations, and your closing with the rule of three in mind.[13] What you select for presentation will depend on the facts and your best judgment of what constitutes a clear, orderly, and logical progression (i.e., what appeals to the *logos*).[14]

Style

The third element of a persuasive case presentation consists of its style. By this I mean the actual words you use, not the delivery (see "Delivery" below). The words we use, the figures of speech we employ, and the images we create all should be selected with care for their potential impact upon the audience. You likely have learned this lesson already and apply it in your brief writing. There, you use simple, declarative sentences rather than complex, convoluted ones. There, you incorporate active voice, not passive voice. And there, you avoid both jargon and adverbs like the plague. Why? Because doing so makes the brief more interesting and more clear. Speaking in court is no different.

Clarity of expression represents a good start in grasping the element of style, but only a start nonetheless. To have a truly persuasive style in your case presentation, you must apply the principle of *pathos*—the stirring of emotions. You can stir those passions with the right word or turn of phrase. To describe a dramatic traffic accident, for example, do not say car A "collided" with car B. "Collided" sounds so mellifluous and relaxing

---

12. For more on effective brief writing at trial, see Chapters 4, 11, and 13.
13. Tigar, *supra* note 1, at 51.
14. For an example of the power of logical arrangement, I recommend reading the speeches of Cicero. One reason they hold up so well after all these years—after the parties and issues on trial are long since dead—is the logical construction of the arguments. *See, e.g.*, CICERO, ORATIONS: PRO MURENA (C. MacDonald trans. 1977).

that it drains all of the drama out of the scene. "Impacted" fares no better. Because an "impact" can be slight as well as severe, such word choice wallows in ambiguity. Instead, say car A "slammed" or "hurtled" into B, to convey the violent energy of the event. For more examples of the power of language to evoke *pathos*, read the speeches of Winston Churchill.[15] If you give serious thought to the words you use, and exercise care in selecting them, your persuasiveness will improve.[16]

Memory

The fourth element of a persuasive presentation is memory. The presentation must be memorable to you, as well as to the jury. Use only a few notes to keep yourself on track, rather than writing out the opening, closing, or witness examinations. Why must you commit so much to memory? For three reasons. The first stems from Aristotle's principle of *ethos*: the personal qualities that you evince to make your presentation credible. When you commit something to memory, you internalize it. And when you repeat it from memory to your audience, your personal credibility is transferred to your message. On the other hand, reading from a script sends a negative message: that this presentation is not important enough to remember. The second reason for relying on your memory is that it allows you to fix your gaze where it should be at various points in the trial. In opening and closing, you should engage the jury (or judge) in direct eye contact—probably the most important form of non-verbal speech. In direct examination, your focus should be on the witness. (For some reason, the jury tends to look where actors in the courtroom are looking. If you are looking down at your notes, the jury will as well. They will not focus on your witness.) So

---

15. *See* HIS FINEST HOURS: THE WAR SPEECHES OF WINSTON CHURCHILL (Graham Stewart ed., 2007). Churchill did not deliver his speeches off the cuff. Rather, he wrote his speeches out, and in doing so sweated and fussed over every word. *See* WILLIAM MANCHESTER, THE LAST LION: WINSTON SPENCER CHURCHILL: ALONE: 1932–1940 32–34 (1988).

16. The same is true with figures of speech. Here, however, you should take care in employing such devices. Emotions can be stirred to your detriment as well as your benefit. Consider this example. Everyone will have heard the expression "turn a blind eye," and understand that it refers to the act of ignoring something or someone. But what if your audience—the judge or a member of a jury—has a close family member or friend who is blind? Would this figure of speech sound pejorative to him or her? Have you unwittingly turned off this member of the audience? Any figure of speech you utter should result from thoughtful deliberation, not from sloppiness or habit.

too in cross-examination, you want the jury to focus on you, not on your notes. The third reason to trust your memory is this: if your presentation is beyond the powers of your memory, it will likely be beyond the jury's as well. And if the jury cannot remember your presentation, then it is not worth giving. Make the presentation memorable to the jury by making it memorable to yourself. Use a logical structure (remembering the power of primacy and recency), keep it simple and clear, and tie it all together with a consistent theme.

Delivery

The final element of a persuasive presentation is the delivery, by which I mean the method of communication—both verbal and non-verbal. Your verbal delivery should be clear and understandable. Do not proceed too quickly, and do not be afraid of silence. Give the audience time to absorb what you say, time to read what you show, and time to think on both. Finally, be conscious of the finite limit of the attention span. The longer you go on with anything—opening, closing, or an examination—the more you will need to vary the pace and tone in order to keep things interesting.[17]

Examples of powerful delivery styles cannot be easily conveyed on a cold record such as this. You will see what I mean, however, if you study some of the great speeches in history. One of my favorites is the keynote address delivered by Barbara Jordan at the 1976 Democratic Party National Convention.[18] Ms. Jordan's delivery makes this a great speech. Her delivery has it all—the cadence, phrasing, and tone are masterful; and it is all her own.[19] Similarly, you must find the delivery style that works best for you.

---

17. To cite Aristotle again, we know things by their differences. Preschool children watching *Sesame Street* will demonstrate this trait during the popular segment "One of These Things Is Not Like the Other." Jurors manifest this trait by tuning out monotone and monotony. Do not get tuned out—mix up your delivery. For example, if a witness who does not want to answer your cross-examination question deflects or provides a non-responsive answer, you will typically repeat the question. You may even have to do so multiple times. You will need to word the question in the same way each time, so the last thing you want to do is deliver it the same way each time. Try slowing down your delivery when repeating the question, or dropping the pitch or volume of your voice.

18. You can find video clips of this speech on YouTube.

19. With a little research, you can find on the Internet many other worthy examples of great speeches. Other masters of delivery include President Franklin Roosevelt and President Ronald Reagan. *See, e.g.*, http://tonguetiedamerica.com.

Do not try to be someone you are not. Instead, try to be more of yourself—by which I mean, let your personality show. Genuine characters usually trump wooden ones.

Most young advocates I see tend to struggle more with the non-verbal elements of communication than with the verbal. How do I stand? What do I do with my hands? How and when should I incorporate gestures? I have no hard-and-fast rule other than this: every movement in the courtroom should be controlled and have a purpose. Otherwise, your movement will create a distraction—or worse, undermine your *ethos* with the audience.[20]

Pay attention to these five elements of presenting a persuasive case, and you will have grasped the first key to trying a case well.

Perception

The second key to trying a case well is understanding the importance of perception. Indeed, trial preparation and presentation consist of a series of inquiries into matters of perception. At most points in the process, I set my course of action by asking myself some form of these three questions:

- How will the judge/jury see it?
- How will the witness see it?
- How will the appellate court see it?

I use these questions of perception like a navigator of the past would use his instruments and charts to guide his ship across the ocean. Time and time again, they point me in the way I need to go.

How Will the Judge/Jury See It?

In preparing for trial, I worry first and foremost about how the judge and jury will see things. I mean this both figuratively (how will they react to the presentation) and literally (how will they receive the presentation).

---

20. For more techniques for effective oral advocacy, *see* BRIAN K. JOHNSON & MARSHA HUNTER, THE ARTICULATE ADVOCATE: NEW TECHNIQUES OF PERSUASION FOR TRIAL LAWYERS (2009).

The Figurative Question

A central question that I consider in trial preparation is how my theme, witnesses, and presentation will play with this audience as factfinder(s). This overarching question leads to further subquestions. What do I need to know about this audience in order to construct a presentation that he/she/they will find persuasive? How do I find this out?

Audience Background

You cannot know how your case will be received if you do not know the audience for whom it will be displayed. If you do not already know the judge well, you need to do some research on him or her. Ask questions of your colleagues that know the judge. Ask questions of the courthouse staff—a good source of information about a judge's procedures and pet peeves. Read opinions or articles written by the judge. Internet research can also provide helpful information about him or her. All these data points can help you construct a profile of your judge, which will in turn help you hone your presentation.

You will also want to find out what you can about your jury pool. If the case warrants it, you will want to engage a jury consultant before trial. A good jury consultant, engaged well in advance of trial, can help you conduct a mock trial, or a survey, in order to test out potential themes and arguments. Once the trial begins, jury selection presents an opportunity to identify the jurors that are likely to be receptive to your arguments (or adverse to them).[21] But I also find it helpful, particularly in a venue outside my hometown, to spend time where the trial will be held, so I can find out about the community firsthand. I read the local newspaper, watch the local news, and eat at the local restaurants—all in an effort to find out what the jury pool is experiencing and what information it is receiving.[22] A lawyer friend of mine in Texas will go to the local barbershop for a haircut the week before trial. Why? Because barbershops (and beauty salons) are good

---

21. It also presents an opportunity to start building rapport with the jury and to start introducing your themes. For more on jury selection, see Chapter 6.
22. At a minimum, you will want to have someone monitoring local coverage of your case and/or your client. In civil cases, you may need to *voir dire* the jury about such coverage to root out preconceived notions and biases. If the pre-trial publicity interferes with your client's right to a fair trial in a criminal case, it may become necessary to seek a change of venue.

sources of local information and indicators of local opinion. In a similar vein, Florida lawyer Willie Gary will sometimes attend local churches in the towns where he will soon start a big trial. The implementation may vary, but the concept is the same: get out of your hotel room and learn what you can about your potential audience.

Content

Keeping the background information on your audience in mind, you will next need to think about what you will present to the judge/jury and consider how it will be received. Usually, the content of your presentation will consist of three discrete segments: preparing the audience to hear your case; making your case; and asking the jury to act in response.

Laying the Groundwork

A message is more easily received when the audience is prepared to hear it. How you will prepare your audience differs depending on whether you have a bench trial or a jury trial. In a bench trial, you want to prepare the judge to accept your narrative by demonstrating that you are a reliable narrator. Of course, everything you say or write to the judge must be accurate. (If you make a mistake, own up to it and correct it immediately.) Beyond that, however, you can demonstrate your ability as a faithful narrator by accurately forecasting what the evidence will show. If the judge allows you to file a trial brief, do so. If not, look for other ways to forecast for the judge what the upcoming evidence will show or what evidentiary issues may arise. When you accurately forecast what develops, you establish for the judge your credentials as a reliable narrator.

In a jury trial, your first interaction with the jury will come during *voir dire*. You will therefore want to think about ways that you can start getting your themes across during *voir dire*, in order to prepare the jurors to receive your narrative. For example, in a construction defect case I tried, one issue was whether the defect existed when the work passed inspection and was handed over to the owner by the contractor. One juror responded to my *voir dire* questioning that he had a similar experience where an inspector had overlooked a problem. This allowed me the opportunity to ask a number of follow-up questions, in front of the entire panel, to make it clear that the performance of the inspector in our case was going to be a significant issue. In another case, where causation of the plaintiffs' business failure was a disputed issue, I worked that into the *voir dire* questions: "Do you think my client should pay damages even if it did not hurt the plaintiffs' business?" and "If we prove to you that my client did no harm, can you find for the defendant?" These techniques lay the groundwork for your narrative and increase the odds of its acceptance by the factfinder.

Telling the Story

The second step is to decide which elements of the narrative to provide to the factfinder, and in what order. As noted above in the discussion on persuasion, the big question here is what to include and what to leave out. Considering how the judge or jury will see the evidence helps answer that question. In asking this question and in making these decisions, keep in mind that you will have lived with, and thought about, your case for a long time. Your audience will not have done so. Think back to when you first became involved in the case. What questions did you have? The judge and jury will likely have the same or similar questions as they are introduced to the case.[23] You should therefore explain issues and concepts in your opening that you had questions about at the beginning of the case. Similarly, in direct examination, ask the questions that you think the jury would ask if they could.[24]

Making the Ask

What will you ask the jury (or judge) to do? What do you need to say to the jury, or give to them, in order to set up a successful ask? If I plan to ask the jury to award punitive damages, for example, I should not simply throw a number out there in closing. Instead, I need to put that number in context (e.g., by comparing it to the defendant's net profits) and discuss how the jury instructions lead the jury to making that award.[25]

---

23. By the time trial arrives, you will likely have forgotten the initial questions you had about the case. It is therefore good practice to keep your notes from your early meetings and review them in preparation for trial.

24. For more on opening statements, see Chapter 7. For more on direct examination, see Chapter 8.

25. For more on jury instructions, see Chapter 3. For more on closing argument, see Chapter 12.

Placing yourself in the position of the audience (judge and/or jury), and asking how that audience will view the evidence, will provide the answer to many of the strategic and tactical questions you will face in a trial.

The Literal Question

In addition to asking the question of how the judge and jury will view the case in a figurative sense, I also worry about how they will see things in a literal sense. What exhibits will I show the jury? Are the documents legible? How will I show them to the jury: in hard copy (via publication) or through trial presentation software? If I choose the latter, can the jury still read the document when it is displayed on the screen? How much time do I need to leave it on the screen in order for it to be read? Do I want the call-outs and highlights for the documents pre-loaded into the trial presentation software, or do I want a member of my trial team to highlight them on the fly during the examination?[26] Will I need hard copies of the exhibits as courtesy copies in addition to the trial presentation software and, if so, do I have enough?[27] How many exhibits will I need to prove my case, anyway? (Usually, less is more.) Am I introducing the exhibits in a logical order that reinforces the narrative I presented in opening statement?

What about demonstrative exhibits? What demonstrative exhibits will I need? Is the demonstrative exhibit a fair summary or depiction of the facts? Is the design of the demonstrative exhibit helpful? Is it too confusing? Does it use the right colors (i.e., green and blue are positive colors, red is negative)? Who will use the demonstrative exhibit to explain the facts to the jury? Is that witness comfortable with it?

---

26. As a general rule, I prefer to have the trial graphic consultant follow my direction and highlight portions of exhibits on the fly during examination, then save them for possible reference later (e.g., during closing). This ensures the jury has enough time to read what is important during the examination, and it makes for a more dynamic presentation.

27. In one of the first cases I tried on my own, I made the mistake of relying on the trial presentation software to publish the exhibits to the jury and the judge. Although I had a hard copy of each exhibit for the witness (and a courtesy copy for opposing counsel), I did not have an additional courtesy copy for the judge. As the trial proceeded, the judge became more and more irritated at me until it boiled over in front of the jury. "I do not know what is going on," he fumed; "I am sitting up here in the dark." Although we made sure to have enough copies the very next day, this error started me off on the wrong foot with the judge. I learned a painful lesson in logistics, one that led to further lessons in dealing with a hostile bench.

I ask similar questions in thinking about what witnesses to put before the jury. Which witnesses do we want to appear live, and which will we allow to appear by deposition? (Live testimony tends to have more of an impact on the jury than does a videotape replay, and much more than a reading of the cold transcript.[28]) For those witnesses appearing by deposition, will I play excerpts of the videotape, read excerpts of the transcript myself, or have a colleague sit in the witness box to read the answers while I read my questions? Of the witnesses that I could call on direct, which are the ones most likely to make a favorable impression with the jury? How do I help them make that favorable impression? What is the logical order in which to call them?[29]

Related questions arise with respect to the selection of the corporate representative, if you are representing a corporate entity. The corporate representative is the face of the client during the trial. As such, you will want to select someone whom the jury will find likeable, who has enough seniority to demonstrate that your client takes this case seriously and has a strong interest in its outcome, and who has the time and interest in the case to be engaged with the trial team (and not with a mobile device) throughout the trial. If your corporate representative gives the jury the impression that he or she does not care greatly about the outcome of the case, the jury will attribute that attitude to the client as a whole—and will not be inclined to act in your favor.

In sum, how your case is received (i.e., "how the judge and jury see it") depends in part on the bias of the audience and in part on how you present the case. Focusing on the issue of audience perception will tell you what you need to do to put your case in the best light.

---

28. For that reason, I will often allow my opponent to introduce deposition testimony, even when the witness is available and could be compelled to testify live. Doing so tends to de-emphasize any damaging admissions the witness may have made in the deposition.

29. A lawyer friend of mine in Knoxville, Tennessee, says this about trying cases: "You want to start strong and end strong. And if you can manage it, try to be strong in the middle as well." I apply that advice by placing my strongest witnesses at the beginning and at the end of my case. If I have to call upon a weaker witness to provide necessary testimony that cannot otherwise be admitted, I order the witnesses to put the weaker one in the middle. If I can find another way to get the evidence in, or if I determine that it is not necessary after all, then I drop the weaker witness.

How Does the Witness See It?

The second question of perception, to which I return again and again in trial preparation, is "How does the witness see it?" Here again, I mean to ask that question in more than one sense:

- "*What* does the witness see?"
- "*How* does the witness come to see it?"
- "*Why* does the witness see it that way?"

These three questions drive the construction of my witness examinations.

Every witness has a story to tell: the factual or opinion testimony he or she contributes for the jury's consideration in determining what happened. How credible that testimony will be depends on the sort of connection that the witness establishes with the jury and the strength of the foundation laid for that testimony. A strong story from a witness become less compelling if it can be shown that the witness did not have a good basis for making his or her observations, or if it can be shown that the observations may be infected with bias.

The following example illustrates what I mean. In constructing a direct examination of an eyewitness to an event, such as a traffic accident, I would first spend time on the position of the witness relative to the parties involved, to establish that the witness had clear lines of sight and ample opportunity to observe what occurred.

Q. Mr. Jones, where were you at approximately 4:00 p.m. on April 15, 2012?

A. I was downtown, on the corner of Trade Street and Fourth Avenue.

Q. How did you come to be there?

A. I was walking back to my office from the post office. I had just been there to mail my taxes.

Q. What was the weather like that day?

A. A typical spring day, bright and sunny.

Q. The jury has already heard from my client, Mr. Blaine Tiff, about how the defendant, Ms. Dee Fendint, hit him with her car that day. Did you see that happen?

A.   Yes.

Q.   I am going to ask you to tell us what you saw in a minute. But first, can you tell us exactly where you were when Dee Fendint hit Blaine Tiff?

A.   I was on the sidewalk, waiting to cross Fourth Avenue.

Q.   Using this diagram, which we have marked as Plaintiff's Exhibit 1, can you show us exactly where you were? Feel free to come down off the stand. Now, please mark on Exhibit 1, with this red pen, where you were when Ms. Fendint hit Mr. Tiff with her car.

A.   [marking] Right there.

Q.   Were you standing still or walking right before Ms. Fendint hit Mr. Tiff?

A.   I was standing, waiting to cross the street.

Q.   Which way were you facing?

A.   This way. [indicating]

Q.   With that same red pen, can you draw an arrow beside the X, marking where you were standing, to show which way you were facing when the crash occurred?

A.   OK. [witness complies]

Q.   So you were facing the intersection of Trade Street and Fourth Avenue?

A.   Yes, that is correct.

Q.   Is that where the crash occurred?

A.   Yes.

Q.   How many feet were you from the middle of this intersection when the crash occurred?

A.   About 20 feet.

Q.   Was there anything between you and the cars when the crash occurred?

A.   No.

Now, having established the foundation for the eyewitness testimony, you get to the critical part of the narrative. In such moments, in order to take the jury to the scene, and to build a connection between the jury and the witness, I typically switch from past tense ("What did you see?") to present tense ("What do you see?") in my questions. In doing so, the witness will (more often than not) respond in kind. The use of present tense in this dialogue sets the scene and allows the drama to play in the mind's eye. This makes the testimony more compelling and more impactful for the jury.[30]

Q. Let's go back to when you are standing on the corner. What happens next?

A. Well, I am standing there waiting for the light to turn so I can cross.

Q. And what do you see?

A. This red Volkswagen Rabbit zooms past me to my left and slams into a gray Ford Focus in the intersection. There is a huge crash, and I remember somebody on the sidewalk screaming in fright.

Q. Let's talk first about the red car.

A. Yes.

Q. It zooms past you.

A. Yes.

Q. Can you see inside the car as it zooms past you?

A. Yes.

Q. Can you see the driver in the car?

A. Yes.

Q. Who is the driver?

A. Her. [indicating] Ms. Dee Fendint.

Q. And what is she doing, as she zooms past you in her car?

A. She has one hand on the wheel, the other on a phone.

Q. Wait a minute. She is zooming past you—how do you know that it's a phone in her hand?[31]

A. I can see the screen—it is lit up.

Q. How is she holding the phone?

A. Kind of off to the side, and down, like this. [indicating]

Q. Holding it in her right hand?

A. Yes.

Q. Above or below the dashboard?

A. Below.

Q. What is she looking at as she zooms past you?

---

30. Professor James W. McElhaney introduced this technique to me. I claim no credit.
31. Remember to ask the questions you think that the jury would want to ask. *See supra* at 10.

[Objection]

A. The phone.

Q. I'll rephrase. Which way is her head turned, as she zooms past you in her car?

A. Down, toward the phone in her hand.

Q. Do you hear anything before the crash, like tires screeching?

A. No, just whoosh and bam.

Q. Bam?

A. Yeah, she slams into the gray Ford.

Q. So what do you do when you see Dee Fendint slam her car into the gray Ford?

A. I run out into the intersection and look in both cars.

Q. Which one do you go to first?

A. The gray one, because it has been smashed pretty badly.

Q. What do you see when you get there?

A. Mr. Blaine Tiff is in the driver's seat, his airbags deployed. Blood is running all down his head. He has these cuts on his forehead, and blood is streaming from his nose. He is unconscious.

Using present tense in this manner builds the connection between the witness and the jury. They literally see it his (or her) way.

Constructing a direct examination for any witness works the same way: you will focus on these three questions. In some instances, you may not need to inquire into issues of bias on direct examination. If, however, some connection exists between the witness and your side of the case, it is better to bring that out on direct rather than to leave it to your opponent on cross.

This method of constructing a direct exam applies as well to expert witnesses. There, you will want to spend a fair amount of time walking the witness through an explanation of how he or she came about formulating his or her opinions, to drive home the point that the process was reliable and likely to produce credible results. If your expert has testified on both sides of an issue (i.e., is not the hired gun for a particular industry or point of view), bring that out on direct to underscore that the opinion is not the product of bias.[32]

Constructing a cross-examination is no different. You will typically focus on some combination of the facts or opinions that help you (the what), the foundation for the testimony that hurts you (the how), and the reasons the witness may be biased or interested in the outcome (the why).[33]

One final thought about cross, which refers back to the issue of jury perception. The tone and delivery you adopt in cross-examination will also depend in large part on how you believe the jury will perceive the action unfolding in the well of the courtroom. You want to project that you are in control, and you want the jury to believe that you are scoring points in your cross. One technique for doing that is to remark, when the witness gives you an answer that you do not want (or is not helpful), "I'll come back to that in a minute," and continue on with your line of questioning. Whether you ever "come back to that" is immaterial: the remark minimizes the damage of the adverse answer and sends the message to the jury that it did not hurt that much.[34]

How Will the Appellate Court See It?

The final question under the heading of perception is "How will the appellate court see it?" You must engage this question in preparation for and during trial. Why? Because the reality is that every time you add to the record, you are addressing multiple audiences—primarily the trial court and the appellate court.[35] Thus, you must constantly consider, as you prepare and

---

32. For more on examining expert witnesses, see Chapter 10.
33. For more on cross-examination, see Chapter 9. As noted there, not every witness requires cross, and not every cross needs to explore all three elements. For example, if the witness can provide several key admissions, then you may not want to attack the foundation for the witness's testimony.
34. A more extreme example exists with an attorney in Alabama who will occasionally respond to an answer given on cross with an enthusiastic "Yes! Thank you for that answer!"—even if the answer was harmful—on the theory that it makes the jury think something good happened for the examining lawyer's side. However, such remarks can also provoke an objection from the other side and an instruction to the jury to disregard the remark; it depends on the trial judge.
35. Other audiences can include the court of public opinion, other clients (or potential clients) similarly situated to the client you represent at trial, and other adversaries (or potential adversaries) in similar disputes. The applicable rules of professional conduct limit the extent to which an advocate can consider how his or her arguments are received by these audiences.

present your case, how the evidence and argument will be perceived by the appellate court. By now, it will not surprise the reader to know that this question has multiple facets as well:

- "Is there a winning legal argument?"
- "What facts will produce a winning argument?"
- "Is the record clear?"

The Winning Legal Argument

Do not abandon what you have identified as a winning legal argument, even if it has not yet won the day. By the time you get to trial, your dispositive motions will likely have been denied. The legal theory you relied upon in those summary judgment motions did not carry the day. But that does not mean that you should abandon that theory. Just because the trial court judge did not agree with the legal theory does not mean that the appellate court will do the same.[36] You will therefore need to be sure not to abandon this legal theory as you proceed to and through trial; you need to avoid waiving it.[37]

The Facts You Need to Win

You will likely have heard the phrase "bad facts make bad law." In your career, you will encounter cases where the result would likely have been different but for the presence of certain facts that appeared to drive the outcome. What does that mean in practice? You must get those facts into the record for potential use on any appeal or, conversely, make sure the record has any context necessary to explain the bad facts your opponent

---

36. I had a case in federal court in Wisconsin a few years back in which the statute of limitations was potentially dispositive. Our client had a good basis to press this theory, in part because the judge had authored an opinion years before in which she supported application of the statute of limitations to identical claims. We therefore filed a motion to dismiss on the basis of the statute of limitations. This time, however, the district judge disagreed—reversing the position she had taken earlier—and denied the motion. We were forced to continue with the case. Although the case settled before trial, the Seventh Circuit in a related case later upheld application of the statute of limitations. The moral of this story: do not abandon your legal argument if it fails upon first hearing. Preserve it as you go through trial, so that you can make the argument on appeal (if necessary).

37. For more on preserving legal issues for appeal, see Chapters 4 and 5 on objections and Chapter 13 on post-trial motions.

will highlight. Make sure that the record is complete, including your proffers on key evidence that the court has excluded.

The Clarity of the Record

Finally, nothing in the trial record will be of any use to you on appeal unless it is clear to a reader who did not attend the trial. Thus, objections must be clearly stated on the record. Similarly, your examination of witnesses must assist them in making a clear record. Think back to the example direct examination of Mr. Jones above.

Q.   Which way were you facing?
A.   This way. [indicating]
Q.   With that same red pen, can you draw an arrow beside the X, marking where you were standing, to show which way you were facing when the crash occurred?
A.   OK. [witness complies]
Q.   So you were facing the intersection of Trade Street and Fourth Avenue?
A.   Yes, that is correct.

Although the answer to the first question in this excerpt may have been clear to everyone in the courtroom, what good does it do the reader of the transcript if the lawyer omits the second and third follow-up questions? In some ways, this may be the most difficult trial skill to master: constantly thinking about (1) how something looks and sounds, and (2) how it reads. As you start out, you may want to have a member of your trial team such as a paralegal specifically tasked with the job of listening for instances when clarification of the record is necessary.

Understanding issues of perception—in all its facets—therefore constitutes the second key to trying a case well.

Preparation

The third key to trying a case well is preparation. Although even the most junior lawyer knows this fact, it is less clear what constitutes adequate preparation. How do you know when you are ready to start trial?[38] I believe that a lawyer is adequately prepared for trial when he or she is able to deliver a presentation that is competent, coherent, and confident.

Competence

You will have attained competence for a task when you know what you need to do and how to do it. Competence represents a key ethical obligation that lawyers owe to their clients.[39] A lawyer should not undertake a representation for which he or she is not able to perform competently.[40] You will not perform competently at trial—even if you know all the basics of lawyering—until you know the case thoroughly (the undisputed facts, the disputes of fact, and the legal issues presented) and what it will take to present the case to the factfinder. Your preparation must be sufficient for you to master this information. You do not need to keep it all in your head, so long as you have it reduced to writing in concise and handy summaries or "cheat sheets" that fit neatly within your trial notebook.[41] If you do not keep these summaries in your notebook, find some other logical and handy place for them. For example, I place a summary of the grounds for admissibility of each exhibit on the inside cover of that exhibit's folder.

Master the facts, and the rules required to present them, and you will have attained the degree of competence required to start your trial.

Coherence

Your job as lawyer is to present to the factfinder a coherent picture of what happened and make a clear request for what he/she/they should do in response. This requires enough preparation to gain a thorough understanding

---

38. No sharp line divides the work of pre-trial preparation from the work of trial itself. Some lawyers will begin working on their closing when they first get the case. Similarly, depositions taken during discovery often come into evidence at trial. On the other hand, I continue to refine and make changes to my trial presentation during trial. I do this not just during breaks or overnight, but even sometimes while standing at the podium. You have to have the flexibility to adjust as necessary as the trial unfolds. In this sense, my trial preparation does not end until I sit down in my chair at the end of the closing. The preparation I discuss here is the work you must do before the trial begins, so that you can effectively do the work required by the trial itself.
39. MODEL RULES OF PROF'L CONDUCT R. 1.1.
40. *Id.*
41. For more on the construction of a trial notebook, see Chapter 4.

of the facts and how they fit together. Putting on a case is a bit like painting in the French impressionist style. You present your facts bit by bit, much like the impressionist paints dot by dot. The overall picture depends upon how the discrete facts (or the tiny dabs of color) fit together. Each item of evidence is relevant—and therefore admissible—only to the extent that it tends to make the existence of any fact of consequence to the determination of the action more probable or less probable than it would be without the evidence.[42] If you select the wrong facts to emphasize, or push theories that conflict with each other, the jury will not see the picture you are trying to paint. You must always have a clear idea of what picture you are trying to paint, and leave out all the rest. When you have developed the coherent picture of the facts and used that picture to identify what facts you will present and the order in which you will do so, then you are prepared.

Confidence

The final stage of preparation is confidence. As Vince Lombardi once said, "Confidence is contagious. So is a lack of confidence." This is true of the courtroom as well as the football field. If you do not believe in yourself and in your client's case, it will show. And if you do not appear to the jury to believe in your case, then why should the jury do so? I worked a sales job one summer in college. I have carried with me ever since a piece of advice given to me by a senior salesman: the acronym that describes the key to successful sales is "IASM." No, that does not stand for "I Am a Sales Man." It means "I Am Sold Myself." You must believe in the product and have genuine enthusiasm for it in order to sell it successfully. So too with trying cases: your belief in and enthusiasm for the case is a necessary condition for success. You therefore need to prepare until you feel ready and have confidence in your knowledge of the facts and your plan for how the trial will unfold.

With that in mind, here is a basic checklist for pre-trial preparation:

1. Make sure all discovery obligations have been satisfied. Supplement the document production and written discovery responses as necessary.

---

42. *See* FED. R. EVID. 401, 402.

2. Identify the key documents to use as exhibits. Become familiar with them. Understand what you need to do in order to establish a foundation for admissibility for each exhibit.

3. Study your opponent's exhibits. Determine which of your opponent's exhibits you will object to and on what basis. Incorporate your opponent's exhibits into your own case presentation as appropriate.

4. Try to reach agreement by stipulation on the admissibility of as many exhibits as you can. If you cannot reach agreement on admissibility, try to stipulate on foundational issues (e.g., authenticity) in order to smooth the trial presentation.

5. Review the depositions to prepare deposition designations and for use on cross. If these include video depositions, review the videotape as well as the hard copy transcript.[43]

6. Synchronize and digitize all videotape depositions so that you can display them through the trial presentation software. Review the clips created for playing before the jury (or for use in cross) to make sure that they are correct and do not capture too much or too little of the underlying record.

7. Share deposition designations and counter-designations with your opponent, and work out with your opponent and the court how depositions will be presented and how preserved objections will be ruled upon.

8. Establish a relationship with the case clerk, and learn all you can about your judge's preferences (both likes and dislikes) and applicable courtroom procedures.

---

43. Sometimes, a picture is truly worth a thousand words. I recall seeing one videotaped deposition of the plaintiff in a personal injury case. The defense lawyer began the deposition by introducing himself, goes through the basic preliminary questions (e.g., "Q. You understand that we are here to take your testimony today? A. Yes."). He then asks his first substantive question: "You are claiming that my client's product caused you injury?" The witness pauses, rolls her chair outside the frame of the camera (to consult with her lawyer), slides back into the camera frame, and answers: "Yes." In another case, a commercial arbitration, I had videotaped an expert witness deposition during discovery. Although I had a recollection that the witness had not performed well in response to my questions, the recollection paled in comparison to the videotape record, which showed the witness pausing for minutes at a time, visibly struggling to come up with a satisfactory answer to certain questions. The point is that you will need to review the videotape for things you may be able to use, but that the written transcript does not pick up.

9. Identify your trial theme, and practice different ways to verbalize it. Think about ways to work that theme into *voir dire*, opening, witness examination, and closing.

10. Draft your direct examination and your cross-examination outlines; organize the materials you need to conduct these examinations in a witness binder.

11. Practice your direct examinations with your witnesses so that they are familiar with the scope of the questioning and the exhibits that you will use.

12. Have another attorney practice cross-examination of your witnesses, to prepare them for what it will entail. Try to eliminate surprise.

13. Identify your trial team. In a small case, that team might consist of just you and the client or client representative. In larger cases, it can also include associate attorneys, one or more paralegals, a trial presentation consultant, and perhaps even a jury consultant. Make sure that every member of the team has a thorough understanding of his or her roles and responsibilities. For example, you may want to designate a paralegal to keep track of which exhibits have been offered, which have drawn objections, and which have been admitted. You may want to have an associate keep track of the order of proof (the key elements you need to prove in order to support a claim or defense) and tick off each element as it is established by testimony or exhibits. (Pre-printed checklists are handy for these tasks.) Finally, consider whether you need some colleagues on standby, back in the office, to prepare written motions and briefs.

14. Brief your trial team on what to expect at trial and—perhaps more importantly—how to act when the unexpected happens. It is important to maintain a calm, professional demeanor at all times. Do not let anyone wince or scowl in reaction to adverse testimony or rulings, or appear to gloat over favorable developments. If a member of the trial team cannot maintain a poker face, he or she does not need to be in the courtroom.

15. Set up a system for your trial team to communicate with you during trial. Personally, I find the passing of notes distracting.[44] You are lead counsel, so act like it. Tell your team that they can make notes and hold onto them for discussion at the next break or recess. Designate one area of the counsel table where your team members can leave notes for you that simply cannot wait until the next break. Instruct your team that they are not to rise while you have the floor, much less interrupt you by grabbing your elbow, touching your shoulder, or whispering in your ear. Why? What we can touch we can control. If you allow others to take the floor and interrupt you in this manner, you send the signal to the jury that you are not in control.

16. Give sufficient thought to the question of logistics. This is particularly important in an out-of-town trial. Where will you stay, where will you work, what will you eat, and how will you get to and from the courthouse? When are your witnesses arriving, and when will they depart? Do they require subpoenas?[45] You will not want to spend time worrying about these issues in the midst of trial. Work out all the details well in advance, then have a paralegal take charge of implementation during trial.

17. Budget your time in the weeks that lead up to trial and in trial itself. Keep in mind that you will likely have to devote time to last-minute settlement discussions. To make effective use of your time in trial, work out a schedule for exchanging information about the order of witnesses that will be called.

---

44. One trial in Pennsylvania comes to mind, in which we represented a company in a suit by several plaintiffs, each with its own set of counsel. The plaintiffs' side of the courtroom was a constant picture of disorder and confusion. Notes flowed continually up and back among the counsel tables, often accompanied with audible sighs or furious scribbling. But the distractions did not stop there. With each witness, the counsel for plaintiffs conducting the examination would leave the podium and run back to the lawyer at the back table for whispered conferences before concluding the examination. The "lead" lawyers were literally looking over their shoulders constantly. Such a display hardly engenders confidence.

45. For witnesses not under your client's control, the answer to this question will be yes more often than you may think. You will not want to take the risk that a key third-party witness decides—at the last minute—not to show up for your trial. If that happens, and you have failed to subpoena the witness, the judge may force you to proceed anyway. In any event, bringing out on direct the fact that a friendly witness has appeared pursuant to subpoena can enhance his or her credibility with the jury.

18. Practice operation of the trial presentation software. Do not try to learn how to operate it on the fly in the middle of trial.

19. Practice delivery of your opening and closing, so that you have memorized each as much as possible (so that you can maintain good eye contact with the audience) and have a rough idea of how long each segment will take.

20. Prepare your trial brief (if a bench trial) or jury instructions (if a jury trial). Make sure that they dovetail with your narrative and case theme, the examination outlines, and the opening and closing.

No pre-trial checklist can cover every possible type of case, but every case should have one. Sit down with your trial team to put one together well in advance of trial, and stick to it. Maintaining order and organization will help you try your best case. Moreover, it will demonstrate the professionalism that boosts your *ethos* with the court and jury and inspire the confidence of your client and trial team.

Summary

Each of the following chapters in this book reflects one or more of the "Three Ps"—persuasion, perception, and preparation—the keys to trying your case well. Note that trying a case well is not necessarily the same thing as trying a good case. A good case—consisting of good facts, strong witnesses, and favorable legal rulings—can be tried poorly; a bad case can be tried well. Good lawyers have lost trials before, and it will happen again. Following the advice provided in this book will not guarantee success in your first trial. Doing so will, however, make you secure in the knowledge that you did the best job possible. And it will make you all the more ready for your next trial.

Chapter 2

The Importance of an Effective Trial Theme

Robert E. Sumner, IV

There are few childhood memories as vivid to me as those of sitting around a campfire with friends and family listening to stories about ghosts, wild animals, and villains on the loose. Perhaps it was the crackling fire, the flickering orange flames, or the deep rusty smell of the smoke, but something seared the stories into my psyche. For years I believed it was the setting that made the experience so compelling. After graduating from law school and beginning a career as a litigator, however, I started to look at storytelling in a different light. Now, after more than a decade of practice, I have a different perspective on what made those stories so real. Sitting in the woods, wrapped in sleeping bags, with our backs to the unknown, we felt vulnerable. As a result, we could relate to the unsuspecting victims in the campfire stories. It was that personal association with the characters in the story, at an emotional level, that caused us to hang on every word.

Trial lawyers are storytellers. It is a trial lawyer's job to capture the jury's attention, captivate them with the case narrative, and, in the end, persuade them to rule in her favor. A trial lawyer makes this happen by creating a connection between the jurors and the story, so that each juror can relate to the characters on a basic, personal level. Trial lawyers must set the tone at trial, decide who tells each element of the story, and bring the details of the case to life. Trial lawyers are ultimately responsible for the message that the jury hears. If a trial lawyer fails to connect with the jury, the jury will not appreciate her message. The key to making that connection with jurors is to establish a powerful theme for trial.

What Is a Trial Theme?

Many possible definitions of trial theme exist. Merriam-Webster defines "theme" as "a subject or topic of discourse or of artistic representation."[1] Noted author on trial practice Stephen Lubet writes that theme is the "moral force" of your message "best presented in a single sentence" that "justifies the morality of your theory and appeals to the justice of the case."[2] Author of *Trial Techniques*, Thomas Mauet, writes that themes are the "anchors that summarize your case."[3] Barbara Hillmer and Bob Gerchen of Litigation Insights write, "themes are intentionally oversimplified concepts that connect complex evidence with jurors' experiences, beliefs and predispositions."[4] There are many definitions of theme, each making a different point about this difficult-to-define but important concept. To borrow from former Associate Justice Potter Stewart, the concept of trial theme is difficult to define, but you know a good trial theme when you see it.[5] It is therefore instructive to define trial theme by examining the attributes of a good one.

What Makes a Good Trial Theme?

The Human Element

First, a good trial theme must be about people. The best stories—the ones that stick with us—give attention to both plot development and character development. A plot-driven story will not connect with a jury unless it

---

1. MERRIAM-WEBSTER COLLEGIATE DICTIONARY 1222 (10th ed. 1996).
2. STEVEN LUBET, MODERN TRIAL ADVOCACY 8 (4th ed. 2009).
3. THOMAS A. MAUET, TRIAL TECHNIQUES 25(8th ed. 2010).
4. Barbara Hillmer & Bob Gerchen, *Using the Story: The Importance of Developing Memorable Themes*, 19 LITIGATION INSIGHTS NEWSLETTER (2010), http://www.litigationinsights.com /case-strategies/using-the-story-the-importance-of-developing-memorable-themes/.
5. *See* Jacobellis v. State of Ohio, 378 U.S. 184, 197 (1964) (Stewart, J., concurring).

focuses on the characters in the story. This is true no matter how compelling the case may be. In other words, if the trial theme only pertains to the documents and words on a page—without involving the persons or thought processes that went into choosing those inanimate words—it will not connect with the jury. Jurors want to understand not only *what* happened and *when* it happened, but *why* it happened. These are questions that can only be answered by focusing on the human aspects of the trial. If jurors do not understand the motivation behind the players' actions, the story will become dull and they will most likely stop paying attention.

Consider a case about a breach of a contract between a manufacturer and his supplier of goods. A dispute arises after the manufacturer discovers that the material delivered by the supplier is substandard and dangerous. Such cases can devolve into tedium, focusing on myriad details buried within pages of legalese. Many lawyers would spend their time at trial introducing the companies, describing the nature of the business, and explaining the mechanical function of the contract. If the trial lawyers stop there, they miss an opportunity to connect with the jury.

To entice the jury to follow the story, a trial lawyer should focus on the individuals involved in the dispute. By focusing on the human elements of the case, such as the dreams of the owner of the company and the countless hours she invested in developing the product, jurors can begin to connect with the people involved in the conflict. Instead of viewing the breach of contract as a technical term, they will feel the disappointment and frustration that followed the unforeseen interruption of business and the lost relationships that resulted from the interruption. It is the emotions—sympathy, anger, disappointment—that will drive a jury to rule for your client. Those emotions arise out of the human elements of the story.

Universal Truths

Second, a good trial theme should focus on universal truths likely to connect with all members of the jury. If a trial lawyer selects a theme that only appeals to persons of a certain political or religious persuasion, he or she risks ostracizing jurors. In the high-stakes game of jury trials, trial lawyers can ill afford to lose a juror because of a flawed message. For an effective trial theme, a trial lawyer must identify a concept that all jurors can understand and appreciate—or would like to be perceived to understand and appreciate. Examples include truth, justice, hard work, and protecting the vulnerable.

This principle is highlighted in the case in which the plaintiff was rendered a paraplegic because equipment designed by the defendants malfunctioned. The plaintiff had a compelling case and presented capable, qualified expert witnesses to support her story. Counsel for the plaintiff, however, employed a strategy from the first day of trial of berating the defendants for how much money they made. Instead of focusing on the tragedy that had occurred and how it could have been prevented, counsel constantly attacked the defendants for being "rich" and accused the wealthy defendants of caring more about money than safety. After weeks of such tactics, the most memorable aspect of trial was counsel's attacks on the "rich" defendants. After a lengthy deliberation, the jury returned a verdict for the defendants. When interviewed after the case, one juror, who himself was a successful businessman, reported that he resented the message that the "rich" defendants did not care about the safety of their customers. He was vocal during deliberations, defending against what he thought was an unfair stereotype of successful people. In the end, this juror persuaded the rest of the panel that the defendants were successful as a result of hard work and that the accident was the result of an unforeseen mistake. By ostracizing one juror, the plaintiff's counsel lost the case.

Solid Foundation

Third, a good trial theme must be supported by sound evidence. A powerful trial theme should be "based on a foundation of undisputed or otherwise provable facts, all of which lead in a single direction."[6] A trial theme is effective if the jury connects the power of the theme to the evidence at hand. Therefore, a trial theme works only when the jury believed the factual basis for that theme. Trial themes built on speculative or unproven facts will cause the jury to discount or disregard the message altogether. There are few moments sweeter for a trial lawyer than when opposing counsel over-promises to the jury, and he or she cannot deliver. Where possible, a

---

6. LUBET, *supra* note 2, at 7.

trial lawyer should take pains to prevent this from occurring at his expense by building the trial theme with only those facts that are uncontested or supported by strong evidence. In short, a trial lawyer should build the trial theme on a solid foundation.

Take, for instance, a trial that I defended in rural South Carolina. We filed numerous motions seeking to strike certain evidence and testimony. Opposing counsel argued vehemently that the court could not properly rule at the pre-trial stage and that he should be given the opportunity to present his evidence in the proper context before the court ruled. The judge was persuaded and instructed the lawyers to make their opening statements.

Much to my surprise and ire, opposing counsel's opening statement focused on the very documents and testimony that we challenged in our motions. Opposing counsel promised the jury that it would see these documents and hear the testimony on critical issues—evidence that counsel claimed would carry the day at trial. It was upon this evidence that opposing counsel built his theme. I was furious. But once I recovered my composure, and we started to present the evidence, I realized that we had been given a gift. One by one, each of the promised documents offered by opposing counsel was ruled inadmissible. The critical testimony was not allowed. During closing, all of my frustration turned to elation as I walked the jury through my opponent's broken promises. When I had finished, my opponent's trial theme had crumbled before his very eyes.[7]

Viscerals

Fourth, a good trial theme should focus on a concept that will connect with jurors at a visceral—or gut—level. Visceral communications trigger "strong emotional and sometime near-physical reactions."[8] Lawyers use

---

7. Of course, the selection and employment of trial theme will depend upon the facts of the case and the hand you are dealt. Sometimes, the only useful theme you have will be based on evidence of dubious admissibility. In that instance, you may want to file a motion in limine to get a preliminary ruling on whether that evidence will be admitted. See Chapter 3. If that does not resolve the issue (and you cannot settle the case), you may have to take a risk, swing for the fences, and hope for the best. If it unfolds that you cannot get your evidence in on the first try, think about alternative ways to do so. Be on the lookout for arguments that the opposition has "opened the door" in some manner. In general, however, it is better to avoid these desperate straits if you can. Build your theme on a solid foundation.

8. DAVID BALL, THEATER TIPS AND STRATEGIES FOR JURY TRIALS 132 (3rd ed. 2003).

"viscerals"—as David Ball calls them—in all aspects of a trial to send a more powerful message with the evidence they present. A trial lawyer will create a more lasting impression if he or she employs a trial theme that reaches the jury on that visceral level.

Consider a case where a trusted employee breaches a covenant not to compete and leaves his company to work for a competitor. An appropriate trial theme for the case might be *accountability* or *broken promises*. Both of these trial themes incorporate human activity and set a proper tone for the trial. But employing a visceral theme such as *betrayal* will elicit a stronger, more emotional response from the jury.

Identifying Your Trial Theme

Know Your Audience

In identifying a powerful trial theme, a trial lawyer must step outside of the role of advocate and into the shoes of his audience. Only by viewing the trial from the jury's vantage point can a trial lawyer truly understand the nuances of a trial theme. The key to viewing the case through the eyes of the jury is learning about the jurors. Who are they? Where are they from? Do they have strong beliefs or preconceived notions about the subject of the trial?

The process of picking jurors makes this a difficult task to be performed in advance; however, a trial lawyer should not wait until a jury is picked before identifying a trial theme. A trial lawyer can test certain themes before trial through surveys, mock trials, or focus groups. For smaller cases, a trial lawyer can test trial themes on co-workers, staff, and family members. A trial lawyer can also learn about his audience by reviewing the list of potential jurors published before trial. With the help of the Internet and jury consultants, trial lawyers can learn additional information about jurors' criminal backgrounds, prior lawsuits, and other publicly available information. A careful analysis of the available information will help a trial lawyer form a reasonable expectation of the makeup of the jury.

Applying psychodrama techniques is an effective method for trial lawyers to identify the predispositions and potential reactions of jurors. In 1921, noted psychiatrist and psychodramatist Dr. J. L. Moreno developed a form of group psychotherapy known as psychodrama.[9] In psychodrama, the patient assumes the role of a different person and acts out an episode employing the other person's perspective. The purpose of psychodrama is to promote personality growth and development through an understanding of one's condition *through someone else's eyes*.[10] The concept of psychodrama has been applied to jury trials for many years.

While a full-blown psychodrama group session is not feasible for the average case, a trial lawyer should consider the concept when trying to understand the jury for purposes of selecting a trial theme. To develop a trial theme, trial lawyers should stop thinking about cases like lawyers and, instead, analyze their cases from the vantage point of their audience:

> It is not just what happens to us that is important and that makes us who we are, it is how we experience what has happened to us. The facts are only a small part of anything that happens. Our experiences are stories, our stories. Together they comprise the story of our lives.[11]

By understanding the story of the jurors' lives, a trial lawyer can select a trial theme that is tailored for a particular audience.

Trial Theory Versus Trial Theme

There exists a common misunderstanding among trial lawyers about the distinction between trial theory and trial theme. A trial lawyer will need both a sound trial theory and a well-crafted trial theme, but the two should not be confused. A trial theory sets out a logical series of events that matches up with the relevant legal issues to be proved or disproved by the parties at trial. "A theory of the case should be expressed in a single paragraph that combines an account of the facts and law in such a way as to lead the trier of fact to conclude that your client must win."[12]

---

9. *See* J. L. MORENO & ZERKA T. MORENO, PSYCHODRAMA: ACTION THERAPY & PRINCIPLES OF PRACTICE (1969).
10. *Id.*
11. John Nolte, *Brochure for the "Psychodrama and Telling the Story" Workshop*, Oct. 23–25, 1998 (Midwest Ctr. for Pyschodrama & Society, Omaha, Neb.).
12. LUBET, *supra* note 2, at 7.

While the trial theme should identify a single fundamental truth that connects viscerally with jurors, the trial theory should be the logical, analytical vehicle that carries the jurors from the start of trial to the finish. Another way to think of the trial theory is as a roadmap for the case. Thus, the creation of a powerful trial theory can be helpful for developing an appropriate trial theme. While a trial lawyer should never wait until the last minute to create a trial theme, as discussed below, it can be very helpful to refine the trial theme after developing the theory of the case.

When to Prepare the Trial Theme?

There is no perfect time to prepare a trial theme. Lawsuits are dynamic, often lasting for years before evidence is presented at trial. The discovery process, which accounts for the vast majority of activity in any given case, is the investigation phase of a case. It is this investigation that enables trial lawyers to frame the facts and disputed issues for trial. As a result, a trial lawyer should not assign a trial theme too early—before the key facts are known—or stubbornly refuse to modify the trial theme as they discover new facts that undermine or contradict the trial theme. Conversely, a trial lawyer should not wait until the last minute to identify the trial theme. The key is to understand the role of the trial theme at each stage of the process.

With Case Intake

A trial lawyer should start thinking about the trial theme as soon as he or she receives a new file. However, trial themes developed early in a case are subject to revision and changes in direction. For each case, a trial lawyer should begin keeping notes about proposed trial themes in one location and revisit these notes at regular intervals. Trial lawyers should think critically about the proposed trial themes and have no loss of pride associated with drastic shifts in the message. A good practice is to consider multiple trial themes and test them against the facts and law as the case progresses.

A benefit of this exercise is to get a trial lawyer thinking about trial *from day one*. If a trial lawyer starts thinking about trial at the beginning of the case and continues to think about trial during each step of the process, he or she will be prepared when the time comes to deliver the theme at trial.

In Discovery

A trial lawyer should also carefully consider the trial theme as he or she conducts discovery. There are two sides to discovery in every case: propounding discovery requests and responding to discovery requests. A trial lawyer should craft discovery that will be useful at trial by seeking to elicit facts that support the trial theme. Blind reliance on form discovery or delegating discovery to an attorney with no knowledge of the case constitutes a waste of time and a missed opportunity. Similarly, a trial lawyer should contemplate trial themes when drafting discovery responses and preparing witnesses for deposition. Cases are often damaged by a discovery response or deposition testimony offered years before trial, because the response or testimony conflicts with the ultimate story at trial. While trial themes are ever-changing, a trial lawyer needs to consider how a discovery response is written and how it will interact with potential trial themes down the road.

For Mediation and Pre-Trial

A trial lawyer should focus on the trial theme at mediation and in the months preceding a scheduled trial date. Mediation represents a rare chance for a trial lawyer to directly address the opposing party. A good trial lawyer should never miss an opportunity to look into the eyes of the party sitting across the table and deliver the key messages of the case. It is not always constructive to hash out every detail of the case, but a trial lawyer should not dismiss the importance of a well-crafted trial theme at mediation.

Rule 408 of the Federal Rules of Evidence prohibits most communications made during settlement negotiations from being admitted as evidence at trial. Nevertheless, the opposing party will remember your position and strategies long after mediation. It is for this very reason that trial lawyers should consider their trial theme and how to use it at mediation.

Trial lawyers are divided on the subject of presenting trial themes and trial evidence at mediation. On the one hand, some trial lawyers play their cards close to the vest, saying little and revealing even less about their trial strategies. This works well when you are in a strong position to defend a case at trial. On the other hand, trial lawyers seeking to resolve the case short of trial may elect to make a more comprehensive mediation presentation. The comprehensive strategy works well for the plaintiff and in cases where the outcome is less than certain. Trial lawyers in the latter category should treat preparation for mediation similar to preparation for trial. A convincing message at mediation supported by a resonant trial theme places a trial lawyer in a better position to negotiate a favorable settlement.

Trial Preparation

A trial lawyer should concentrate on the trial theme as he or she prepares for trial. Many trials involve a team of partners, associates, paralegals, and legal assistants. For a trial team to operate efficiently, team members must divide trial preparation tasks. This division of labor frustrates many trial lawyers because there is a risk that the case presentation will become disjointed.

To avoid this result, the team leader should work diligently to create an effective trial theme at the outset of trial preparations and communicate the trial theme to all team members. Clearly communicating the trial theme during trial preparation will minimize the risk of an inconsistent presentation and ensure that a common message is being delivered to the jury throughout the trial.

Using Your Theme at Trial

Voir Dire

The use of trial themes during *voir dire* can be difficult. Different states, and different courts within each state, have unique rules for jury selection. In some states, a trial lawyer submits questions to be asked by the trial judge. Judges will rarely ask any but the most innocuous *voir dire* questions, leaving little room for introduction of a trial theme. However, a purposeful *voir dire* question can help a trial lawyer test the jurors' prejudices and how they may react to certain trial themes. In other states, trial lawyers conduct *voir dire* by asking questions and interacting directly with the jury venire. The system in these states provides an excellent chance to develop rapport with the jury. A trial lawyer should not miss this opportunity to introduce and cultivate the trial theme.

A trial lawyer should be careful, however, in introducing the trial theme during *voir dire*. At this point in the process, jurors have seen no evidence and heard from no witnesses. Juror opinions are based only on their observation of the judge and counsel. This fact can be positive, but it can also be a liability. If a trial lawyer chooses to emphasize honesty as the trial theme, he or she must be prepared to be scrupulous with the truth, never giving the adversary an opportunity to accuse her of violating the trial theme. A trial lawyer is on stage from the moment he or she walks into the courtroom. A prudent trial lawyer must personify the trial theme at all times.

Opening Statement

A trial lawyer has many decisions to make about using the trial theme during opening. Foremost is whether to (1) state explicitly one's theme at opening; or (2) allow the jury to arrive at the theme through the use of carefully orchestrated suggestions. The most popular method is to *tell* the jury the theme and then return to the theme repeatedly during the trial. This method reduces the risk that the jury could misunderstand the trial theme. As Mauet explains, trial themes "are the psychological anchors that jurors instinctively create to distill and summarize what the case is about."[13] Thus, a trial lawyer may want to establish the psychological anchors early on, to help the jury understand the "whys" of the case.

The downside to *telling* the jury the trial theme is that many jurors do not want to be *told* how to think. Jury research confirms that jurors are more inclined to defend conclusions that they have reached on their own. For these reasons, a trial lawyer may want to be subtle about introducing the trial theme.

There are methods for presenting trial themes in order to allow jurors to reach their own conclusions that are consistent with a selected trial theme. For instance, a skillful trial lawyer may deliver an opening by setting the stage, introducing the characters, and telling the story—all in a way that supports the trial theme. In this scenario, a trial lawyer can end the opening

---

13. MAUET, *supra* note 3, at 62.

statement with the trial theme as the logical conclusion that most jurors have already reached on their own.

One effective way of employing this strategy is to ask questions such as "Where is the eyewitness?"; "What happened to the deleted e-mail?"; or "What motivation did this woman have to harm her employer?" When you pose questions, jurors will begin to focus on the evidence or lack of evidence that drives your trial theme. I once had the opportunity to observe a criminal case in which the defendant was accused of breaking and entering into a medical office building. The prosecutor's case was built solely upon circumstantial evidence. Counsel for the defendant gave a three-sentence opening statement. All three sentences were questions, each pertaining to the lack of evidence to be produced at trial by the prosecutor. By the time he sat down, in the brief span of his short opening, everyone in the courtroom had formed the answers to his questions and arrived at his intended trial theme on their own.

During Trial

After introducing the theme at the start of trial, the trial lawyer can use many persuasive techniques to increase the effectiveness of the message. The first is using a tagline or catchphrase. Some themes are expressed in one simple word, while others are comprised of a phrase or sentence. A trial lawyer should always use the same terminology to express the trial theme. There may be many ways to articulate the trial theme, but a trial lawyer should choose one and stick with it. The power of disclosing the trial theme early comes from repetition.

There are often one or two pieces of evidence that come to symbolize the trial theme. A trial lawyer should consistently return to these symbols to reinforce the message of the trial theme. At the end of trial, the jury will associate the key pieces of evidence with the trial theme. During deliberations, supportive jurors can refer to the symbols to advocate for your side of the case.

Consider the use of the famous glove in the O. J. Simpson murder trial. At trial, defense attorney Johnnie Cochran baited the prosecutor into requesting that Simpson try on the glove. As we all know, the glove did not fit. The glove and Cochran's famous quip ("If it doesn't fit, you must acquit.") were referred to multiple times during the presentation of other evidence and at closing. While we may never know what ultimately propelled the verdict in Simpson's favor, there is no question that the repeated use of the phrase and references to the glove made a lasting impression.

Closing Argument

By this final stage of trial, jurors should be intimately familiar with the trial theme and the pieces of evidence that symbolize the trial theme. However, this does not mean you can ignore the theme at closing. It is imperative to end with a strong message that emphasizes the trial theme. During the opening statement, a trial lawyer forecasts the evidence that will support the trial theme. At closing, the jurors have seen the evidence. A savvy trial lawyer should remind the jury of what was promised in opening and walk through the evidence that supports the trial theme. It is good practice to refer to documents and audiovisuals to reinforce associations with the trial theme at closing. Reiterating the trial theme at closing is another way to prepare the jury for deliberations and lead them to the logical, moral outcome that is supported by the trial theme.

Closing argument is a trial lawyer's last chance to connect with the jury. Although most jurors have made up their minds by the time of closing arguments, some may be undecided. Delivering a strong closing will help your supporters on the jury to defend your position and champion your case to the other jurors during deliberations. For this reason, a trial lawyer's closing should be memorable.

Consider the case of a young girl who died because her family physician failed to diagnose her with a deadly disease. From the beginning, counsel for the girl's family employed a theme about lost opportunities and "what might have been." Counsel elicited the story about the promising young girl's life. He touched on the things she had done and the joy that she brought to her family. He also focused on those milestones the girl would miss. Counsel questioned the girl's mother and asked her to go through a memory box that the mother had created for keeping special items from the girl's life. After concluding the questioning, the box was empty. For the rest of the trial, that empty box sat at counsel's table, a grim reminder of the loss.

At closing, counsel spoke to the jury about those things that the girl had done and, more importantly, those things that she had not done—things that she would never do because her life had been cut short. When counsel finished the closing argument, the empty box was left in the middle of the floor. There was not an eye in the courtroom that was not staring at the box and thinking about "what might have been."

Risks and Pitfalls

Active use of a trial theme is not without risks, and I have alluded to some of them already. A trial lawyer should be aware of these risks and take steps to minimize them. First, a trial lawyer should consider whether a potential trial theme could be turned around by one's adversary and used against her case. It is damaging at trial when opposing counsel twists the trial theme and uses it for a contrary purpose. The effect of such a reversal of fortune can be catastrophic in front of a jury. A prudent trial lawyer should therefore choose her words carefully, to avoid falling prey to this technique. It is good practice to test trial themes on co-workers and family members, asking them if they perceive a downside. A trial lawyer may be pleasantly surprised at the valuable insights non-lawyers can provide on proposed trial themes.

Consider the case in which an appraiser was sued for making an appraisal that did not accurately reflect the market value of the property in question. Defense counsel employed a trial theme about judgment. In essence, defense counsel sought to prove that the alleged mistake was the result of a judgment call and that the defendant had impeccable judgment. During opening and throughout much of the trial, the theme was effective. This all changed when plaintiff's counsel presented a document on cross-examination that had been forged by the defendant. While the forgery was innocent and only made out of convenience, suddenly the defendant's judgment was called into question. With the introduction of one document, the balance of the trial turned on its head. From that moment forward, it was plaintiff's counsel, and not defense counsel, who was the champion of judgment.

A second risk is whether opposing counsel can break down or neutralize the trial theme. This risk relates to basing the trial theme on undisputed evidence. If the evidence supporting a trial theme is solid, the chances of having the trial theme neutralized are small. But a trial lawyer should think through the risk. If there are critical factual or legal points that are necessary for a trial theme to work, a trial lawyer must emphasize those points at trial.

A final risk is that the trial theme will upset a juror. Jurors are everyday people with opinions about politics, religion, and everything in between. It would be shortsighted to employ a contentious concept as a trial theme. While a trial lawyer cannot always choose which side of the battle he or she is fighting on, he or she should be realistic about common juror perceptions. At a jury trial, a prudent trial lawyer should be conservative with the trial theme and the language used to communicate it.

Summary

The effectiveness of your trial theme can make or break your case. As demonstrated in this chapter, trial theme plays a role in every aspect of a trial, including the months and years leading up to trial. By thinking about trial themes from the start of a new case, a trial lawyer will be prepared to identify a trial theme that connects with the jury. Creating a real connection with the jury is the cornerstone to effective storytelling and obtaining a favorable outcome for the client.

Chapter 3

Jury Instructions

Philip N. Elbert

"After the arguments are made, I will instruct you on the rules of law that apply to this case. . . . [Y]ou are required to accept the rules of law that I give you whether you agree with them or not."
—Tennessee Pattern Jury Instructions—Civil, 12th ed., § 1.02

A lawyer cannot prepare a case for trial without understanding the rules of law that apply to it. In a case to be tried to a jury, those rules will be stated as instructions to the jury. Because you should be thinking about jury instructions at the start of a case, not as an afterthought (or a box to check) the week before trial, this chapter comes toward the beginning of this book. You need to understand how the jury is likely to be instructed before you first frame the issues and settle on your theme for the case, a topic that should be in the front of your mind from the outset of litigation.

What's the Big Deal?

There is a popular belief that jury instructions do not matter, that jurors do not listen to them and, even if they did, could not possibly recall and correctly understand them.

But, contrary to popular belief, experienced litigators will tell you that jury instructions *do* matter. In fact, in a jury trial, the outcome of your case often hinges on how well the jury understands and applies the instructions it receives from the court. No doubt jurors frequently misunderstand or fail to correctly apply the instructions. This, however, is not a flaw in the system; it is an opportunity for you, the trial lawyer, to be of assistance.

Take it as an article of faith that the jury is likely to give more credence to what the judge tells them than to what you or your adversary contends. When you connect your arguments and the evidence you present with the judge's instructions, you not only reinforce rules for decision that a jury is likely to latch onto, you also cloak *your* side of the case with the approval of the central authority figure in the courtroom.

Begin to think about jury instructions from the beginning of a case. They contain the very elements of proof necessary for successful litigation. Ask questions in deposition and at trial that incorporate language you expect to see in jury instructions. Everything a lawyer does—evaluating a case, framing his theory of a case, assembling evidence, presenting the case—should be framed in the context of what the jury instructions will be. The jury is going to be told to decide your client's fate based on those instructions.

The key point is: *Start early!* Examine your case to see the issues that will likely arise, and then start assembling instructions that appropriately address those issues. Crafting jury instructions is not a chore to be endured, but a chance to speak through the judge to the jury.

This chapter will first define jury instructions and identify their sources. Second, it will describe the various types of jury instructions, providing examples of their use and formulation. It will then provide a step-by-step guide to drafting and submitting jury instructions and corresponding verdict forms, and it will cover the steps to take if the judge rejects your proposed instructions or gives incorrect instructions. Finally, the chapter sets forth some practical guidance about how you can weave the instructions the judge will give into argument and advocacy. Because I practice in Tennessee, most of my examples are from Tennessee's pattern instructions; however, most jurisdictions have comparable pattern or standard instructions upon which you may rely.

What Are Jury Instructions?

Jury instructions guide the jury in deciding your case. They are basic instructions telling the jurors what their job is and cautioning them about what they may or may not consider in rendering their verdict. The judge will instruct the jurors on the substantive law and what to look for in assessing the evidence, and will also provide guidance as to how the jurors are to deliberate. More specific instructions tell the jurors what the burden of proof is and which side bears the burden of proof as to which issue.

Where Do I Find Them?

Pattern Jury Instructions from Your Jurisdiction

Most states have standard jury instructions, also known as pattern instructions or jury instruction guides. For example, Tennessee has the Tennessee Pattern Jury Instructions—Civil and the Tennessee Pattern Jury Instructions—Criminal, both prepared by the Committee on Pattern Jury Instructions of the Tennessee Judicial Conference.

Most federal courts also have pattern jury instructions. Some, such as the Sixth Circuit, have only issued pattern criminal jury instructions. Others, such as the Eleventh Circuit, have issued both criminal and civil pattern instructions.

Pattern instructions are only suggestions. While appellate courts often recommend their use, they are not mandatory. Courts attempt, as a general rule, to tailor the pattern instructions to fit the facts of the case before them. You should always submit a specifically crafted instruction when there is a critical issue in your case not covered by pattern instructions. As the Sixth Circuit has cautioned, courts should not use pattern instructions without carefully considering their applicability to the facts and theories of the specific case being tried.[1]

A great way to use pattern instructions is first to prepare a checklist of the evidentiary and procedural issues you want the judge to emphasize

---

1. United States v. Wolak, 923 F.2d 1193, 1198 (6th Cir. 1991).

to the jury. Then, scan the index or table of contents of the jurisdiction's pattern instructions to find the draft instructions that address the issues on your checklist. If, for example, the case involves eyewitness testimony, search for instructions telling the jury how they are to consider such testimony. If you represent the defendant in a personal injury case and intend to prove that the plaintiff contributed to his injury and failed to mitigate his losses, you should locate the pattern instructions on comparative fault and the duty to mitigate.

Example 1

In a civil trial in the Eleventh Circuit, the opposing side has three experts testifying on a certain issue. You only have one. You want the judge to give an instruction that the jurors may be persuaded by your expert and disregard the other three. If you searched the table of contents of the Eleventh Circuit Pattern Civil Jury Instructions, you would see the following expert witness pattern jury instruction:

> When scientific, technical or other specialized knowledge might be helpful, a person who has special training or experience in that field is allowed to state an opinion about the matter.

But that doesn't mean you must accept the witness's opinion. As with any other witness's testimony, you must decide for yourself whether to rely upon the opinion.[2]

But this instruction does not actually tell the jury that more witnesses do not equal more weight, so you also need to ask the court to combine this instruction with the following instruction:

> The number of [expert] witnesses testifying concerning a particular point doesn't necessarily matter.[3]

---

2. 11th Cir. Pattern Civil Jury Instr., § 3.6.1.
3. *Id.*, § 3.4

In *voir dire,* in opening, and in your closing argument, remind the jury that this is the law—and that the judge will tell them so.

Example 2

You represent a physician in a medical malpractice case. There is evidence that the physician acted reasonably, despite the resulting injury to the plaintiff. As such, you want an instruction that explains the physician's standard of care and tells the jury that a physician is not negligent simply because treatment was unsuccessful. Check the index to the pattern jury instructions for instructions regarding the duty of a physician. If there are none, you may tailor instructions on the duty of a specialist or professional to fit your case. For the Tennessee Pattern Jury Instructions—Civil, the instruction is as follows:

> A physician who undertakes to perform professional services for a patient must use reasonable care to avoid causing injury to the patient. The knowledge and care required of the physician is the same as that of other reputable physicians practicing in the same or a similar community and under similar circumstances. . . .
>
> By undertaking treatment a physician does not guarantee a good result. A physician is not negligent merely because of an unsuccessful result or an error in judgment. . . . It is negligence however if the error of judgment or lack of success is due to a failure to have and use the required knowledge, care and skill as defined in these instructions.[4]

This instruction, or the substance of it, should become a central theme of your case.

The Judge's Standard Charge

Many judges have a standard charge on basic issues, some more comprehensive than others. Law clerks are often happy to provide both sides with a copy of the judge's standard charge. You may wish to inquire in advance or at the pre-trial conference. Also, attorneys should ask about the timeline

---

4. Tenn. Pattern Jury Instrs., Civil, 12th ed., §§ 6.10 & 6.12.

for submission of jury instructions and about how amenable the judge is to proposed instructions from each side. If you have never done so, go and listen to a judge charge a jury, preferably the judge presiding over your case. Listen to the lawyers to see whether they ignore or embrace that charge in arguments.

Analogous Jury Instructions from Other Jurisdictions

If there is no pattern jury instruction on an issue arising in your case, or if the pattern instruction is unsatisfactory for some reason, you may resort to analogous jury instructions from another jurisdiction to guide you. The goal is to craft complete and accurate jury instructions that support your theory of the case.

Tailor Pattern Instructions to Your Case

Whenever possible, offer simplified versions of pattern instructions that concisely address the issues in *your* case, as opposed to generic instructions that perforce address all issues that might have arisen in the same *type* of case, but are not matters of dispute in the case you are actually trying. For example, a generic instruction that addresses the defense of comparative fault should be pared down to address only the comparative fault allegations actually raised. If there is no third party alleged to be at fault, delete language about consideration of third-party fault. If there is no allegation of fault on the part of the plaintiff, do not confuse the jury with an instruction about consideration of a plaintiff's fault.

Substantive Rules of Law on the Issues Arising in Your Case

If your case is unusual or involves an undeveloped area of law, there may be no suitable pattern jury instructions. In such a case, you will need to craft the suggested instructions from the substantive law. Research the law in your jurisdiction and craft a proposed instruction that accurately states the law and fits your theory of the case. A specially tailored instruction on the critical issue in your particular case can contribute to a win or can serve as a ground for reversal if refused by the court.

In cases alleging negligence per se or statutory violations, it is crucial for you to base the instruction on the substantive rule in the relevant statute.

The statute will provide an authoritative, clear, and objective rule to guide the jury. The jury is likely to view the instruction as the law and apply it rigorously. In these cases, carefully craft the jury instruction based on the elements of the statutory violation and cite to the statute. Then, in your *voir dire*, opening, and closing, tell the jury to listen for and apply the statutory standard as you expect them to be instructed by the court.

Types of Jury Instructions

While the main charge to the jury will come at the close of all proof and often after closing argument by counsel, there are jury instructions issued at various stages of the jury trial. Some are general and basic, providing little room for your input; others are more specific to your case and present a great opportunity to reinforce the theory of the case you advanced in your opening statement, evidence, and closing statement. The following are four types of jury instructions.

Preliminary/Introductory/Basic Instructions

The goal of the initial instructions, given at the start of the trial, is to acquaint jurors with the type of case, the attorneys and parties, and the role that the jury will play in the trial. The court will inform the jury about the course the trial will take and instruct them how to conduct themselves during the trial.

There will usually be a preliminary instruction in which the judge tells the jury, or the panel from which the jury is to be chosen, what the case is about. If you are given any opportunity to provide input, this is your chance to frame the issues in your favor. And when you first speak and tell the jury what your case is about, link your words back to what the judge told them.

The court may also instruct that the jury is the sole arbiter of the facts and may explain direct and circumstantial evidence, factors to consider in assessing whether a witness is credibile, how to evaluate expert testimony, and what the jury may consider as evidence.

Example 3

You must decide what the facts are in this case only from the evidence you see or hear during the trial. Sworn testimony, documents, or anything else may be admitted into evidence. You may not consider as evidence anything that you see or hear when court is not in session, even something done or said by one of the parties, attorneys, or witnesses. . . . What the attorneys say during the trial is not evidence.[5]

While the preliminary instructions are generally standard, circumstances may make it necessary for you to request additional preliminary instructions. For instance, if you represent a corporation and the other side is an individual party, you should request that the judge give an instruction on impartial treatment of corporations. Or, if the issue of insurance coverage came up during *voir dire*, you could request the following:

Whether or not insurance exists has no bearing upon any issue in this case. You may not discuss insurance or speculate about insurance, based on your general knowledge.[6]

Cautionary Instructions

Before recesses and adjournment, judges normally remind jurors about the rules of conduct that apply to them. These are cautionary instructions.

Example 4

We are about to take our first break during the trial, and I want to remind you of the instruction I gave you earlier. Until the trial is over, you are not to discuss this case with anyone, including your fellow jurors, members of your family, people involved in the trial, or anyone else. If anyone approaches you and tries to talk to you about the case,

---

5. Cal. Civil Jury Instrs., § 106.
6. Tenn. Pattern Jury Instrs.—Civil, 12th ed., § 1.05.

do not tell your fellow jurors but advise me about it immediately. Do not read or listen to any news reports of the trial.

Finally, remember to keep an open mind until all the evidence has been received and you have heard the views of your fellow jurors.[7]

Give some thought to what an enterprising juror might decide to do that might sabotage your case. Consider, for example, asking the judge to add an instruction that jurors not visit the scene of an accident and that they refrain from Internet research.

Curative Instructions

The judge will issue curative instructions during the trial to try to limit the impact of attorney misconduct, inappropriate argument, or improperly offered evidence. A curative instruction is the preferred remedy for correcting error when the jury has heard inadmissible evidence, as long as the instruction adequately addresses the resulting prejudice.

Judges often issue curative instructions *sua sponte*. If the judge fails to do so, the attorney may make a motion for curative instruction. Curative instructions raise competing interests. On the one hand, if you fail to object and request a curative instruction, you waive the right to challenge it on appeal. On the other hand, a curative instruction may also reinforce the jury's memory of the improper material. You should therefore weigh the value of requesting curative instructions.

Example 5

I instruct the jury to disregard the last comment about the defendant's conviction for possession of marijuana. That is irrelevant to this case and should not be considered by you in any way.

Final Instructions—General

Final instructions are wide ranging. General instructions include charges that apply to all cases and may repeat some of the preliminary instructions. The

---

7. Fed. Civil Jury Instrs. of the 7th Cir. (Rev. 2005).

judge will instruct the jury on its role, the burden of proof and who bears it for particular issues, and the credibility of witnesses. General instructions are often included in the pattern jury instructions of the court or jurisdiction.

Example 6

> The indictment or formal charge against a defendant is not evidence of guilt. Indeed, the defendant is presumed by law to be innocent. The defendant begins with a clean slate. The law does not require a defendant to prove his innocence or produce any evidence at all. . . . The government has the burden of proving the defendant guilty beyond a reasonable doubt, and if it fails to do so, you must acquit the defendant.[8]

Final Instructions—Specific

Specific instructions address the elements of the legal claims in the case. If the claim is common, the pattern instructions probably contain the relevant instruction. If not, you may have to resort to another of the sources listed above.

Example 7

You defend a manufacturer of small kitchen appliances in a product liability case. The plaintiff alleges he purchased a toaster manufactured by your client, and defective wiring in the toaster led to a kitchen fire. You elicit expert testimony that someone tampered with the toaster's wiring prior to the fire. The judge's final instructions should address the issue of subsequent alteration.

> The manufacturer of a product that is not defective or unreasonably dangerous at the time it leaves the manufacturer's control, is not at fault if the product becomes defective or unreasonably dangerous

---

8. Pattern Jury Instrs., Criminal Cases, Prepared by the Comm. on Pattern Jury Instrs., District Judges Ass'n, 5th Cir., 2012 ed.

by subsequent unforeseeable alteration, improper maintenance or abnormal use.[9]

Selecting and Submitting Jury Instructions

The jury instructions are the only source of law that the jury can rely on in its deliberations. Therefore, it is imperative that they contain an instruction on every important issue and theory advanced in your case. The jury cannot rely on attorney arguments or objections. An appellate court will review the judge's charge to the jury to see if it was an accurate and complete statement of the law. What you have said in argument will not substitute. For this reason, you should select and construct the jury instructions you wish to propose early in your trial preparation.

The court or local rules generally set the deadline for submitting proposed jury instructions. Often, this deadline will be before the trial even begins. However, judges are generally receptive to additional requests that take into account the proof as it actually develops at trial. A charge conference to discuss and attempt to resolve disagreements about the instructions to be given to the jury is usually held shortly prior to closing argument; therefore, you will generally know exactly what the jury instructions will be and can tailor your argument accordingly.

Select the instructions with three main purposes in mind: (1) creating a road map as to the elements you need to prove, the evidence you need to introduce, and the arguments you will make in opening and closing; (2) providing the jury with simple rules that support your theory of the case, and emphasizing those rules so the jury will remember them during deliberations; and (3) preserving issues for appeal. Here is a 10-step guide to submitting proposed instructions:

1. Create a checklist of all the issues on which the court should instruct the jury, based on the facts and legal theories of your case. The set of instructions should be complete in that it covers all factual and legal

---

9. Tenn. Pattern Jury Instrs.—Civil, 12th ed., § 10.03.

issues of the case. As a guide, a party usually has the right to a jury instruction on an issue once there is evidence in support of that issue.

2. Once you have identified the areas for jury instruction, you may begin to draft your instructions. Check the index of the jurisdiction's pattern jury instructions for relevant instructions.

3. If you find relevant instructions but they are unsuitable, inaccurate, or outdated, then make the necessary modifications. If there is no applicable pattern jury instruction on the issue, you may have to rely on the other sources previously mentioned or draft an instruction yourself.

4. Proposed modifications to pattern instructions, or instructions you have drafted, must be supported by citation to case law or statutory authority. Citations should be listed at the bottom of the last page of a proposed instruction.

5. Draft instructions that are clear, concise, correct, and complete—the "four Cs." Can the jury easily comprehend the instructions? Do they adequately address the nuances of your case? The draft instructions should support your theory of the case, but they should not be overtly biased or imbalanced. They should also comply with ethical rules. Therefore, they should not include false statements on the law or fail to disclose unfavorable controlling authority. Your instructions should be drafted to withstand appellate scrutiny.

6. Try to make the portions of the jury instructions that support your theory of the case stand out. Provide examples within an instruction to help the jury make the necessary ties between the evidence, your arguments, and the jury instructions. Jurors are likely to remember and correctly apply an instruction that was emphasized and clearly explained using concrete examples.

Example 8

You represent the plaintiff in a personal injury suit against a commercial trucking company. Your client alleges that an employee of the company negligently swerved the company's trailer into the path of his car, causing him significant damage and injury. The trucking company proposes the following jury instruction on the duty of care owed by the driver of a commercial truck:

Each driver has a duty to drive with reasonable care, considering the hazards of weather, road, traffic, and other conditions. All drivers have the same duty to drive with reasonable care.

However, a jury may interpret this instruction to mean that the driver does not have a duty to exercise more care when he drives a tractor trailer, compared to when he drives a compact car. You may want to propose the additional instruction to explain that:

In deciding whether the defendant exercised reasonable care, you must consider the particular activity he was engaged in. The care that a person must exercise in a particular situation is in proportion to the degree of danger of injury to oneself or to others in the act to be performed. The greater the danger, the greater is the care required.

You may then argue to the jury that because the more difficult handling characteristics and mass differential make an 80,000-lb. trailer far more dangerous to other vehicles than a passenger car, it is to be expected that a reasonable and prudent person driving a tractor-trailer will exercise special caution when proceeding on the highway.

7. Prepare two sets of proposed instructions: one with separate instructions on each page with the relevant citations and authorities (to assist the judge in reaching a decision), and one without citations and authorities (for the jury).

8. Also, prepare a verdict form. Determine which form is most appropriate: (1) a general verdict form on which the jury simply states its verdict; (2) a special verdict form on which the jury makes findings on issues of fact and nothing more; or (3) the hybrid general verdict form accompanied by answers to special interrogatories. In the latter two, the questions or interrogatories should mirror your jury instructions. Similar to the jury instructions, draft the verdict form so that it is simple and easily understood, and so it reflects your theory of the case in a logical sequence. If the forms are too complex, they may

confuse the jury and jeopardize your case even if the jury ultimately decides in your favor.

9. Submit your proposed jury instructions and verdict form in accordance with the judge's orders or the jurisdiction's applicable rules of procedure. Usually, the court will accept proposed instructions up until the close of evidence. For example, under Tennessee Rule of Civil Procedure 51.01, attorneys should generally submit their proposed jury instructions at the close of the evidence, or at such earlier time during the trial as the court reasonably directs.

10. After the attorneys have submitted their proposed instructions, the court will decide which instructions to give. The court will inform the attorneys of its choice before summation and before it gives the charge (instructions and verdict form) to the jury. Typically, the judge will have a conference with counsel on the record. The judge will issue an order specifying the instructions and verdict form to be given to the jury. Not every jurisdiction automatically makes proposed instructions part of the record, so attorneys should make sure their proposed instructions are included in it. This will become important if the attorney later wishes to challenge an instruction on appeal.

What If I Disagree with the Jury Instructions?

If you disagree with a jury instruction that the judge chooses, speak up! If the judge gives an incorrect jury instruction, or gives an instruction on an issue for which there was no evidentiary support, this is a ground for appeal. Make the objection in a timely fashion and before the jury begins to deliberate. Your objection must be on the record and outside the presence of the jury. The purpose of the objection is to allow the correction of errors in the charge while there is still time to do so.

You must specifically state the nature and grounds for your objection. If, for example, there was no admissible evidence in support of an issue, then an attorney may object on the ground that no factual support exists in the record for the proposed instruction. Check the case law in your jurisdiction to see what is required to preserve an objection for appeal. Jurisdictions have different requirements regarding the timing, formality, specificity, and details of objections to jury instructions.

Address, at Every Opportunity, the Key Instructions You Expect the Court to Give

In jurisdictions where the attorneys conduct *voir dire,* begin in *voir dire* to introduce concepts you expect to be reflected in the jury instructions at the end of the trial. For example, if you represent the plaintiff in a civil case, you may want to ask a few questions about burdens of proof. Ask the jurors if they understand that this is a civil and not a criminal case. Ask them if, should the judge instruct them that the plaintiff need only prove her case by a preponderance of the evidence—a more-likely-than-not standard—they will agree not to hold her to a higher standard.

Whenever possible, address preemptively instructions you expect your adversary to emphasize. For example, if you represent the plaintiff, do not leave an opening for defense counsel to undermine your credibility and deflate your case by reminding the jury, at the end of your stirring closing argument, that, as the judge will instruct them, this is a court of law and decisions based on emotion have no place in it. Tell the jury you expect the judge will instruct them that they are to decide the case based on the evidence, and that passion or sympathy should play no part in their deliberations. Tell them your client does not want their sympathy—rather, the plaintiff wants justice. Then make an impassioned plea for justice!

In your opening statement, tell the jurors you expect the judge will instruct them that what lawyers say is not evidence, and describe to the jury the evidence by which you intend to prove your case. If you allege a statutory violation and expect a negligence *per se* instruction at the end of the case, show the jury the statute and tell them about the evidence you expect to put on to prove it was violated.

In closing argument, tell the jury about the instructions for which you want them to listen. Pick one or two—certainly no more than three—phrases from the instructions that you want the jury to key on, and hammer home how the evidence applies to the instructions. Remember how abstract some of the legal concepts you learned in your first year of law school were. How long was it before you understood the "reasonable and prudent person" standard for negligence? How does a jury decide whether a product is "unreasonably dangerous"? Did a party to a contract exercise "reasonable efforts to mitigate damages"? Read the instructions to be given to the jury. Highlight with a yellow marker key phrases in the instructions such as the definition of "reasonable care," upon which your case will turn; then tell the jury how you expect the court to define these terms and why the evidence meets or does not meet the definition.

Tie Your Theme of the Case to the Instructions

Chapter 2 talks about the theme of a case—the central point of the story you want to tell, the picture you want to paint of how the evidence fits together. Convincing the jury that your theme of the case rings true represents only half the battle. To prevail at trial, you must tie your theme to the judge's jury instructions.

For example, in a case in which you seek to establish the terms of a contract by course of dealing (or in which a written agreement was tendered but never signed by the party you claim breached it), a simple theme might be "Actions speak louder than words." In closing, you want to tie this theme and the evidence that fits it to a specific jury instruction. For example, in Florida, you would expect the judge to give Florida Standard Jury Instruction 416.6:

> CONTRACT IMPLIED IN FACT
> Contracts can be created by the conduct of the parties, without spoken or written words. Contracts created by conduct are just as valid as contracts formed with words.
> Conduct will create a contract if the conduct of both parties is intentional and each knows, or under the circumstances should know, that the other party will understand the conduct as creating a contract.

In deciding whether a contract was created, you should consider the conduct and relationship of the parties as well as all of the circumstances.

Now think about developing your argument to the jury in light of this instruction. Here is an example argument:

You recall the testimony of the witnesses. Mr. Smith never signed a contract. His lawyer points out that he and my client, Mr. Jones, never spoke about any terms under which work would be done. But, between these people in this business, there was never any question about what was agreed. Remember, in opening statement I mentioned that old adage your parents may have used, "Actions speak louder than words." When I sit down, the judge will instruct you as to the law. Listen carefully for the instruction about Contract Implied in Fact. The law, as she will tell you, is, "Contracts can be created by the conduct of the parties," by their actions, and that "spoken or written words" are not required. That's in the first sentence of the instruction the judge will give you titled "Contract Implied in Fact." That instruction tells you all the law you need to decide this case. That instruction tells you it does not matter that no paper was signed. It does not matter that nobody talked about how payment would be handled. It is your duty to apply the law to the facts before you. The judge will instruct you that contracts created by conduct are just as valid as contracts formed with written or spoken words. When you retire to deliberate, apply the law as the judge instructs you. Actions speak louder than words. Listen to what the parties' past actions tell you about what the expected financial arrangement between the parties was in this instance, and enforce that expectation as the law requires.

Final Thoughts

Be prepared to rebut your adversary's attempts to argue from the jury instructions. For example, in a medical malpractice case, the jury may be instructed that medicine is "an art, not a science," and that an exercise of "reasonable medical judgment," even if proven in hindsight to have been an error, is not malpractice. In a missed diagnosis case, the defense will emphasize this instruction. The jury will agree it would be unfair to second guess the defendant doctor with the benefit of 20/20 hindsight. You must have an answer for this argument. Plaintiff's counsel could respond, for example, that there can have been no reasonable exercise of judgment when a doctor refused to come and examine a patient.

When you make a closing argument, always review the verdict form, or what you anticipate the form will look like, with the jury. You need to tell the jury how you want them to fill it out and why you contend the evidence and the law compel the result you want. If you do not tell the jury what you want, do not expect them to give you what you want.

A closing argument should have passion, but the emotion of the moment is often short-lived. When a jury retires to deliberate, they will attempt to understand and follow what they perceive to be the law. The judge will read them the law. It is your job, as an advocate, to explain and frame it to your advantage.

Finally, remember to consider jury instructions on the front end of your litigation, throughout discovery, and at every stage of the trial. The framework of proof should match up to the instructions the jury will be bound to follow.

Key Sources

Dennis J. Devine, Jury Decision Making: The State of the Science 183, 229 (2012).

Rick Friedman & Patrick Malone, Rules of the Road: A Plaintiff Lawyer's Guide to Proving Liability 32–36 (2nd ed. 2010).

Roger Haydock & John Sonsteng, Advocacy, Bk. 5, Jury Trials 71–88 (Professional Education Ed.) (1994).

Robert E. Corlew, III, Tennessee Practice § 1.2 (2012–13 ed. 2012).

Chapter 4

Assembling the Trial Record, Pre-Trial Objections, and Motions in Limine

Jason P. Eckerly and Elaine M. Stoll

After many years of a case working its way through the judicial system, mountains of discovery, and countless hours of work, the eve of trial approaches. Despite the numerous hours already invested, the months and weeks leading up to trial can often make or break a case.

The use of the final weeks in preparing the trial record and motions in limine is time well spent. Preparing the trial record requires the distillation of all that has gone on with the case since its inception. Assembling trial notebooks gets you organized for trial. Finally, drafting motions in limine provides an opportunity to get sticky issues out of the way prior to the jury becoming part of the process. All are important steps explored in this chapter.

Assembling the Trial Record and Your Trial Notebooks

Formal assembly of the trial record varies from jurisdiction to jurisdiction and can even vary from judge to judge. Insight from colleagues familiar with the assigned judge, as well as court staffers, is invaluable in determining what, if anything, needs to be filed or available for use at trial and determining how it should be marked ahead of trial. While the Rules of Civil Procedure and your jurisdiction's local rules may be helpful, they are often incomplete.

Among items to be considered are the following:

- Operative pleadings (e.g., the latest complaint, the answer to it, and so on)
- A complete set of all motions and/or orders filed in the case
- Certified copies of deposition transcripts
- Copies of key discovery responses (e.g., responses to contention interrogatories)
- Pre-marked exhibits

If the case is pending in federal court, these preparations will make the drafting of the final pre-trial statements[1] much easier. Even if the court does not require the submission of any particular record prior to the beginning of the trial, it is wise to assemble case notebooks to have accessible in court every day. This will enable you to quickly access any material you may need during trial. The only thing to expect at trial is the unexpected, so it is best to be overprepared.

One way to organize the case notebooks is as follows:

- **Notebook Set #1—The Court Record.** This notebook should start with the complaint and should include all motions, responses, replies, and orders issued by the court during the pendency of the case. An index should be compiled with corresponding tabs and should include a short summary of the issues raised or the court's ruling.
- **Notebook Set #2—Transcripts.** This notebook should include all transcripts and exhibits from the depositions in the case. There should be at least two copies of each transcript—one copy that can be used as a working copy and a clean copy in case the transcript needs to be used for impeachment or any other purpose during trial. Page-line

---

1. FED. R. CIV. P. 26(a)(3).

summaries of the transcripts are also very helpful, allowing testimony to be located quickly.

- **Notebook Set #3—Exhibits.** This notebook should contain any documents that may be used as exhibits during trial. For each exhibit, determine ahead of time how the exhibit can be introduced into evidence and include with it in the notebook case law or rules of evidence supporting its admissibility. Anticipate any objections opposing counsel may raise, and be prepared to rebut such arguments. To keep the flow of trial moving, bring extra copies of all exhibits for the judge, jury, and all other counsel. The judge and jury will appreciate the seamless introduction of the exhibits.

- **Notebook Set #4—Witness Binders.** For each witness you plan on calling at trial or that you anticipate opposing counsel will call, assemble a separate binder. Each binder should include (1) your outline for the examination of the witness, including cites to the transcript for purposes of impeachment; (2) the deposition transcript; and (3) the exhibits you plan on using during the examination of the witness in the order you plan on using them. If there are any evidentiary issues you anticipate arising while you are examining the witness, also include any case law or specific rules of evidence so that they can be addressed seamlessly.

While the trial record in your first case will likely be relatively manageable, the principles set forth herein apply to cases of all sizes and complexity. Being organized with the various trial notebooks will help to ease the nerves that invariably accompany trials, as well as provide a sense of confidence that the case is ready to be tried. The judge, jury, and clients will all appreciate the effort to move the trial along as expeditiously as possible.

Demonstrative Exhibits

Demonstrative exhibits, sometimes called demonstrative evidence, can be useful tools at trial to help a jury understand a witness's testimony, visualize a product or event, or see where a critical document or occurrence fits on a timeline.[2] Demonstrative exhibits are not offered as substantive proof and will not be admitted into evidence or be available to the jury during deliberations, but they can be valuable—and persuasive[3]—aids in presenting your case. Perhaps you will be calling a medical expert whose description of an injury or a surgical procedure could be clarified with a three-dimensional model or diagrams. Maybe your accident reconstruction expert has a theory of how the accident occurred that could be shown on an animation. Or, in order to understand your engineer's testimony in a product design case, perhaps you need the jury to understand a critical scientific principle that can be demonstrated or illustrated. These are all examples of demonstrative exhibits.

If you plan to use demonstrative exhibits at trial, you'll need to plan ahead as you do for your substantive exhibits. Consider what testimony or other substantive evidence you will need in the record to establish the appropriate foundation for your demonstrative exhibit[4] and when you will plan on showing the exhibit. Demonstrative exhibits are usually offered and formally marked as such at trial. You should be familiar with your jurisdiction's case law governing admissibility criteria for demonstrative exhibits. If a demonstrative exhibit has been created especially for trial—for example, an animation of how a crime, vehicle accident, or workplace injury may have occurred—there is a good chance your opponent may challenge the admissibility of the exhibit, and you will need to be prepared to show that it conforms with the requirements for demonstrative exhibits in your jurisdiction.

Check all applicable procedural rules and your judge's scheduling order to make sure you follow any requirements for the disclosure and exchange of demonstrative exhibits in advance of trial. For example, if your case is in federal court, demonstrative exhibits prepared by an expert or that support

---

2. *See, e.g.,* Baugh v. Cuprum S.A. De C.V., 730 F.3d 701, 706–09 (7th Cir. 2013).

3. *See, e.g.,* Burchfield v. CSX Transp., Inc., 636 F.3d 1330, 1338 (11th Cir. 2011) (explaining that "demonstrative evidence is highly persuasive").

4. *See Baugh,* 730 F.3d at 707 (quoting Robert D. Brain & Daniel J. Broderick, *The Derivative Relevance of Demonstrative Evidence: Charting Its Proper Evidentiary Status,* 25 U.C. DAVIS L. REV. 957, 961 (1992) for proposition that demonstrative evidence "serves only to explain or clarify other previously introduced, relevant substantive evidence").

an expert's opinions are subject to the disclosure requirements of Fed. R. Civ. P. 26(a) and the court's deadlines for Rule 26(a) disclosures.[5]

Motions in Limine

What They Are and When to Use Them

A motion in limine is a "request that certain inadmissible evidence not be referred to or offered at trial."[6] "In limine" means "at the threshold."[7] Motions in limine are usually filed in the lead-up to trial.[8] They are occasionally used during trial if an unanticipated evidentiary issue arises, in which case the motion would be filed before the evidence in question is offered.[9] Motions in limine are used for the same purpose as evidentiary objections at trial: the exclusion of inadmissible evidence.[10] Like evidentiary objections at trial, motions in limine are properly targeted at particular evidence—a specific document, for example, or certain conclusions by an expert witness—and not at all of your opponent's evidence on a particular claim or defense.[11]

The rules of evidence, case law, and, to some extent, rules of civil procedure and local rules applicable to the jurisdiction where your trial is pending provide the ground rules for trial, including the evidentiary issues raised by motions in limine.

There are a number of reasons not to wait until trial to object to certain evidence that you anticipate your opponent will offer. For example, some evidence might be so inflammatory that even a brief reference to its existence could prejudice the jury against your client.[12] A motion in limine provides

---

5. Estate of Thompson v. Kawasaki Heavy Indus., 291 F.R.D. 297, 314–15 (N.D. Iowa 2013).
6. A.E.C. v. J.R.M., Jr., 46 So. 3d 481, 497 (Ala. Civ. App. 2009) (quoting BLACK'S LAW DICTIONARY 1038 (8th ed. 2004)); see also Mansur v. Ford Motor Co., 129 Cal. Rptr. 3d 200, 217 (Cal. Ct. App. 2011).
7. Massengale v. State, 894 S.W.2d 594, 595 (Ark. 1995).
8. See A.E.C., 46 So. 3d at 497; Mansur, 129 Cal. Rptr. 3d at 217.
9. See State v. Amidon, 967 A.2d 1126, 1128 n.1 (Vt. 2008) (quoting Luce v. United States, 469 U.S. 38, 40 n.2 (1984)).
10. See Duran v. Hyundai Motor Am., Inc., 271 S.W.3d 178, 192 (Tenn. Ct. App. 2008).
11. See Johnson v. Chiu, 131 Cal. Rptr. 3d 614, 618 (Cal. Ct. App. 2011); Lewis v. Buena Vista Mut. Ins. Ass'n, 183 N.W.2d 198, 201 (Iowa 1971).
12. See State v. Pitt, 352 Ore. 566, 573 (2012).

an opportunity for the parties to argue about and the judge to determine the admissibility of such evidence before trial, outside the jury's presence.[13]

Sometimes rules and case law pertaining to certain evidence are generalized or ambiguous, leaving areas of uncertainty as to how they apply to the evidence in your case. Motions in limine and pre-trial objections can be used to clarify any gray areas by seeking pre-trial guidance from the court on how it plans to apply the rules or on whether particular evidence will be admitted or excluded at trial.[14] Obtaining a pre-trial understanding of evidentiary "ground rules applicable at trial"[15] allows time to adjust trial strategy accordingly.[16] Most of the time, motions in limine seek exclusion of certain evidence that the opposing party is expected to introduce, but they may also be used by the proponent of particular evidence to confirm its admissibility.[17]

Narrowing the evidence ahead of trial by motions in limine can help you shape the focus of trial. For example, in a product liability case, the court's decisions about which evidence of other occurrences will be admitted and which will be excluded will determine whether the focus remains on what happened to the plaintiff or the trial turns into a series of mini-trials on what happened to people who are not parties to the case. Likewise, whether a criminal defendant's prior convictions are admitted or excluded might significantly affect the focus of trial.

Another advantage of a written pre-trial motion, rather than a contemporaneous objection to evidence as it is introduced at trial, is that the former gives the judge more time to carefully consider the evidentiary issues.[18] This tends to be less important if the evidence or the reason for its inadmissibility is of a type a judge will be familiar with—a hearsay objection or a relevancy issue, for example. But the opportunity to explain the evidence and the reasons for its inadmissibility in an articulate way, and to give the

---

13. *See* Benson v. Shuler Drilling Co., 871 S.W.2d 552, 555 (Ark. 1994); Dep't of Transp. v. Taylor, 440 S.E.2d 652, 655 n.2 (Ga. 1994); Geuder v. State, 115 S.W.3d 11, 14–15 (Tex. Crim. App. 2003).
14. *See Duran*, 271 S.W.3d at 192; State v. Horn, 407 N.W.2d 854, 860 (Wis. 1987).
15. Hercules, Inc. v. AIU Ins. Co., 784 A.2d 481, 500 (Del. 2001) (quoting 3 MOORE'S FEDERAL PRACTICE § 16.77[4][d] (3d ed. 1997)).
16. *See Duran*, 271 S.W.3d at 192.
17. People v. Owen, 701 N.E.2d 1174, 1178 (Ill. App. Ct. 1998).
18. People v. Clark, 833 P.2d 561, 601 (Cal. 1992).

judge time before a decision is required, can become very important when the evidence you are objecting to or the reasons it is objectionable are complicated—for example, as with scientific or technical evidence[19] requiring "a potentially lengthy factual inquiry."[20] When certain evidence or the legal argument for its inadmissibility is especially complex, your motion in limine might request a hearing or attach an expert's affidavit in support. There will not be time at trial for the same sort of consideration.

Identifying Evidence for Exclusion or Admittance

An obvious first step in writing a motion in limine is identifying which evidence you will be asking the court to exclude or admit. This will become second nature as you gain more trial experience, but might seem daunting before your first trial. To help you think through the possibilities for motions in limine, some categories of evidence that are frequent subjects of motions in limine are discussed in this section. Of course, your own trial strategy and priorities, the evidence you anticipate your opponent will seek to introduce, and the rules and case law governing the admissibility of evidence in the jurisdiction where your case is pending will all be important factors in choosing the evidence on which to focus your attention—and the court's—before trial.

Expert Testimony

One of the most common uses of motions in limine is to seek the limitation or exclusion of an expert's testimony. Some of the numerous grounds for seeking exclusion or limitation of expert testimony include the following:

- A witness designated as an expert does not have the necessary qualifications to testify as an expert. Knowledge, skill, experience, training, or education can qualify a witness to give expert testimony,[21] but attending

---

19. *See* Tennant v. Marion Health Care Found., Inc., 459 S.E.2d 374, 389–90 (W. Va. 1995).
20. *Id.* at 389.
21. FED. R. EVID. 702.

a few seminars that briefly covered a subject, for example, is not enough to make someone an expert on that subject.[22]

- Certain opinions of the witness or certain subject matter about which the witness is prepared to testify are outside the scope of her expertise. An expert may be qualified as an expert, but opinions outside the scope of her particular expertise will be inadmissible.[23] For example, an expert qualified to treat and testify about an injury may be unqualified to give an opinion about its cause.[24]

- The subject matter of the expert's proposed testimony is within the common knowledge of the average layperson. When jurors are competent to determine a particular factual issue based on their ordinary knowledge and experience, without the assistance of expert testimony, expert testimony on that issue may be inadmissible.[25]

- One or more of the expert's opinions are speculative. An expert's opinion is inadmissible if the "expert fails to demonstrate that a particular opinion is more than a mere subjective belief, unsupported speculation, or a bald conclusion."[26]

- The expert cannot render the opinion with the degree of certainty required for the opinion to be admissible. Related to the rule that experts may not base their opinions on speculation, some jurisdictions have requirements about the degree of certainty with which an expert must hold an opinion in order for the opinion to be admissible. For example, an expert's opinion may be admissible if he can render the opinion to a degree of "probability" but not if the opinion is expressed in terms

---

22. Turner v. Home Depot U.S.A., Inc., No. 108069, 2009 Mass. Super. LEXIS 208, at *6–9 (Mass. Super. Ct. June 26, 2009) (order on defendant's motion to exclude testimony and opinion of plaintiff's expert).

23. *See* Carnegie Mellon Univ. v. Marvell Tech. Grp., Ltd., No. 09-290, 2012 U.S. Dist. LEXIS 120555, at *14 (W.D. Pa. Aug. 24, 2012).

24. *E.g.,* Hollingsworth v. Norfolk S. Ry. Co., 689 S.E.2d 651, 652–54 (Va. 2010); Parmentier v. Novartis Pharm. Corp., No. 1:12-CV-45 SNLJ, 2012 U.S. Dist. LEXIS 84574, at *9–11 (E.D. Mo. June 19, 2012) (order granting defendants' motion to exclude testimony of plaintiff's causation experts) (citing Turner v. Iowa Fire Equip. Co., 229 F.3d 1202, 1208 (8th Cir. 2000)).

25. *See* Baroud v. Wal-Mart Stores, Inc., No. 10-2048 Section "L"(5), 2011 U.S. Dist. LEXIS 91572, at *5–6 (E.D. La. Aug. 17, 2011) (order granting plaintiffs' motion to exclude expert testimony) (quoting Vogler v. Blackmore, 352 F.3d 150, 156 n.5 (5th Cir. 2003)).

26. Hardesty v. Barcus, No. CV 11-103-M-DWM-JCL, 2012 U.S. Dist. LEXIS 167477, at *11–12 (D. Mont. Nov. 26, 2012) (order granting in part and denying in part parties' motions in limine).

of "possibility."[27] The opinion of a medical expert may be inadmissible if the expert does not express his opinions "to a reasonable degree of medical certainty or probability."[28]

- The expert bases an opinion on data insufficient to render that opinion. If insufficient data is available to reach the conclusion that the expert has reached, or if there is "too great an analytical gap between the data and the opinion proffered," the opinion will be inadmissible.[29]

- The expert's methodology is flawed. An expert purporting to use a recognized methodology, but who either fails to employ the recognized standards or follows the prescribed method but performs it on flawed or insufficient data,[30] may not be allowed to render her resulting opinion. An expert is expected to "employ[] in the courtroom the same level of intellectual rigor that characterizes the practice of an expert in the relevant field."[31]

- The expert opines on what the law requires, interprets a statute or regulation, or concludes that a defendant in fact violated a law or breached a particular duty. As a general rule, "matters of law are inappropriate subjects for expert testimony."[32]

- The expert bases testimony upon standards that the expert created without proof that they are accepted in the expert's field or have been peer reviewed, or the expert testifies to a supposed "industry standard" without sufficient proof it is in fact a standard in the applicable industry. A standard or theory created by the expert—or advanced by just a few individuals—may be deemed an insufficient basis for an expert's

---

27. *See* Millium v. New Milford Hosp., 20 A.3d 36, 47 (Conn. App. Ct. 2011).
28. *Hardesty*, 2012 U.S. Dist. LEXIS 167477, at *36–37.
29. *See* Ratner v. McNeil-PPC, Inc., 91 A.D.3d 63, 75 (N.Y. App. Div. 2011) (quoting Gen. Elec. Co. v. Joiner, 522 U.S. 136, 146 (1997)).
30. *See* Rondigo, LLC v. Michaels, 537 F. Supp. 2d 891, 895 (E.D. Mich. 2008) (order granting and denying defendant's motions in limine); Parmentier v. Novartis Pharm. Corp., No. 1:12-CV-45 SNLJ, 2012 U.S. Dist. LEXIS 84574, at *11–14 (E.D. Mo. June 19, 2012) (order granting defendants' motion to exclude testimony of plaintiff's causation experts); Hixon v. Houston Indep. Sch. Dist., No. 4:09-cv-3949, 2011 U.S. Dist. LEXIS 91824, at *18–19, 24–36 (S.D. Tex. Aug. 17, 2011) (order granting defendant's motion to strike plaintiff's statistical expert).
31. Kumho Tire Co. v. Carmichael, 526 U.S. 137, 152 (1999).
32. Hooper v. Lockheed Martin Corp., 688 F.3d 1037, 1052 (9th Cir. 2012); *accord* Southern Pine Helicopters, Inc. v. Phoenix Aviation Managers, Inc., 320 F.3d 838, 841 (8th Cir. 2003); Bartlett v. Mut. Pharm. Co., 742 F. Supp. 2d 182, 188, 197–98 (D.N.H. 2010) (order granting in part and denying in part parties' motions to exclude or limit expert testimony).

opinion without some other proof that it has gained acceptance in that field.[33] Likewise, an expert's testimony describing or relying upon an industry standard that purportedly governed a party's conduct or product is inadmissible absent evidence that such a standard existed.[34]

- The expert bases her opinion on or is merely parroting the conclusions or opinions of others, or is presented for the sole purpose of describing other evidence about which she has no personal knowledge. An opinion that simply restates the opinions of others or that is based on the conclusions or opinions of others is inadmissible.[35] It is similarly impermissible to present an expert for the sole purpose of describing, rehashing, or presenting in narrative form evidence about which the expert lacks personal knowledge.[36]

- The expert opines on what another person knew, believed, or intended, or on a criminal defendant's mental state. An expert may not offer an opinion on what another person actually knew, believed, or intended, because to do so would require speculation,[37] does not require expertise, and invades the jury's role.[38] Federal Rule of Evidence 704(b) expressly bars an expert from offering an opinion on whether a criminal defendant was in a mental state constituting an element of a crime or a defense.[39]

- The expert offers an opinion on the credibility of another witness or party. Determinations about the credibility of witnesses are for the jury

---

33. *See* Fernandez v. Spar Tek Indus., Inc., No. 0:06-3253-CMC, 2008 U.S. Dist. LEXIS 41520, at *29–32 (D.S.C. May 23, 2008) (order on motion to exclude expert testimony); Turner v. Home Depot U.S.A., Inc., No. 108069, 2009 Mass. Super. LEXIS 208, at *10–11 (Mass. Super. Ct. June 26, 2009) (order on defendant's motion to exclude testimony and opinion of plaintiff's expert).

34. *See* Gable v. Nat'l Broad. Co., 727 F. Supp. 2d 815, 830 (C.D. Cal. 2010), *aff'd*, 438 F. App'x 587 (9th Cir. 2011); *Fernandez*, 2008 U.S. Dist. LEXIS 41520, at *34–35.

35. Gunkel v. Robbinsville Custom Molding, Inc., No. 2:11cv07, 2013 U.S. Dist. LEXIS 4020, at *38 (W.D.N.C. Jan. 10, 2013) (citing FED. R. EVID. 703).

36. Levinson v. Westport Nat'l Bank, No. 3:09-cv-00269 (VLB), 2012 U.S. Dist. LEXIS 140909, at *13–14 (D. Conn. Sept. 28, 2012).

37. United States v. Lopez, No. H-09-342, 2012 U.S. Dist. LEXIS 141385, at *9 (S.D. Tex. Oct. 1, 2012).

38. Robinson v. Hartzell Propeller, Inc., 326 F. Supp. 2d 631, 647–48 (E.D. Pa. 2004).

39. FED. R. EVID. 704(b); United States v. Morales, 108 F.3d 1031, 1033 (9th Cir. 1997).

alone to make,[40] and "expert opinions that constitute evaluations of witness credibility, even when such evaluations are rooted in scientific or technical expertise, are inadmissible."[41]

- One of the jurisdiction's requirements for admission of expert testimony in that expert's particular field has not been met. Certain jurisdictions have articulated requirements or limitations specific to experts in a particular field—for example, criteria for the admissibility of accident reconstruction[42] or human factors[43] testimony or limitations on testimony by a life care planner.[44]

- The proponent of the expert's testimony failed to comply with civil procedure requirements or the court's deadlines for disclosing expert witnesses and their opinions. An expert may be barred from testifying, or from testifying as to particular opinions, if the proponent of his testimony fails to comply with disclosure requirements imposed by the applicable rules of civil procedure or by the court.[45] Similarly, a witness disclosed only as a lay witness but whose testimony is actually in the nature of expert testimony may be barred from testifying.[46]

In *Daubert*[47] jurisdictions, which include federal courts and the majority of state courts, courts have a special obligation to scrutinize expert testimony.

---

40. Jordan v. City of Chicago, No. 08 C 6902, 2012 U.S. Dist. LEXIS 3473, at *11–12 (N.D. Ill. Jan. 11, 2012) (citing United States v. Hall, 165 F.3d 1095, 1107 (7th Cir. 1999)).
41. Nimely v. City of New York, 414 F.3d 381, 397–98 (2d Cir. 2005) (citing FED. R. EVID. 702 and numerous cases).
42. *E.g.*, People v. Ethridge, 610 N.E.2d 1305, 1320 (Ill. App. Ct. 1993) (describing four elements necessary to admit accident reconstruction testimony).
43. *E.g.*, Florida Power Corp. v. Barron, 481 So. 2d 1309, 1310–11 (Fla. Dist. Ct. App. 1986) (holding human factors testimony admissible only when "there are enough unusual circumstances present to support the admission of expert testimony" on "how these unusual circumstances would affect the human response").
44. *See, e.g.*, First Nat'l Bank v. Kansas City S. Ry. Co., 865 S.W.2d 719, 738–39 (Mo. Ct. App. 1993) (holding life care planner's testimony regarding need for and cost of certain future care inadmissible due to lack of medical testimony establishing need for such care).
45. *See, e.g.*, Southard v. State Farm Fire & Cas. Co., No. 4:11-cv-243, 2013 U.S. Dist. LEXIS 7283, at *12–17 (S.D. Ga. Jan. 17, 2013) (order granting and denying various pre-trial motions); Klazak v. Consol. Med. Transp. Inc., No. 96 C 6502, 2005 U.S. Dist. LEXIS 13607, at *44–47 (N.D. Ill. May 26, 2005).
46. *See, e.g.*, *Gunkel*, No. 2:11cv07, 2013 U.S. Dist. LEXIS 4020, at *28–29, 34–39.
47. Daubert v. Merrell Dow Pharm., 509 U.S. 579 (1993).

They act as gatekeepers,[48] admitting expert testimony only when it is sufficiently reliable and relevant and when the expert is sufficiently qualified.[49] Courts have latitude in deciding how to perform their gatekeeping function and, for example, are not required to hold an evidentiary hearing on the admissibility of expert testimony.[50] Nevertheless, challenges to expert testimony under *Daubert* are frequently resolved after a *Daubert* hearing before trial.

A minority of states[51] have not adopted *Daubert*. Most of these instead employ some version of the *Frye*,[52] or "general acceptance," test. In *Frye* jurisdictions, scientific evidence that is novel is scrutinized and must have gained general acceptance in the relevant field in order to be admitted at trial. Expert testimony that does not qualify as novel scientific evidence is not assessed under *Frye* in these states, meaning it need not be generally accepted to be admissible. But non-novel expert evidence is still subject to the jurisdiction's evidentiary rules and foundational requirements governing expert testimony.

When your motion in limine concerns expert evidence, be sure to determine whether *Daubert* or *Frye* governs your evidentiary issue, and to thoroughly research your jurisdiction's case law and rules of evidence, to ensure that you are advancing your argument under the appropriate legal standard.

Hearsay

Hearsay is a common subject of motions in limine. It is defined as an out-of-court statement offered into evidence for the purpose of proving the truth of the matter asserted in the statement.[53] Hearsay is inadmissible

---

48. *Id.* at 597.
49. *See* Schneider *ex rel.* Schneider v. Fried, 320 F.3d 396, 404 (3rd Cir. 2003); Quiet Tech. DC-8, Inc. v. Hurel-Dubois U.K. Ltd., 326 F.3d 1333, 1340–41 (11th Cir. 2003).
50. United States v. Fama, No. 12-CR-186 (WFK), 2012 U.S. Dist. LEXIS 174887, at *10–11 (E.D.N.Y. Dec. 10, 2012) (citing Kumho Tire Co. v. Carmichael, 526 U.S. 137, 152 (1999)).
51. *E.g.,* Donaldson v. Cent. Ill. Pub. Serv. Co., 767 N.E.2d 314, 323–24 (Ill. 2002); People v. Wesley, 633 N.E.2d 451, 454 (N.Y. 1994).
52. Frye v. United States, 293 F. 1013 (D.C. Cir. 1923), *overruled by Daubert,* 509 U.S. at 589.
53. FED. R. EVID. 801(c).

as a general rule[54] but can be admissible if of a type permitted by statute or evidentiary rules.[55]

Sources of hearsay you may wish to challenge by motion in limine could include, for example, an expert's account of informal conversations he had with others to investigate an incident or industry practices,[56] a lay witness's testimony about what a doctor told the witness about his medical condition,[57] descriptions in records of medical providers of how an accident occurred,[58] or "other incident" reports maintained by a product manufacturer based on customer reports.[59]

Statement by Lay Witness with Lack of Personal Knowledge

A lay witness lacking personal knowledge of a matter may be precluded from testifying on that basis.[60] Arguing for exclusion of such testimony is easiest when the witness admits she has no personal knowledge of the matter,[61] although such an admission is not essential if other circumstances demonstrate the witness's lack of knowledge.

Demonstrative Exhibits

Photographs, videos, animations, reenactments, and exemplar products, when they are used not as substantive proof but to illustrate testimony or evidence already admitted, all fall under a category of evidence known as demonstrative exhibits. Demonstrative evidence is not substantive evidence but rather is presented for the purpose of illustrating or aiding the jury's understanding of substantive evidence, such as an expert's testimony. Case

---

54. FED. R. EVID. 802.
55. *See, e.g.*, FED. R. EVID. 803, 804 & 807.
56. *See, e.g.*, Korsak v. Atlas Hotels, Inc., 3 Cal. Rptr. 2d 833, 835–40 (Cal. Ct. App. 1992).
57. *See, e.g.*, Holt v. Olmsted Township Bd. of Trustees, 43 F. Supp. 2d 812, 819 (N.D. Ohio 1998); Brewer v. Brewer, No. M2005-02844-COA-RC-CV, 2007 Tenn. App. LEXIS 639, at *25–26 (Tenn. Ct. App. Oct. 15, 2007).
58. *See, e.g.*, Benson v. Shuler Drilling Co., 871 S.W.2d 552, 554–57 (Ark. 1994); Saul v. John D. & Catherine T. MacArthur Found., 499 So. 2d 917, 918–20 (Fla. Dist. Ct. App. 1986); Wagner v. Thomas J. Obert Enters., 396 N.W.2d 223, 227–28 (Minn. 1986).
59. *E.g.*, Wielgus v. Ryobi Techs., Inc., No. 08 CV 1597, 2012 U.S. Dist. LEXIS 98867, at *11–13 (N.D. Ill. July 17, 2012) (order granting in part and denying in part defendants' motions in limine).
60. *See* FED. R. EVID. 602.
61. *See, e.g.*, Charles v. Lizer, No. 02C-03-039 WLW, 2003 Del. Super. LEXIS 251, at *1–2 (Del. Super. Ct. July 10, 2003).

law from the relevant jurisdiction will outline when demonstrative evidence is and is not appropriate, and may even set out specific admissibility criteria for particular types of demonstrative evidence.[62]

Demonstrative exhibits can be particularly persuasive (and may be designed especially for trial with that aim[63]), so be sure to obtain and carefully review any demonstrative exhibits your opponent plans to use in advance of trial, and consider challenging your opponent's ability to use a demonstrative exhibit if it fails to conform with the applicable requirements for demonstrative exhibits. A motion in limine may target demonstrative evidence based on its lack of relevance, on its potential to mislead the jury, on an inadequate or inaccurate factual foundation for assumptions incorporated into the exhibit, on its potentially disproportionate persuasive effect, on the proponent's failure to disclose the exhibit, or on other grounds.[64] You may also ask for a limiting instruction reminding the jury that the exhibit is not substantive evidence.[65]

Do not object to an opponent's demonstrative exhibit simply because it is persuasive or shows a theory of the case at odds with your client's. Just as each party is entitled to offer expert testimony that conforms with his theory of the case and conflicts with his opponent's theory, demonstrative exhibits may illustrate the testimony or other substantive evidence supporting the party's theory and does not need to account for or incorporate an opponent's evidence or theory. However, it is appropriate to object to a demonstrative exhibit that is designed to be especially prejudicial or that is not sufficiently tied to the facts of the case. For example, in an auto accident

---

62. *See, e.g.*, Lau v. Allied Wholesale, Inc., 922 P.2d 1041, 1047–53 (Haw. Ct. App. 1996) (discussing use-dependent criteria for admissibility of videotape).

63. *See* Baugh v. Cuprum S.A. De C.V., 730 F.3d 701, 706–07 (7th Cir. 2013) (recognizing "adversarial," "persuasive," and "less neutral" nature of demonstrative exhibits as compared to exhibits admitted as substantive evidence).

64. *See, e.g.*, State v. Hall, No. M2003-02326-CCA-R3-CD, 2005 Tenn. Crim. App. LEXIS 87, at *30–36 (Tenn. Crim. App. Feb. 8, 2005); Hutchison v. Am. Family Mut. Ins. Co., 514 N.W.2d 882, 890 (Iowa 1994) (both discussing admissibility criteria for, and ultimately excluding, computer animations); Robenhorst v. Demantic Corp., No. 05 C 3192, 2008 U.S. Dist. LEXIS 30040, at *19–20 (N.D. Ill. Apr. 14, 2008) (denying plaintiff's unsupported motion to exclude two demonstrative exhibits but permitting a subsequent argument "that the benefit of the demonstrative exhibits is substantially outweighed by the danger of unfair prejudice, that the exhibits should be excluded due to lack of foundation, or that their use should be limited to a specific purpose and the jury provided with a limiting instruction").

65. *See Robenhorst*, 2008 U.S. Dist. LEXIS 30040, at *20.

case, one of the authors successfully moved to exclude an opponent's animation that depicted pitch-black light conditions very different from the morning light witnesses consistently described, depicted a vehicle driving across a street that all witnesses agreed it turned onto, and included a foreboding soundtrack not illustrative of any fact in evidence.

Convictions or Citations

Evidence of a person's prior or subsequent convictions or bad acts can be "highly prejudicial,"[66] and for that reason, such evidence is a frequent subject of motions in limine.[67] Admissibility will depend upon a number of factors, such as the purpose for which the evidence is offered, the timing of the convictions in relationship to the occurrence at issue in the present trial, the similarity of the prior and present acts, and the probative value versus prejudicial effect of the evidence.[68]

Evidence that a party or non-party was or was not cited in connection with an incident is also a common subject of motions in limine. For example, in a civil action related to a motor vehicle collision, a party who received a traffic citation in connection with the same incident may move to exclude evidence of the citation.[69] Sometimes statutes, in addition to case law, address the admissibility of citations.

Accident Causation Conclusions by Investigating Officer

Jurisdictions differ on whether and when an investigating officer's opinion on what or who caused an accident is admissible.[70] Due to the weight a jury may accord such testimony, a party may wish to use a motion in limine to

---

66. Cappara v. Schibley, 709 N.E.2d 117, 119–20 (Ohio 1999).
67. *See* State v. Pitt, 352 Ore. 566, 573 (Or. 2012).
68. *See, e.g.*, State v. Garrett, 248 P.3d 965, 967–70 (Or. 2011); State v. Mattatall, 603 A.2d 1098, 1116–18 (R.I. 1991); Dyce v. State, 582 A.2d 582, 584–86 (Md. Ct. Spec. App. 1990).
69. *E.g.*, Nixon v. Chapman, 288 S.W.3d 266, 267–68 (Ark. Ct. App. 2008).
70. *Compare* Peterson v. Foley, 931 N.E.2d 478, 482–84 (Mass. App. Ct. 2010) (holding trial court erred in admitting officer opinion on cause of accident), *and* Johnston v. Lynch, 574 A.2d 934, 939–40 (N.H. 1990) (holding trial court properly excluded investigating officer's opinions on fault and on manner and cause of collision), *and* Talley v. Tri-State Waste Solutions, Inc., No. 05C-08-311-PLA, 2007 Del. Super. LEXIS 570, at *1–7 (Del. Super. Ct. June 26, 2008) (excluding officer testimony as to "primary contributing circumstance" of collision), *with* Fortner v. Town of Register, 657 S.E.2d 620, 622–23 (Ga. Ct. App. 2008) (holding officer may testify as to which driver caused accident but not on ultimate issue of a party's negligence).

seek exclusion of such causation testimony by an officer designated as a trial witness. Related questions of whether an officer possesses the necessary qualifications or knowledge of the facts to testify about how an accident occurred[71] may also be addressed by motion in limine.

Tests and Experiments

Case law will set forth a jurisdiction's admissibility requirements for evidence of a test or experiment.[72] The criteria for admitting evidence of a test or experiment may depend upon the purpose for which it is introduced. The admissibility of experiment-based testimony is also connected to the qualifications and methodology used by the expert who conducted the experiment.[73] Whether an experiment conducted by one party's expert has satisfied the criteria necessary for testimony or other evidence of the experiment to be admissible is a subject the opposing party may wish to address ahead of trial via motion in limine. This allows for a more detailed explanation of why the evidence is inadmissible, which can be critical if the experiment or the explanation of why it is objectionable is particularly technical or complicated. It also gives the judge time to understand and weigh the arguments and to inform the parties of her initial determination before trial.

Other Occurrences

In a product liability, premises liability, or other negligence action, the plaintiff may wish to introduce evidence of other accidents as proof that a product or condition was dangerous or that the defendant had notice of the alleged danger. Similarly, the defendant may wish to introduce evidence of a lack of other occurrences as proof of a lack of danger or of notice. When such evidence is and is not admissible may vary depending on the jurisdiction and on the purpose for which the evidence is introduced,[74] but many

---

71. *See, e.g.*, Scott v. Yates, 643 N.E.2d 105, 106–07 (Ohio 1994).
72. *E.g.*, Pannu v. Land Rover N. Am., Inc., 120 Cal. Rptr. 3d 605, 622 (Cal. Ct. App. 2011); First Midwest Trust Co. v. Rogers, 701 N.E.2d 1107, 1113–14 (Ill. App. Ct. 1998).
73. *See, e.g.*, State v. Calise, 2012-Ohio-4797, at ¶ 9–25 (Ohio Ct. App. Oct. 17, 2012).
74. *See, e.g.*, Turgeon v. Commonwealth Edison Co., 630 N.E.2d 1318, 1322–23 (Ill. App. Ct. 1994) (describing different criteria for other occurrence evidence to be admissible in premises liability case, depending on purpose for which it is offered).

jurisdictions require a showing of "substantial similarity" as a prerequisite to admitting such evidence.[75] Challenges to other occurrence evidence on grounds of insufficient similarity are frequently made before trial via motion in limine.[76] This affords the parties an opportunity to prepare detailed arguments about which occurrences or products are sufficiently similar to be admissible and which are not and gives the judge time to consider the issue and make an informed preliminary decision before trial.

Subsequent Remedial Measures
A change made after an accident that would have made the accident less likely to occur had it preceded the accident is commonly referred to as a subsequent remedial measure. A subsequent remedial measure could include a product modification, the addition of a warning, or the termination or additional training of an employee involved in an accident. Evidentiary rules[77] and case law[78] limit the admissibility of evidence of subsequent remedial measures, depending upon the purpose for which such evidence is offered and, sometimes, upon the nature of the claims asserted.[79]

Speculative Damages
Depending upon the jurisdiction, damages must be reasonably certain[80] or more likely than not[81] to be recoverable. In a personal injury case, for example, testimony predicting future consequences of a plaintiff's current injury will be admissible only insofar as the potential consequences iden-

---

75. *E.g.*, Walden v. Dep't of Transp., 27 P.3d 297, 303 (Alaska 2001); Claveloux v. Downtown Racquet Club Assocs., 717 A.2d 1205, 1207–08 (Conn. 1998); Farrell v. John Deere Co., 443 N.W.2d 50, 61–63 (Wis. Ct. App. 1989).
76. *E.g.*, Blevins v. New Holland N. Am., Inc., 128 F. Supp. 952, 954, 960–61 (W.D. Va. 2001) (order granting motion in limine to exclude evidence of other hay baler accidents).
77. *E.g.*, FED. R. EVID. 407.
78. *E.g.*, Precise Eng'g, Inc. v. LaCombe, 624 So. 2d 1339, 1341 (Ala. 1993); Robles v. Shoreside Petroleum, Inc., 29 P.3d 838, 845 (Alaska 2001); Duckett v. Mausness, 546 N.E.2d 1292, 1293–94 (Ind. Ct. App. 1989).
79. *See* Forma Scientific, Inc. v. Biosera, Inc., 960 P.2d 108, 111–18 (Colo. 1998) (holding evidentiary rule limiting admissibility of subsequent remedial measures inapplicable in design defect case premised on strict liability); Scott v. Dutton-Lainson Co., 774 N.W.2d 501, 503–08 (Iowa 2009) (distinguishing between product liability theories for purposes of applicability of rule limiting admissibility of subsequent remedial measures).
80. *See, e.g.*, Marzullo v. J.D. Pavement Maint., 975 N.E.2d 1, 6–7 (Ohio Ct. App. 2011).
81. *See, e.g.*, Davidson v. Miller, 344 A.2d 422, 427–28 (Md. 1975).

tified are sufficiently probable.[82] If some damages asserted are speculative, a motion in limine could be used to limit evidence of damages at trial to reasonably certain damages.

Evidence of Settlement Offers and/or Insurance Coverage

Parties frequently move to exclude any evidence or mention at trial of settlement offers or communications[83] and/or of insurance coverage.[84] For cases in federal court, Federal Rule of Evidence 408 bars evidence of compromise offers and negotiations when offered for certain purposes, including as proof of the validity or invalidity of a legal claim.[85] Evidence of liability insurance coverage may be prejudicial to a defendant,[86] and Rule 411 bars "[e]vidence that a person was or was not insured against liability" when offered "to prove whether the person acted negligently or otherwise wrongfully."[87] A plaintiff may wish to exclude evidence that a collateral source, such as medical insurance, covered a portion of medical bills incurred as a result of a defendant's tort.[88] States recognizing a "collateral source rule" by common law or statute differ on what evidence is admissible versus inadmissible. If these are issues in your case, check your jurisdiction's rules.

---

82. *See id.*
83. *See, e.g.,* Brand Mktg. Group, LLC v. Interek Testing Servs. NA, No. 12cv1572, 2013 U.S. Dist. LEXIS 10299, at *19–23 (W.D. Pa. July 23, 2013) (granting motion to exclude settlement agreement under Fed. R. Evid. 408); United States v. St. Bernard Parish, No. 12-321, 2013 U.S. Dist. LEXIS 64918, at *9 (E.D. La. May 7, 2013) (granting motion in limine to exclude settlement evidence on grounds of irrelevance and the danger of juror confusion).
84. *See, e.g.,* Lee v. Small, 829 F. Supp. 2d 728, 740 (N.D. Iowa 2011) (granting parties' cross motions to exclude evidence of liability insurance coverage or lack thereof, as "evidence of the existence or lack of insurance coverage is generally inadmissible"); Riano v. Heritage Corp., 665 So. 2d 1142, 1143 (Fla. Dist. Ct. App. 1996) (declining to review trial court's interlocutory order granting motion in limine to preclude testimony regarding insurance coverage on grounds that insurance coverage was collateral issue).
85. Fed. R. Evid. 408.
86. *See, e.g.,* Arnold v. Eastern Air Lines, 712 F.2d 899, 906–07 (4th Cir. 1983).
87. Fed. R. Evid. 411.
88. *See, e.g.,* Barnes v. Commerce & Indus. Ins. Co., No. 11-0041, 2013 U.S. Dist. LEXIS 165660, at *1–7 (W.D. La. Nov. 20, 2013) (explaining Louisiana's collateral source rule and granting the plaintiffs' motion in limine to exclude evidence of their health insurance and disability insurance policies).

Unfairly Prejudicial Evidence

Even otherwise admissible evidence may be excluded if its probative value is substantially outweighed by the danger of unfair prejudice, confusing the issues, or misleading the jury.[89] A motion in limine may be used to seek exclusion of otherwise admissible but "intensely prejudicial" evidence that threatens to become the focus of trial despite its remote relevance.[90]

Prioritizing Evidentiary Issues

These categories are merely examples of the kinds of evidence that might be addressed ahead of trial by motions in limine. If evidence could be the subject of a trial objection, it could also be the subject of a motion in limine.

However, you will want to be selective about the evidence to target with a motion in limine. For one thing, time constraints before trial—including the time it will take to respond to your opponent's pre-trial motions—make it impossible to cover all of your anticipated evidentiary objections by motion. Give thought to which issues are most important to you and which will require more detailed explanation or a pre-trial hearing.

Another important consideration is the strength of the legal authority in support of your position. Courts are reluctant to decide evidentiary issues ahead of trial under the rationale that "questions of foundation, relevancy and potential prejudice may be resolved in proper context" at trial, and "a court is almost always better situated during the actual trial to assess the value and utility of evidence."[91] Consequently, the evidentiary motions most likely to be granted before trial are those with the strongest, clearest legal authority for the evidentiary ruling requested. Not only will motions with a thin legal foundation likely be denied or a decision deferred until trial, but motions without adequate support could harm your credibility with the court.

---

89. FED. R. EVID. 403.
90. *E.g.*, Haralampopoulos *ex rel.* Haralampopoulos v. Kelly, No. 10CA0668, 2011 Colo. App. LEXIS 1645, at *2–3, 31–35 (Colo. App. Oct. 13, 2011) (holding trial court erred in admitting "intensely prejudicial" evidence of plaintiff's alleged cocaine use more than a decade prior to incident at issue in case).
91. Morford v. Wal-Mart Stores, Inc., No. 2:09-cv-02251-RLH-PAL, 2011 U.S. Dist. LEXIS 61650, at *10 (D. Nev. June 9, 2011) (quoting Hawthorne Partners v. AT&T Techs., Inc., 831 F. Supp. 1398, 1400 (N.D. Ill. 1993); Wilkins v. K-Mart Corp., 487 F. Supp. 2d 1216, 1219 (D. Kan. 2007)).

Determining the Appropriate Type of Motion in Limine
There are several styles of motion in limine. They are described briefly here.

The General Motion in Limine
The general motion in limine style is sometimes referred to as a "string" or "omnibus" motion in limine. The motion addresses numerous unrelated types of evidence in a single motion, with a very brief description of each item of evidence and of the applicable authorities for excluding or admitting it. In courts that allow great latitude in the filing of motions in limine, general motions in limine are a very effective way to set some additional ground rules for the trial. Given the quantity and nature of the issues raised, the court will likely ask the parties to meet and confer to see if agreement can be reached as to the issues raised. The court will then hear argument and rule on the remaining issues. Oral argument is usually very brief, but the court may request more complete briefings on an issue that is more complicated. Because general motions in limine, and the court hearings that follow, resolve so many evidentiary objections before trial, they allow the trial to run more efficiently.

The Issue-, Witness-, or Document-Specific Motion in Limine
While the general motions in limine discussed above may be useful in helping to set the generalized ground rules for *voir dire* and trial, motions in limine specific to a single issue, a single witness, or a single document or document category can be used to address an evidentiary argument in greater detail. An issue-specific motion should be fully briefed, including the same caliber of legal analysis as would be expected in a motion for summary judgment. Response and reply briefs should be filed when allowed by the court.

In determining the length and complexity of the argument presented in the motion, brevity is often the rule of the day. On the eve of trial, judges are dealing with the logistics of trying the case, which can include shuffling other hearings, obtaining a jury pool, holding settlement conferences, and any number of other logistical matters. On top of these issues, a court could have upwards of 20 motions in limine to review prior to holding hearings and ruling on the motions. Thus, it is often best to keep motions in limine as succinct as possible so as to assist the court in getting to the heart of each issue. That said, a motion must give the court enough factual background and legal authority to understand the specific evidence in question and to make a pre-trial determination on its admissibility.

Review the local rules or the court's pre-trial order to determine if there will be oral argument on the motions and prepare accordingly. If the issue of oral argument is not addressed in either, contact the court's clerk or inquire of the judge at the final pre-trial conference.

The Daubert or Frye Motion

A motion challenging the admissibility of expert witness testimony on grounds such as reliability or methodology, or challenging the admissibility of a novel scientific technique or theory, would be brought under the *Daubert* or *Frye* standard applicable in the jurisdiction where your case is pending. In many ways this resembles an issue- or witness-specific motion. However, the motion should emphasize the applicable standard for admissibility and the court's gatekeeping function, and—in the case of complicated technical or scientific evidence—must explain in lay terms the background necessary for the court to understand what the evidence is and why it is objectionable or admissible. If the complexity of the issue warrants additional explanation, the motion might include a supporting affidavit from an expert in the field who can attest to, for example, the reason a methodology is flawed or the fact that a new technique or theory has not yet gained acceptance in the relevant field. And the motion might request a court hearing on the subject, at which both parties would have an opportunity to offer evidence, including expert testimony, in support of the admissibility or inadmissibility of the evidence.

The Permissive Motion in Limine

The most common use of a motion in limine is the prohibitive variety—a motion that seeks to exclude evidence. However, "permissive" motions in limine may be used to advocate for the admissibility of certain evidence. Unlike the more traditional prohibitive motions seeking to exclude evidence, the permissive motion requests a pre-trial determination that certain evidence will be admitted at trial. This could include, for example, a motion to take jurors to view an accident location or a facility where a plaintiff worked, or a motion to admit specific evidence for a particular purpose.

Drafting the Motion

Once you have identified the evidence on which your motion in limine will focus, researched the jurisdiction-specific evidentiary rules and case law governing the admissibility of that evidence, and determined the type of motion in limine you are writing, you are ready to draft your motion. The advice in this section assumes you are writing an issue- or witness-specific motion in limine, the most common type.

Structure Your Motion Effectively

The rules and prevailing practices in your jurisdiction will affect the format of your motion. In some jurisdictions, the motion is very brief—perhaps a page—and is limited to a short description of the evidence to be excluded and the rule supporting its exclusion. A separately titled memorandum in support accompanies the motion and contains all the factual grounds and legal authority supporting the motion. In other jurisdictions, both the request for exclusion and all the factual and legal support are contained in a single document titled as a motion.

Under either format, the very first text the judge reads after the case caption and document title should be a strong one-page summary that identifies the evidence you are targeting, describes the rule of evidence and/or common law rule governing the admissibility or exclusion of that type of evidence, and explains why application of that rule requires exclusion of the evidence. This summary will be your entire motion, if your jurisdiction calls for factual and legal grounds to be set forth in a separate memorandum, and it will be under the heading "Introduction" if your motion and support are to be filed as a single document.

The body of the motion—or memorandum in support—should contain two main sections. First, a factual background section should set forth, in as concise a manner as possible, the factual background necessary to put the evidence in context and to understand the arguments for or against its admissibility. Motions in limine are often a judge's first detailed look at a case. Although you have been living with the case for years, the judge has not. Include basic background on the incident giving rise to the legal action and a concise summary of the nature of the parties' claims or theories of events, as well as details necessary to understand the content and context of the specific evidence in question. Do this as briefly as possible while still giving the judge the information that a person heretofore unfamiliar with your case and evidentiary concerns would need to understand and make a preliminary ruling on the admissibility of the evidence that is the subject of your motion.

A legal argument section should follow the background section. The structure of the legal argument section of a motion in limine resembles the structure of a legal argument section of a summary judgment motion. You may wish to begin this with a brief summary of the jurisdiction's favorable language on motions in limine or with the jurisdiction's criteria for granting a motion in limine prior to trial. If you are filing a *Daubert* or *Frye* motion, the legal argument section should begin with a brief summary of the applicable standard. Then, under separate headings for each legal argument if your motion advances more than one theory of inadmissibility, set forth the legal authority in support of your argument, including applicable rules of evidence and case law that is on-point. If there is conflicting authority, be sure to distinguish unfavorable case law.

End your motion with a conclusion repeating your specific request for court action: identify the evidence and the ruling you wish the court to make and, if applicable, whether you are seeking a *Daubert* or *Frye* hearing or other hearing or opportunity for oral argument.

Precisely Identify the Evidence You Are Targeting

A concise, precise summary of the exact evidence you want the court to rule on should be included at the outset of the motion. Courts cannot rule on the admissibility of evidence they cannot identify, and a judge will deny or defer a ruling on a motion that fails to adequately specify the evidence at which it is aimed.[92]

---

92. *See, e.g.*, Gracia v. Volvo Europa Truck, N.V., No. 87 C 10005, 1996 U.S. Dist. LEXIS 3372, at *29–32 (N.D. Ill. Mar. 21, 1996).

Stick to Your Best Arguments

One common mistake is to throw every possible argument for the exclusion of a particular piece of evidence into your motion. Not only will this make your motion much longer than necessary, but it will also draw attention away from—and thereby weaken—your best argument for exclusion. Focus on your primary argument and resist the urge to list more, but much weaker, reasons for the judge to rule in your favor.

Know Your Audience

Your motion will turn out best if you always keep your audience in mind while you draft it. Your motion is addressed to a busy trial judge largely unfamiliar with your case. Accordingly, do not dwell on details unrelated to the issue addressed in your motion, but also do not omit any information critical to an informed decision on the admissibility of the evidence that is the subject of the motion. The trial judge may be reluctant to decide an evidentiary issue before trial for reasons summarized in a recent Oregon case.[93] Your goal is to demonstrate why the evidence is clearly inadmissible[94] (or admissible, if you are writing a permissive motion) such that a pre-trial determination is appropriate.

Invest in Your Writing

Writing the motion should not be an afterthought. If you have identified certain evidence as so critical that it is worthy of a motion explaining why it should be excluded or admitted, take the time and use the tools to make your argument as effective as it can be.

---

93. *See* State v. Pitt, 352 Ore. 566, 573 (Or. 2012), explaining:
    > A challenge during trial to an offer of evidence provides greater context for the trial judge to assess issues concerning the admissibility of the proffered evidence in light of what has occurred in the course of the trial. In contrast, a trial judge ruling on a motion *in limine* must rely on the parties' representations and arguments about what they expect the evidence, including the challenged evidence, will demonstrate during trial. Those representations and arguments can be hypothetical and abstract. Moreover, as trial progresses, new circumstances may arise that directly or indirectly alter the admissibility or evidentiary value of certain pieces of evidence.

94. *See* Jonasson v. Lutheran Child & Family Servs., 115 F.3d 436, 440 (7th Cir. 1997).

Numerous books focus on good writing and persuasive argument. Several favorites in the legal writing category are Richard C. Wydick's *Plain English for Lawyers*,[95] Steven D. Stark's *Writing to Win*,[96] and Bryan A. Garner's *The Winning Brief*.[97] Resources such as these can help you distill arguments to their essence and convey them efficiently and persuasively. Find a good editor among your colleagues to help you polish your motions and to ensure that your arguments make sense to someone unfamiliar with your case.

After You File: Judge's Ruling and Preserving Issues for Appeal

Once you file a motion in limine, the judge has several options for ruling on the motion. He may grant the motion, determining ahead of trial that the evidence will be excluded (or, in the case of a permissive motion in limine, that the evidence will be admitted) at trial. The judge may deny the motion, overruling your objection to evidence (or disallowing its admission, in the case of a permissive motion). Or the judge may defer a ruling on the motion until trial, necessitating objection to the evidence as it is presented.[98]

When a motion is granted or denied, a written order should be entered memorializing the court's decision. If opposing counsel violates the order on a motion in limine, object to the evidence immediately and present the relevant order. Depending upon the nature of opposing counsel's actions, the court may instruct jurors to disregard the evidence, sanction the offending attorney, declare a mistrial, or take any other remedial actions necessary to address the violation.[99]

While motions in limine can be very useful in obtaining pre-trial guidance on the admissibility of evidence, you should keep in mind that the judge is not bound by such pre-trial determinations and may reconsider the admissibility of evidence during trial.[100]

Many jurisdictions require a formal objection to be made during trial to evidence that was the subject of a previously decided motion in limine

---

95. 5th ed. 2005.
96. 2d ed. 2012.
97. 2d ed. 2004.
98. *Massengale v. State*, 894 S.W.2d 594, 595 (Ark. 1995).
99. *See* Susan E. Loggins, *Motions in Limine, in* 2 LITIGATING TORT CASES § 19:37.
100. *See* Luce v. United States, 469 U.S. 38, 41–42 (1984); Geuder v. State, 115 S.W.3d 11, 15 (Tex. Crim. App. 2003).

in order to preserve the evidentiary issue for appeal.[101] Be sure to know the law on this issue in your jurisdiction prior to trial so that important evidentiary issues are preserved for appeal, if necessary.[102] Likewise, your pre-trial motion in limine setting forth your arguments for the admissibility or inadmissibility of particular evidence may not be part of the record on appeal unless you renew the motion during trial or otherwise reference it as you orally object to evidence.

Summary

In assembling the trial record, you are assembling the building blocks of your case. With your pre-trial evidentiary objections, you are attempting to weaken your opponent's case and to clarify the scope of trial to better focus your preparation. Those who take full advantage of these tools will enjoy the advantage heading into trial. The trial lawyer should remain closely involved in these steps and avoid over-delegation of the work to paralegals or junior associates. Mastering the trial record and the rules of evidence will make you a more effective advocate at trial.

---

101. *See, e.g.*, Hunt v. CIT Group, No. 03-09-00046-CV, 2010 Tex. App. LEXIS 2767, at *17 (Tex. App. Apr. 15, 2010) (quoting Kauffman v. Comm'n for Lawyer Discipline, 197 S.W.3d 867, 873 (Tex. App. 2006) for proposition that trial court's ruling on motion in limine "preserves nothing for review"); Quad City Bank & Trust v. Jim Kircher & Assocs., P.C., 804 N.W.2d 83, 89–90 (Iowa 2011) (explaining general rule that trial court's ruling on motion in limine does not preserve evidentiary issue for appeal and that issue is waived on appeal without timely objection at trial when evidence is offered).
102. *See* Annot., 76 A.L.R. Fed. 619 (1986).

Chapter 5

The Basic Science and Art of Trial Objections

J. Todd Spurgeon

And yet there is not a more fatal error to young lawyers than relying too much on speech-making. If any one, upon his rare powers of speaking, shall claim an exemption from the drudgery of the law, his case is a failure in advance.
—Abraham Lincoln, notes for a lecture, July 1, 1850

Many times when non-lawyers think of a trial, they usually envision the dramatic portrayals seen on television and in the movies. Those scenarios often play out in the stereotypical manner and include the obligatory "I object!" Most often these boisterous objections are immediately sustained or overruled and end with the objector either proudly sitting down having conquered the opponent's attempted injustice or sheepishly retreating having been dealt a devastating, humiliating blow.

As anyone who has seen an actual trial will attest, reality is much more mundane and technical. A lawyer learning to try a case must learn the science and art of objecting. Knowing the what, when, why, and how of trial objections can have a drastic, if not dramatic, effect on the outcome of a case. What follows is not intended to be an exhaustive list of trial objections (some examples are included in the appendix to this chapter). Rather, this chapter is designed as a reference for an attorney trying that first case, focusing on the how and why of lodging objections at trial, as well as how to respond properly to objections raised by opposing counsel. Those skills are an essential part of any trial attorney's tool kit.

Preliminary Thoughts—The Purpose of Objections

As a younger attorney, I was advised by my mentors that everything I did at trial—including every question I asked and every exhibit I introduced—had to have a purpose. If something did not fit that purpose, I should seriously reconsider whether it needed to be part of my trial presentation. I have carried that bit of advice with me throughout my career, and it has served me well. That reasoning is easy to apply to an exhibit or line of questioning. But what about objections? What purpose do they serve at trial?

Trial objections are not part of our system of justice simply to add drama to an otherwise mundane trial process. Objections serve a crucial role as a multipurpose tool that can alter the course of a trial or even determine a subsequent appeal. Learning the art and science of trial objections is essential to becoming a good trial lawyer. Like a Swiss army knife on a camping trip, the tool of trial objection skills is helpful in countless situations.

Objections serve many purposes at trial. Their primary function is, of course, to bring error to the judge's attention so that it can be prevented or remedied at the earliest opportunity. Similarly, objections serve to preserve arguments for appeal (if done properly). Using objections in this technical manner is the science of trial objections.

Trial objections also serve less technical, more artful purposes. This includes advancing your trial strategy by preventing harmful or unfavorable evidence from reaching the jury or by getting a point across to the jury. Objections can also serve tactical purposes. More seasoned attorneys will often use objections to test younger adversaries by attempting to disrupt the rhythm of an opening statement or to break up the flow of a crushing cross-examination. Objections can be used to rattle an opponent, disrupt an opponent's flow, or shift the focus away from a particularly damaging witness or evidence. If successful, this can be disruptive or even devastating to an opponent's case. If not, one runs the risk of being seen by the jury as a bully or as someone desperate to shift the focus away from some problem in the case. None of this is meant to suggest frivolously objecting for no reason, but simply to reinforce the multipurpose nature of objections.

Mastering the art of trial objections also requires knowing when *not* to make an objection. Realizing when to keep the gun holstered is a key trial skill with which many young lawyers struggle. Sometimes it is better to let something objectionable go. Opposing counsel may be asking your client an objectionable question, but maybe the answer to that question is one that you could not properly elicit from your client. In addition, you do not want to flood the court with objections. A judge may grow weary of nickel-and-dime objections that serve no real purpose and that are easily overcome with a mere rephrasing of a simple question. A jury may grow just as annoyed. Knowing when to use objections and when not to is just as important as to learn as knowing which objections to use.

A key part in successfully trying your first case is realizing there is an art and science to making, and meeting, trial objections. The following are a few points to keep in mind before and during your first trial.

Know *Why* You Are Objecting

Do not object just to object, and do not object just because something is objectionable. As stated above, you should always have a purpose in everything you do at trial. Each exhibit, each witness, each question should be another step down that path toward your goal of a verdict in your client's favor. Anything that does not lead down that path just wastes time or—worse yet—could lead to defeat.

Knowing why you are objecting is more important than knowing how to object, knowing when to object, or knowing how to respond after an objection. If you know the ultimate purpose of your objection, the rest of the trial objection skills are more likely to fall in line.

Therefore, there is no need to take the court's and jury's time to object merely because a harmless question was poorly phrased or the exact foundation was not laid to authenticate a photograph of the scene. An objection should fit in the general scheme of your trial strategy. It should be another step toward your ultimate goal. If it is not, you need to ask yourself whether you really need to make that objection, no matter how well made or timely it may be.

Making a Proper Objection

Once you know why you are objecting, making a proper objection is critical. This is a skill that must be mastered before that first trial. Failing to make a proper objection can lead to the admission of harmful or erroneous evidence and lost opportunities for appeal.

Imagine yourself defending your first personal injury trial arising from an automobile accident. Plaintiff's counsel asks his client, "John, what did your doctor tell you at that first visit about your injuries and what caused them?"

Evidence 101 tells you that counsel's question asks for hearsay. Counsel is asking his client to tell the jury what his doctor told him (an out of court statement) and is in all likelihood attempting to use it for the truth of the matter asserted (that the accident caused the claimed injuries). In those few seconds that it took counsel to ask the question, you have realized the question is not proper. Now, before John answers, you have to figure out why it was improper and get the objection out of your mouth as you rise to address the court. However, that objection must be made properly, or it will all be for naught, and that jury will hear that a doctor has related the injuries to the accident.

In most courts, simply stating "I object" is insufficient to accomplish anything. Such a statement will usually be met with a judge questioning why you are objecting, or you may fall victim to an immediate overruling in front of the jury. If the goal is truly to have the error addressed, a proper objection must be made.

There are three elements of a proper objection: (1) the objection, (2) the basis, and (3) the explanation. First, you must state your objection. Second, you must give the legal basis for your objection, that is, what rule the challenged material violates. Finally, you must explain why the challenged material violates that rule. Here is sample objection to the example scenario:

Objection, Your Honor. The question calls for hearsay. Counsel is asking the witness to relate what he was told by his doctor to establish the truth of what he claims he was told.

Simply stating, "Objection, calls for hearsay," does not constitute a complete objection—although it has a better chance of being sustained if the judge is following along and is on the same page as the objector.

All three elements of the objection must be used to make the objection properly and, more importantly, to preserve any error for appeal. Using all three elements makes it easier for the judge to sustain your objection, and the easier it is to sustain, the more likely it is the objection will be successful. The objection itself stops the proceedings and allows you a chance to make your argument. Sharing the basis of the objection alerts the judge as to why you are objecting. The explanation tells the judge why you are right, and why she should sustain your objection.[1]

Knowing how to lodge a proper objection is one of the few trial skills you can master before you try your first case. (And doing so will free you of one more worry going into your first trial.) Surprisingly, however, many veteran attorneys either have not learned this skill or have forgotten it. If you have this skill down before your first trial, you already have a leg up. The judge, and jury, will appreciate it as well.

Making a Timely Objection

Timing is everything. Object too soon, and you can look silly in front of the jury. Object too late, after the cat is out of the bag, and you may have waived an error (and by the action of objecting emphasized the importance of the testimony). Knowing when to object is just as important as knowing how to do so.

---

1. Of course, you should discuss with the trial judge, preferably at the pre-trial conference, the judge's particular preference for stating objections during witness examination. Some judges do not allow "speaking objections," particularly in front of the jury. In that case, you may need to call for a sidebar to state the objection properly.

Obviously, making the objection before the challenged information gets in front of the jury is the goal. Being timely and preventing an unwanted elephant from entering the room is a lot easier than asking the jury to ignore that elephant they just saw. However, you have only, at most, a few seconds to hear the question, decide whether it is objectionable, formulate your objection, and rise to voice your objection. You want to make sure the jury is not exposed to the objectionable evidence or statements. If you are objecting to a question being asked by counsel, making the objection before the witness can answer the question is critical. Although making an objection too soon may make you look a bit silly when opposing counsel explains to the judge that where he was going with the question was not quite where you thought it was, that is usually a better result than trying to "unring the bell." It is a fine balance to learn. However, the key to remember is that it is better to object too soon than too late.[2]

The task becomes a bit more complicated when the objectionable material is contained in the answer to a perfectly proper question. What do you do now? This is when you have to figure out a way to get the jury to forget that elephant in the room or a way to have the judge tell them to ignore the elephant. There are a couple of options when a witness blurts out an objectionable answer.

First, of course, you must object as soon as possible. From there, you can treat it as a typical objection, putting your objection on the record in front of the jury. Sometimes, however, you may not want the jury to know why that answer they just heard was so improper or damaging to your case. Learning when to ask to approach to make your objection is another aspect of the art and science of making objections. Certainly, the procedures to be used when approaching the bench will vary from judge to judge, but there are times when making an objection to the judge, out of the hearing of the jury, is the more effective way to go about correcting

---

2. Anticipation is key. Consider what objectionable testimony the witness may offer before he takes the stand. Game plan how the testimony may develop. When one of your prepared scenarios starts to unfold, you pounce. Similarly, if you anticipate that you may have a problem with the admissibility of a witness's expected testimony, bring that to the judge's attention at a break before the witness takes the stand. Highlight the issue and you will be more likely to get a thoughtful ruling when you rise to make your objection. Perhaps the very act of airing the potential objection will lead opposing counsel away from the objectionable matter.

an objectionable answer blurted out by a witness. Usually, simply rising and asking to approach is an acceptable way to bring up the objection. Counsel can then approach the bench and make their arguments on the objection. The jury is none the wiser as to why that last answer was out of order, or, more importantly, why it may have been so harmful to your case. For example, they will not know that it was you who filed that motion in limine to keep that information from them.

If the judge sustains your objection, your work is not yet over. The testimony has been given and is on the record. If the judge does not *sua sponte* strike the offending testimony from the record and instruct the jury to disregard it, then you must make a motion to do so. *See infra.*

As opposed to knowing how to make an objection, properly timing your objections is a skill that cannot be mastered without trial experience. Although depositions can provide valuable practice time, they are not a perfect substitute for the flow and dynamics of a trial. However, going into your first trial armed with the basic premises of timing your objections gives you a better opportunity for a more successful outcome.

After the Objection

In the few seconds allotted you by counsel's question, you have figured out why you are objecting and delivered a perfectly phrased and timed objection. Now what? There are generally three options for a judge when faced with an objection: sustain it, overrule it, or take it under advisement. When your objection is sustained, no response on your part is needed. Simply sit down at the counsel table and continue with the trial. There is no need to thank the judge. The judge is following the law, not doing you a favor. For countless reasons, obviously, no retort to opposing counsel is needed. Although having a hard-fought objection sustained can make you feel like rubbing it in a bit, gloating is the last thing you want to do. Remember, the jurors are always watching. Presenting a calm, focused demeanor is critical. You do not want to give the jury any reason to question your professionalism. Act as if the result is exactly what you thought it would be and exactly what it should have been.

A measured reaction is also best when your objection is overruled. The last thing the judge or jury needs to see is a whiny or sulking lawyer at counsel table. Opposing counsel will also be emboldened if your reaction is anything but a calm, measured acceptance of the ruling. You do not want counsel to think you are easily flustered or brought to anger. It is fine to feel that way on the inside. However, as is the case with most jury trial tactics, portraying a professional demeanor to the judge and jury is crucial.

You must keep focus following a ruling on an objection. If your objection is sustained, the likely response by opposing counsel is an immediate attempt to get the challenged evidence or challenged testimony in through another means or through a slightly rephrased question. If you are gloating or enjoying your successful objection, the challenged, yet rephrased, question could fly right into evidence without your noticing. If you are pouting after being overruled, your opponent will likely be hammering away with additional questions and evidence of the same variety to which you objected, while you are busy sulking. Even if you are right with your objection, you have now waived that issue by failing to object to the follow-up questions as well. (*See infra.*)

Many times the sustaining or overruling of an objection is not the end of the exercise. One of the most difficult aspects of trial objections is knowing what to do once your objection is overruled or sustained. Knowing what to do if counsel continues to offer up similar objectionable evidence, when to make an offer of proof, and when to ask the judge to admonish the jury are just a few of the nuances that young trial lawyers need to be aware of to successfully try that first case.

The Continuing Objection

If you are overruled and opposing counsel continues to attempt to introduce the same or similar evidence that you find objectionable, you have a couple of options. First, you can simply object each time. Alternatively, you can ask to lodge a continuing objection. Many jurisdictions will allow continuing objections, so long as the judge had been apprised of the alleged error and has had an opportunity to alleviate that error. (The Federal Rules of Evidence state that once a court has definitively ruled on an objection on the record, a continuing or renewed objection is not needed.)

Preserving objections to repeated attempts to introduce evidence you find objectionable must be done carefully, so as not to waive any appealable error. A continuing objection allows the flow of the trial to continue and does not force you to waste your time, or the court's time, repeatedly objecting and being overruled in front of the jury. In the case of the continuing objection, always request the judge to note your continuing objection on the record, and make sure it is a proper objection, as discussed above. Then, when the challenged exhibits arise, simply remain silent. If asked by the judge, simply note your previous continuing objection. If the judge does not recognize the continuing objection, then you have no choice: you must object each time the evidence is offered.

The Offer of Proof

Suppose opposing counsel successfully objected to the admission of your expert's opinion or the eyewitness testimony of that witness that came forward at the last minute. What do you do now? If you want to appeal the exclusion of that evidence, often you will need to inform the trial court, and ultimately an appellate court, as to what that evidence would have been. Sometimes, the objection is not enough, and an offer of proof is required. An offer of proof allows you to get the proffered evidence into the record, outside the presence of the jury. This gives the trial court the opportunity to hear the specific proposed evidence, gives the judge a chance to change the ruling, and creates a record for any appellate court reviewing the case. Without an offer of proof placing the opinion in the record, any appellate courts will not have a basis upon which to reverse the evidentiary ruling.

- **Content:** An offer of proof must be sufficiently specific to allow the trial court to determine whether the evidence is admissible and to allow an appellate court adequate review of the trial court's ruling. Sometimes a summary of the anticipated evidence will be sufficient; in other cases more is required. The offer must also be made on the record to preserve any error.
- **Timing:** This is generally up to the trial judge. However, the sooner the better is generally the best course of action. Of course, you will make the offer outside the presence of the jury.

- **Tips:** Procedures and requirements for offers of proof are found in Federal Rule of Evidence 103 and its state counterparts. Additionally, if you know that exclusion of certain evidence is possible, be prepared ahead of time with an offer of proof. You can put it in writing and attach relevant documents so it is ready to be filed with the court, or you can have a pre-planned line of questions for examination of a witness if the offer of proof deals with testamentary evidence.

Instructing the Jury

Sometimes, despite the best intentions of all involved, inadmissible evidence gets in front of the jury. Perhaps a witness does not stop talking when the objection is raised, a witness blurts out something unexpectedly, or an insufficiently redacted exhibit gets shown on an overhead. In cases such as these, you may need to ask the judge to instruct the jury to ignore the evidence or the statement. Trial lawyers will always debate the ultimate effectiveness of such after-the-fact admonishments, but all will agree that they must be requested if you wish to preserve any error.

The procedure is similar to a normal objection. At the first opportunity, stop the proceedings, state the objection properly, and, if it is sustained, ask to approach the bench. There you can request the jury be instructed to ignore the evidence. The judge will then likely confer with both counsel on the appropriate wording and will then instruct the jury to ignore the improper evidence as if they had never heard it. On occasion, an instruction will not be sufficient to cure the issue. If you feel that is the case, a mistrial must be requested to preserve error.

Properly Responding to an Objection

Until this point, this chapter has focused on making objections. However, knowing how to properly react when an objection is lodged against you during your questioning or your argument is just as important as knowing how to make objections to an opponent's case. Much of the science is the same when responding to an objection. However, the art of responding to objections raises some additional considerations.

Whereas there are three general parts of an objection, there is generally only one component to the response. You "simply" need to make your case as to why your question was proper or why your exhibit is admissible. There may be some back and forth between counsel (depending on the judge's patience), but the procedure is fairly simple.

There are also a few keys to remember while trying your first case regarding the art of responding to objections. First, do not show fear. Seasoned attorneys often use an objection to try to knock a rookie off of her game. Being prepared and confident in your tactics can ensure a more successful first trial. Second, stay on track. Do not let an objection distract you from your purpose or redirect you from your goal in your line of questioning. If you let the objection get you flustered, your opponent has a leg up. Finally, it is acceptable to take a pause after a successful objection is lodged against you. This does not necessarily mean asking for a recess, but it does mean that if you need a moment or two to collect your thoughts or regroup, you can take those few extra seconds to get re-centered or to calm down. Doing so will allow you to make sure you stay on track and to make sure you are calm and collected, and that you continue to appear professional and prepared in front of the jury. This brief respite will also allow you time to think about alternative ways to get your point across to the jury or get your exhibit introduced.

Conclusion

Certainly one short chapter in a book will not teach you how to master the art and science of trial objections. That takes years of trial experience. However, learning the basics of making and responding to trial objections before you head in to select your first jury is part of being prepared to successfully try your first case. If you are armed with that knowledge, it is more likely your first trial will ultimately be successful, and you will want to come back for more.

Appendix

When thinking in terms of trial objections, most civil trials can be divided into four general parts: *Voir Dire*, Opening Statements, Witness Examination, and Closing Arguments. Each of these has a distinct purpose in the overall scheme of a trial. As a result, different objections are particularly suited to each stage. Of course the number of possible objections is almost infinite, but below is a basic listing of some of the more common objections encountered at each stage of a trial.

- *Voir Dire*
  - Counsel misstates the law
  - Counsel argues the case
  - Counsel violates a motion in limine
  - Counsel asks jurors to commit to a particular outcome
- Opening Statement
  - Counsel argues the case
  - Counsel refers to inadmissible evidence
  - Counsel misstates the law
  - Counsel violates a motion in limine
- Witness Direct/Cross-Examination
  - Hearsay
  - Improper form of question, including
    - Leading (direct examination)
    - Calls for speculation
    - Misstatements of evidence
    - Calls for legal conclusion
    - Argumentative (cross exam)
    - Calls for improper opinion
    - Assumes facts not in evidence
    - Compound question
    - Improper impeachment
  - Irrelevant matter
  - Non-responsive answer
  - Insufficient foundation (expert qualifications)

- Beyond the scope of direct examinations (cross exam)
- General evidentiary issues (Rules of Evidence)
- Privilege (attorney/client, physician/patient, and so on)
- Rule 403 prejudice vs. relevance
- Violates prior order (e.g., motion in limine, pre-trial order)
- Violates a discovery obligation (e.g., the evidence should have been produced during discovery, or attempts to change Rule 30(b)(6) testimony).
- **Closing Argument**
  - Counsel violates the "Golden Rule" by asking jurors to put themselves in a party's position
  - Counsel misstates the law
  - Counsel misstates the evidence
  - Counsel improperly vouches for a witness's credibility
  - Counsel asks jury to "send a message" rather than decide this case
  - Counsel improperly appeals to jurors' sympathy, passion, prejudice, and so on
  - Counsel uses abusive or inflammatory language

Chapter 6

Jury Selection for Your First Trial

Cynthia R. Cohen, Ph.D.

Voir dire will set the stage for trial. True, the outcome of jury deliberations will depend upon both the jurors seated and how well you present
the evidence and communicate your themes during trial. But it all starts
with jury selection. Yet despite its importance, the subject of jury selection
is not well understood and has become shrouded in myth. The goal of this
chapter is to shine a light on the jury selection process and dispel the myths
that surround it.

Mechanics of Jury Selection

Terminology

The first step in understanding jury selection consists of mastering the terminology. Jury selection begins with a jury list, a list of persons who may
be summoned to serve as jurors.[1] A jury commissioner typically manages
the jury process, the procedure by which jurors are summoned and their
attendance is enforced.[2] The venire is the panel of persons who have been
summoned for jury duty and from among whom the jurors are to be chosen; each venire member is a prospective juror.[3]

---

1. BLACK'S LAW DICTIONARY 862 (7th ed. 1999).
2. *Id.*
3. *Id.* at 1553.

After initial processing by the court clerk or jury commissioner, the venire is brought to the courtroom, where *voir dire* will take place. *Voir dire* is a preliminary examination of a prospective juror by a judge or lawyer to decide whether the prospect is qualified and suitable to serve on the jury for the case at hand.[4] Preliminary questions are directed to the venire as a whole, followed by individual questions to individual jurors. The order in which individual jurors are questioned is determined by use of a jury wheel, a physical device or electronic system used for storing and randomly selecting the names of individuals in the venire.[5]

Based upon the answers given by the prospective jurors during *voir dire*, the parties may make challenges to individual jurors. There are two types of challenges to individual jurors: challenges for cause and peremptory challenges.[6] A challenge for cause is a party's challenge supported by a specified reason, such as bias or prejudice, that would disqualify that potential juror from sitting in the case at hand. For example, close kinship with a party would render a potential juror incompetent to serve in that case. Other reasons a person may not be allowed to sit on a jury include alienage (although this is changing in some states), infancy, non-residence, or criminal conviction.[7]

The other type of challenge a party may exercise, a peremptory challenge, is one of a party's limited number of challenges that need not be supported by any reason, although a party may not use such a challenge in a way that discriminates against a protected minority or class.[8]

After the parties have exercised all of their challenges for cause and all of the allotted peremptory challenges that they care to use, the result is a petit jury (the trial jury).[9] The Sixth Amendment does not specify jury size. Most

---

4. *Id.* at 1569.
5. *Id.* at 863.
6. Technically, one may also make a "challenge to the array," which is a challenge to the manner in which the entire venire is selected, usually for some failure to follow the procedures prescribed for the selection of impartial juries. *Id.* at 223. Because such challenges are rare, they will not be discussed further in this chapter.
7. *Id.*
8. *Id. See also* Batson v. Kentucky, 476 U.S. 79 (1986); Edmonson v. Leesville Concrete Co., 500 U.S. 614 (1991) (extending *Batson* to civil cases); J.E.B. v. Alabama, 511 U.S. 127 (1994) (extending *Batson* to gender discrimination).
9. BLACK'S LAW DICTIONARY, *supra* note 1, at 861.

state courts use 6, 8, or 12 jurors in civil matters and 12 jurors in criminal matters.[10] Federal courts seat at least 6 and no more than 12.[11]

After the trial jury is seated, the clerk will typically administer the jury oath and the judge will deliver his initial instructions, or charge, to the jury. These initial instructions will cover the basic expectations for jurors and define what constitutes juror misconduct, such as communicating with others about the case; bringing into deliberations information not placed in evidence; or conducting experiments regarding theories of the case outside the court's presence.[12]

Now that we have the basics down, let us examine in more detail the mechanics of jury selection.

Questioning Formats

Voir dire may consist of questioning of the venire by the judge, by counsel for the parties, or by both.[13] Judge-conducted *voir dire*, the norm in federal court, has the advantage of eliminating the risk of improper questioning by counsel. The downside, however, is that the questioning by a judge is not likely to be as useful in identifying the hidden biases that jurors may hold. Here, we encounter the first myth about jury selection:

Myth: Attorneys get no *voir dire* in federal court.

Reality: The reality is more complex. Judges in federal court typically conduct *voir dire* of jurors from submitted questions from the

---

10. The National Center for State Courts maintains a complete list of the number of jurors to be seated and the number required for a verdict in each state (www.ncsc.org).

11. In my experience, 6-member panels do not perform as well as 12. *See also* Shari Seidman Diamond, *Zimmerman Trial: Time to Reconsider Six-Member Jury*, Miami Herald, July 15, 2013.

12. Black's Law Dictionary, *supra* note 1, at 1013–14.

13. In each of these formats, however, there exists a list of basic questions that the judge will typically cover with the jurors:
Name
City of residence
Spouse
Occupation
(Spouse's Occupation)
Education
Children
(Adult Children's Occupations)

trial lawyers. Many federal judges, however, will give each side some limited time for attorney *voir dire*, upon request.

Do not simply assume you will not get *voir dire* in federal court. As one state court judge in Illinois advises, "Don't let the judge cut you out."[14] Even if the judge tells you that she will conduct the *voir dire*, that does not mean that you cannot participate. Some judges ask the lawyers to submit, prior to trial, *voir dire* questions for the judge to ask. After the judge completes *voir dire*, he may allow the parties to suggest other questions to pose to the panel, on the basis of the answers previously given. The selection by the judge of which, if any, questions to pose from among those suggested by the parties rests firmly within the judge's discretion. The judge may even allow attorneys to conduct some *voir dire* after she has completed the bulk of the questioning.

Lawyer-conducted *voir dire* represents an opportunity for the litigants to elicit the information they need to identify favorable and unfavorable jurors, to test out trial themes, and to develop rapport and credibility with the jury. The remainder of this chapter will therefore focus on attorney *voir dire*.

Procedures for *Voir Dire*
Preliminary Statements

Once the venire enters the courtroom, the presiding judge will typically welcome them with an explanation of the jury selection process and the nature of the case for which they will be examined. The judge may also introduce the parties and their counsel or may allow counsel to make their own introductions.

The next step consists of some general questions to the entire venire. These typically need yes or no answers, and the judge or lawyer asks venire–persons to raise their hand and identify themselves if the answer is yes. These questions may include the following:

- Is anyone related to either (or any) of the parties?
- Is anyone related to counsel for either (or any) of the parties?

---

14. Mark A. Drummond, *Practice Points:* Voir Dire, *Don't Let the Judge Cut You Out,* 37(3) LITIG. NEWS 16–17 (Spring 2012).

- Has anyone worked in the [insert relevant industry] industry?
- [If a criminal case] Has anyone been a victim of a crime?
- The judge will typically follow up on any positive responses to these questions.

After these basic questions, the next layer of selection process deals with jurors' hardship. Often, for judicial economy, the jury commissioner time-qualifies jurors. Other judges conduct hardship screening with the lawyers present in the courtroom. Trial lawyers may agree with the judge's time-qualification in advance, or they may ask the judge not to prequalify in order to see the entire pool. It is often advisable to request that the judge time-qualify the jurors in court. Jurors expressing hardship may soften their stance once in the courtroom. Furthermore, what jurors say during this questioning can be telling. Because many hardship requests are denied, this presents an additional source of information to the trial lawyer.

More jurors get dismissed for hardship during a recession, which can impact the unemployed and partially employed the most. Whether jurors have a job makes a difference in their outlook on the world. Chronically unemployed people tend to project problems onto corporations or corporate officers. If you are defending a corporation in a civil case, it is generally best to let those with hardship go. But that is not always the case. In a recent civil case of mine, the public defenders' information technology (IT) manager claimed hardship because he had major projects to oversee. The judge rejected that claim, stating that because the public defenders use the courts service so frequently, they need to give this court this juror. I encouraged my client to keep this juror—the plaintiff's case was weak and I felt that the IT manager would hold it against the plaintiff for sitting in this trial. Sure enough, my client prevailed. As it turned out, the IT manager served as foreperson for the jury.

Questions to Individual Jurors

After questions addressed to the entire venire, next comes more follow-up questions addressed to individual jurors. Most courts will call the entire number of jurors needed to the jury box, and individual questions will be addressed to this subset of venirepersons. Other courts question venire–persons singly, one by one.

How judges seat jurors during selection varies. There are two basic methods of jury selection: (1) the "struck" system where all panel members participate in *voir dire*, and (2) the "strike and replace" procedure where only the minimum number of jurors needed for strikes participate.

The struck method calls for all of the members to be sworn in and to answer *voir dire* and standard questions. After *voir dire*, outside the jurors' presence, the judge rules upon requests for excusal due to undue hardship and hears and rules upon cause challenges. Using the randomized list of jurors, strikes are made counting from the top of the list. After the peremptory strikes, the judge resolves any *Batson* issues.[15] The names remaining on the "roll list" constitute the trial jury plus alternates, and the list is then read in open court in the jurors' presence.

The strike and replace system begins by the judge calling into the box a number of jurors equal to the size of the trial jury, plus alternates, and the number of peremptory challenges allowed by law. Those jurors are then examined by the judge and counsel, while the rest of the venire observes from behind the bar. Some judges question only the jurors in the box. Others include those in additional seats or rows at the same time. Generally, a juror will be excused for hardship, for cause, or on a peremptory challenge in front of the other jurors. Another juror will then be called forward to replace the departing juror. The replacement is asked for her answers to all previous questions. This process continues until cause and peremptory challenges are exhausted and the required number of jurors (plus alternates) remains. Allocated peremptories do not need to be used. When both sides accept the panel, you have a jury.

Although the strike and replace method is more common, each method has merits. It is easier for the trial team to visualize the composition and keep track of the jurors in the strike and replace method. While jury selection actually represents de-selection, the struck method makes it appear that jurors were selected rather than rejected when the judge calls jurors forward who remain on the list.

---

15. *See supra* note 8.

Exercising Challenges

How the parties exercise challenges depends upon which mode of questioning the court prefers. If the jurors are called up and questioned one by one, then the parties usually have to challenge them one by one. If, on the other hand, a group is called up and seated in the box for questioning, then the challenges come at the end of the questioning of that group.

Use a strike list to decide which jurors to challenge. During *voir dire*, write down jurors' responses, then rate whether to keep (+, + +) or strike (– , – –) each juror, and make note of neutral jurors (ø) and possible leaders. Listen to jurors' responses to both sides in *voir dire* before making final decisions about the strike list. Developing a strike list with an order of whom to strike (and whom you expect opposition to strike) will drive the strategy of executing challenges. Before making final strikes, remember to look down the line to see who may be coming into the box. Do not just focus on the people currently sitting in the box.

During breaks, lawyers can discuss potential strikes with clients and consultants. Although judges usually give jurors a mid-morning and mid-afternoon recess, when *voir dire* concludes you may not have any such break. If you do not have any such opportunity, you can use a technical aid such as iChat to get input from a social media/records investigator or advice from a trial consultant not at counsel table.

Planning and Conducting *Voir Dire*

Basic Tips

When trying your first case, be prepared and ready for jury selection. Be at counsel table on time and ready to proceed. Knowing the procedures, conducting an effective *voir dire*, and not wasting time will have you on the good side of the judge. Judges often allow more time for *voir dire* when you are direct with jurors, on target with the issues, and respectfully listening to juror responses. Because procedures for *voir dire* can vary across courts, ask the judge in advance about his procedures, including the number of allocated peremptory challenges.[16] Some judges prefer jury innovations such as mini-openings before jury selection.[17] You should be well-versed in your judge's preferences before you begin.

Give some thought to whom the prospective jurors will see at counsel table as they enter the courtroom and throughout the *voir dire*. If you are representing a single person or party, the decision regarding who sits at counsel table is easy. In multi-party cases, you will have to decide whether to use multiple representatives and how many trial lawyers to seat in front of the bar at any one time. Who in the trial team will conduct *voir dire*? Who will observe? Deciding whether you have a jury consultant seated at counsel table is a case-by-case decision. While the trial consultant can sit unobtrusively behind the bar, sometimes logistics make it more advisable for her to sit at counsel table. Furthermore, the consultant sitting at counsel table can add value in terms of viewing jurors. While the trial lawyers engage the jurors verbally, consultants trained in observational methods can spot non-verbal clues. If you opt to seat a consultant at counsel table, ask the judge's permission first. If the judge knows it is your first trial, he may appreciate anything that you do to make the process move quickly. That can include using a trial consultant.

Consider whether to seat the parties at counsel table during *voir dire*. If you choose a corporate representative to be at counsel table, pick someone who humanizes the company and connects with the jurors. Jurors watch everyone in the courtroom. If the corporate representative never speaks, jurors will view the representative as less involved and draw negative inferences. Sometimes it is better to forgo having a corporate representative at the counsel table. Wherever you seat your client, advise him to write notes rather than whisper comments about jurors to you at counsel table. Whispers often are louder than you intend—and the jurors' hearing may be better than yours.

Before you begin, you must also ensure that you have the tools necessary for *voir dire*. This includes the jury box seating chart, the randomized jurors list, any jurors' summons information, the completed jury questionnaires

---

16. Most judges will answer your questions of this sort pre-trial.
17. JURY TRIAL INNOVATION (G. Thomas Munsterman, Paula L. Hannaford & G. Marc Whitehead eds., National Center for State Courts 1997).

(if any), and, if the number of questionnaires merits it, a questionnaire management system.

Jury Box Seating Chart

You will want to write down the jurors' names (unless you have an anonymous jury in a criminal matter); this will help keep track of information and serve as a prompt for you in addressing each juror. Courts typically provide a jury box seating chart to each side before the jurors enter the courtroom. The seating chart matches seat numbers in the jury box and has a tiny square or rectangle on each seat. You can add sticky notes to this chart, create your own paper-version seating chart, or use an application such as Jury Box. Be sure to note whether the juror #1 seat is in the back row or the front row and whether the numbers ascend from left to right or right to left.

Sticky notes are a tried and true way for keeping track of jurors called into the jury box. In the strike and replace method, it is critical that you move notes when a juror is moved to an earlier seat or replaced. Most trial lawyers and consultants therefore use handwritten sticky notes during *voir dire*.

Randomized Jurors List

Most courts give the trial teams a list of jurors' names before they enter the courtroom. Either the randomized list is sent with the jurors to the courtroom or the court clerk does the randomized ordering "bingo style" from a container in the courtroom. The court's list of jurors' names has little information but may include political affiliation, city of residence, and number of days available for jury duty.

Jurors' Summons Information

Some states, such as Illinois, use an intake juror questionnaire that the prospective jurors complete before coming to the courtroom. I know of one judge in Illinois who suggests that trial lawyers ask for the jury service questionnaires, as they can reveal important information.[18]

Jury Questionnaire

A jury questionnaire consists of a series of written questions that the trial lawyers agree to submit to the entire venire, for the venire to complete before *voir dire* begins. Whether or not your judge permits a jury questionnaire is a matter of discretion.

In the 1980s, when jury questionnaires began to surface, the defense team on a bad faith case dealing with the failure of satellites asked me, "What do you make of this questionnaire submitted from the plaintiffs?" Our client, an insurance company, was going to trial. Twelve other insurance companies had previously settled out of this case. Reading the other side's proposed questionnaire, I had intuition about jurors for this bad faith case. We tested the opponent's questions to confirm what would make a difference with the jurors. Our client's case hinged on the jurors' understanding of the difference between partial loss and total loss. At jury selection, we identified those likely to favor our position through a few questions in the jury questionnaire:

- Do you like reading science magazines?
- Do you feel insurance companies use fine print to avoid paying claims?
- Do you feel policy owners claim bad faith against insurance companies?
- Are you familiar with quality control procedures?
- Do you think NASA created wonderful opportunities for our children?

The defense team won the trial and was later recognized as one of the best insurance defense cases for the year.

Today, jury questionnaires are more common. New methods in online jury studies make it easier to recruit larger numbers of mock jurors, producing more robust studies to identify predictors and unfavorable jurors.

---

18. Hon. Mark A. Drummond, ABA Webinar, Voir Dire: *Finding and Ferreting Out Good and Bad Jurors*, ABA Webinar (July 9, 2013). As Judge Drummond noted, it tells you a lot when, in response to the question "Can you follow the U.S. Constitution?," the juror handwrites: "Yes, especially the Second Amendment."

An online study of 400 randomly sampled mock jurors can generalize to the venue and statistically identify predictors. It is easier to recognize in *voir dire* a juror who favors plaintiff or defense positions when you have obtained jury research predictors. Demographics such as race, gender, age, or socio-economic status are not sufficient predictors—nor is it legal to eliminate prospective jurors based on gender or race.[19] You will need to look at jurors' prior experience and attitudes for informed and successful de-selection.

When judges limit time for *voir dire*, quick assessments must be made with minimal information. For that reason, a jury questionnaire can be quite useful. Do not forget, however, that you will need to process what you get back on the questionnaires for this exercise to mean anything. When asking the judge to permit a jury questionnaire, you should also ask for sufficient time to read the collected questionnaires. What constitutes adequate time to read and analyze the questionnaires depends on the number of questionnaires collected as well as the length of the questionnaire.

Questionnaire Management System

In addition to the questionnaires themselves, you may also need a questionnaire management system. In one case of mine in San Diego, over 600 prospective jurors answered a 25-page questionnaire. The defense team devised a system to focus on each individual that allowed them to recall individual comments and follow-up questions for each juror during *voir dire*. For example, your trial consultant can scan the questionnaires and maintain a database with jurors' responses on either index cards or a computer. Such a system will focus on responses to the most important experiences (e.g., banking history, home ownership, or foreclosures in a lender liability case).

Juror questionnaires can provide the in-depth background that reveals bias even before the jurors speak. You should prepare to address during *voir dire* any red flags found in the written comments or answers marked private in the juror questionnaires.[20] Evaluate the written responses for emotions and experience that can bias perceptions. If a juror had a family

---

19. *See supra* note 8.
20. Ask the juror who marked answers as private to speak in chambers or a sidebar.

member injured, for example, that incident will affect jury deliberations in a personal injury case. The closer the jurors' experiences are to the epicenter of the trial, the more difficult it will be to reduce their bias. A functional questionnaire management system helps manage the responses, so that you can formulate your strategy to address that bias during *voir dire*.

Areas of Inquiry

Now that you have all the tools and have determined the seating arrangements for your team, where do you start? Unless the judge has already done so, you should respectfully introduce anyone in front of the bar, as well as others on the trial team. If your trial consultant is at counsel table, introduce him as part of the team. Jurors can accept the role of trial consultants as looking for bias. (Indeed, jurors often recognize bias in others jurors' comments in *voir dire*.) If the jury consultant and/or other members of the trial team are behind the bar, introductions are not expected.

Following introductions, you will want to ask about every venireperson's background, in an attempt to understand the type of juror they may make for the case at hand. Ask about their work, their life experiences, and listen to what they consider important. Ask if they have heard anything about the case. For more on the areas of inquiry, see the next section, "*Voir Dire* Strategies." Stay away, however, from argument about the case, such as, "If we prove to you that Plaintiff has suffered no injury or damage, can you find for the Defendant?" That will likely draw an objection and perhaps a rebuke from the judge. For more on the areas to avoid, see the section "Ethics and Objectionable Conduct." As you question the jurors, keep your cards close to the vest. It is best not to expose a juror that you want to keep. Do not ask too many questions of a juror that you have already identified you want to keep.

Question Form

There are two types of questions that you might pose to a venireperson: content questions and process questions. Content questions deal with the specific case issues; you ask them to elicit some sort of reaction that you can weigh in the selection process. For example, if you know that the other side will rely upon a certain piece of evidence (a "bad fact" for your side), bring it out early in *voir dire* and try to inoculate the jury against it. If you cannot successfully inoculate the jury against that fact, then you may at least have the chance to challenge the juror that responded most strongly to that concept.

Process questions, on the other hand, are open-ended questions (or statements) designed to get the venirepersons to talk. For example: "Tell me more about . . . ." You need to elicit information from jurors in order to flush out those you want to dismiss. Examples of process questions include:

- Deeper demographics: Occupational status is important. If retired, what was your profession? Have you ever had a job that you really liked or disliked? Why? What do you do at work? What is your workday like? Is there anything else that we need to know about you before we pick you as a juror?
- If you were the opposing party, would you want someone like you as a juror on this case?
- Is there anything in your own current life or past experiences that reminds you of this case? How does this affect your perceptions of this case?
- Is there anything that you have seen or heard that makes it difficult for you to judge my client the same as the other side?
- Is there anything you'd prefer to discuss in private?

Sometimes jury questionnaires—or the judge's questions—may reveal an area that requires further exploration. If this is a sensitive area, ask the judge to have the juror questioned separately: "Your honor, perhaps we could have a sidebar with this juror?" This lowers the risk of embarrassing the juror or alienating other jurors. After the sidebar concludes, the juror may return to his seat (in the strike and replace method) or may be challenged.

Stereotypes and Generalizations

Some attorneys believe that because group identification can be a proxy for life experiences, it can reliably predict how a juror will react. They may therefore look for jurors that will "identify" with the client and key witnesses. This is the myth of a "jury of your peers." The reality is that it is nearly impossible to have a jury of your client's peers. In any event, jurors most similar to your client can be the most critical of your client. For example, a mother of a two-year-old injured by an exploding bottle in a product liability case may be more harshly judged by another mother, especially if the plaintiff mother could have exercised precautionary measures that would have prevented the injury.

Similar overgeneralization occurs with generational differences. "[D]on't trust anybody over thirty."[21] This reflection on generational differences could well be repeated by today's Generation Y (also known as Millennials). The concept of a generation gap persists through the ages. While generation cohorts or peer groups have developmental milestones in common, other factors such as family, culture, learning style, and socio-economic status influence jurors just as much as—and sometimes more than—the peer cohort. Thus, peremptory challenges based on age alone are fraught with stereotypes. To get beyond stereotypes, jury consultants will examine many factors within each cohort, attempting to correlate individual experiences with responses to specific issues in the case. Individual differences within generation cohorts are the spice of life. Stereotypes, on the other hand, do not scratch the surface.

Juror Profiles

In contrast to reliance on stereotypes and generalizations, jury profiling represents the science of testing hypotheses about jurors to develop a list of "predictors"—factors indicative of a plaintiff-oriented or defense-oriented juror for the case at hand. To find reliable jury selection predictors, a study usually needs more mock jurors than in the typical mock trial. To get a large enough sample (n=400) to measure predictors reliably, you will need to use an online survey. An online survey allows trial lawyers to tap the venue economically and to test case contentions and obtain juror profiles. Such jury studies can effectively reveal jurors' perceptions of the case strengths and weaknesses, compare alternative strategies, and obtain more valid measures of jurors' perceptions of liability and damages.

---

21. Interview with Jack Weinberg on Free Speech movement at University of California, Berkeley (1964), reprinted in BARTLETT'S FAMILIAR QUOTATIONS 835 (17th ed. 2002).

A juror profile developed through such a study will help you identify good jurors during *voir dire*. With different facts and issues, there is no one characteristic that makes for a good juror in every trial. Predictors will vary with the evidence. In a personal injury case, for example, experience indicators for a plaintiff-oriented juror could include loss of a child or caretaking for an invalid parent.

Because jurors focus on the issues rather than the law, you will want to develop a profile of jurors or guide of the factors that tend to favor your case (and those that do not). In pre-trial jury research, you may uncover clues to critical factors that make a difference in your case. Those clues will drive your strategies in *voir dire*.

Voir Dire Strategies

Voir dire is about four things: (1) gathering information, (2) making proper use of challenges, (3) introducing your trial themes and testing the jurors' reactions, and (4) developing rapport and credibility with the jury.

Gathering Information

First and foremost, you need to find out what kind of juror each venire-person would make. The main tools that you will need to gather this information are your empathy and your listening skills.

Empathy as a Tool

Trial lawyers need insight and empathy when talking with jurors. Many jurors are afraid of public speaking—and that includes in open court. You will therefore need to empathize with the jurors in order to draw them out. Before you ask jurors to be in your clients' shoes, step into the jurors' shoes and know how the layperson sees the issues in your case. Become a student of the world, observing everywhere. In traveling into new venues, put down your iPhone, Blackberry, or Droid and observe people. Hop onto local transportation or shop at the local CVS, 99¢ Only Store, or Walmart. You must be able to connect with people outside of your social circles. One good way to connect with jurors is to craft reflections on their comments. That will often lead to more revealing experiences.

For sensitive issues, such as their experiences as victims of a crime, respect the juror's privacy. Invite the juror to speak at a sidebar, rather than in open court.

Listening

Great lawyers never let ego get in the way of listening to jurors. There are six basic forms of communication; one can

1. ask questions,
2. give advice,
3. control silence,
4. reflect,
5. interpret, or
6. self-disclose.

In the early 1970s, Dr. Gerald Goodman, a UCLA psychology professor, posited that with each form of communication, there are both "responses" and "intentions."[22] Responses are the actual words used in the communication. Intentions are the thoughts or behavior that the speaker wants to provoke in the listener by the use of those words.

In Goodman's framework, one tool is silence. The best piece of advice in conducting *voir dire* is to wait for responses. If you give jurors time, they often continue to talk and reveal more about themselves. After asking a question, waiting five seconds allows the juror to respond with below-the-surface answers. Waiting five seconds for a response may seem interminable, but in the long run allowing the juror to speak and discovering cause issues may save a costly mistrial. On the other hand, "advising" a juror will shut down the conversation. Giving advice generally makes people clam up. Thus, responding to a juror's statement with the advice that she "should

---

22. Gerald Goodman & David Dooley, *A Framework for Help-Intended Communication*, 13 PSYCHOTHERAPY: THEORY RESEARCH & PRACTICE, no. 2 at 106–17 (1976).

not consider XYZ" will prevent the juror from vocalizing her true feelings about prior experiences. Ask, do not instruct.

So what are you listening for in the venirepersons' responses? Primarily, two things: (1) hidden biases and preconceptions, and (2) personal qualities that will impact deliberations.

Identifying Bias and Preconceptions

Intuition is like common sense: we all have it to a certain degree. Our intuition or gut feeling tells us to trust our instincts. Intuition gives us confidence. Without feedback, however, our own intuition may miss the mark. For example, we sometimes believe that those we like will like us in return. This is not always true. What is in the minds of the jurors is an important—and sometimes unpredictable—factor in the outcome of the case. Intuition alone will not unlock what lies in the minds of the jurors. You have to uncover the hidden biases.

How do you reveal hidden bias? Address the issue of bias head on. One judge described bias by self-disclosing to jurors, "I went to UCLA Law School. When UCLA is playing USC in football, I obviously have some bias." Getting jurors to understand bias is a first step toward getting them to admit bias. Jury consultants are trained to identify hidden bias. Everyone has bias. Bias is found in emotions and culture; it can be tied to school rivalry, among other things. Simply asking, "Can you tell me about your experiences regarding your relationship with UCLA Medical Center?" may not suffice. Here is a quick checklist for uncovering hidden biases.

1. *Examine for relevant experiences*. Experience leads to stronger convictions (or bias) than attitudes alone. Thus, you should first focus on ferreting out the most compelling jurors' experiences that will influence your case. Then, and only then, will you examine attitudes.

   For example, if your case involves a drunk driving accident, examine jurors' experiences in accidents and experiences with alcohol. Being in an accident involving a drunk driver is never forgotten unless the person is severely injured or comatose. It is more revealing to ask about jurors' *experiences* with automobile accidents or drinking than their *attitudes* about drunk driving. A mother whose child died in a traffic accident caused by a drunk driver has a stronger experience and attitude than someone with the attitude alone. On the other hand, mere attitudes can change over time and with experience. A college student's attitude that drivers who drink should be given second chances is likely to change with maturity.

As another example, consider a personal injury case involving automobiles or tires. Here, jurors might be sympathetic to plaintiffs since virtually everyone has experience in an auto accident. Uncovering jurors' experiences with tires, driving practices, and maintenance routines is useful. Older jurors may have experience purchasing retreads for tires in their youth. They may have experienced that tires can separate without the event turning deadly. Those who successfully dealt with auto accidents could be less inflamed by the incidents in the trial.

Similarly, firsthand experience is stronger than observation. If a person was a passenger in a deadly accident, he will never forget that experience. A passenger in a deadly crash has a stronger experience than a bystander witnessing a crash. A bystander witnessing a fatal accident is more affected by the incident than someone seeing images of devastation on television or YouTube.

As a practical matter, use open-ended questions such as "How do you feel about . . . drunk driving?" Doing so will reveal experience as well as attitude.

2. *Ask about membership in relevant advocacy groups.* Membership in an advocacy group can signal that a venireperson holds strong convictions about a particular topic. Membership in an advocacy group such as Mothers Against Drunk Drivers, Heal the Bay, the National Rifle Association, Occupy Wall Street, Sierra Club, and others does not happen by accident—it develops from one's life experiences. Moreover, collective experience as a member in an advocacy group can form strong bonds between the venireperson and others who have such strong convictions. Consider whether there are any advocacy groups relevant to the issues in your case and ask about them in *voir dire.*

3. *Ask about occupational status.* While there is no silver bullet predictive of a verdict in all cases, the factor that may come closest is occupational status or occupation. The effect of occupational

status—disabled, employed, retired, unemployed—is more pronounced during a difficult economy. Occupational status is a good indicator of the jurors' experiences. Follow-up questions are necessary, however, to get a better picture of the individual. There is a difference between those chronically unemployed and those temporarily unemployed. There are differences as to whether the person is retired by choice. A person who chooses early retirement to travel the world is different from a person forced into retirement by a mandated company retirement-age policy.

4. *Ask about occupation—but do not stop with the label.* We ask about a juror's occupation because his job will contribute to his expertise. Common myths or stereotypes about teachers, nurses, artists, and business owners exist. Trial lawyers used to automatically see teachers as favoring plaintiffs in a personal injury case. Why? At the core of a teacher's qualifications exists the ability to empathize and take care of young people's needs. During *voir dire*, ask the teacher about daily tasks or curriculum. There are greater expectations for teachers today than for teachers in the 1950s. Moreover, there are a wide variety of teachers today. A yoga teacher might be a good plaintiff's juror in a case against a corporation—or that individual instructor might have a strong view about responsibility and reject plaintiff's claims.

How a particular person in any occupation sees a case depends upon individual experiences pertaining to case issues. Although occupation can define a person, what she does within that profession matters. Stereotyping teachers, artists, nurses, and others is what people do in the absence of other information. Stereotypes attribute characteristics to someone within that group when not much is known about individual differences. Consider your own profession as a lawyer and the vast differences among yourself and your colleagues or lawyers at other firms. A solo practitioner has different experiences than a lawyer from a large law firm. There are also commonalities between the solo practitioner and the big firm lawyer. From a juror's perspective the two look alike—especially if jurors don't have family members or friends who are lawyers. Think of your own stereotype before relying on stereotypes of other occupations.

5. *Examine for job satisfaction.* In order to truly understand a juror's work experience, you need to ask questions about their job satisfaction, such as what they like about their job. Ask what their workday is like or what their responsibilities are at work. Jurors in management, or who have supervisory experience, are more likely to facilitate deliberations. Ask about what kind of training jurors have on the job and how they got the job. Was it something they trained for or acquired by knowing someone in the industry? People who choose their careers enjoy more job satisfaction. Disgruntled jurors, on the other hand, are often more plaintiff-oriented.

6. *Examine for attitudes about the economy and the "ME" Factor.* The state of the economy will affect trials, by shaping jurors' "ME" factor—that is, the tendency for jurors to wonder how the decision in the case will affect them personally. In civil cases, for example, perceptions of corporate America and the state of the nation will affect jurors' outlooks and perceptions on liability and damage awards. In employment cases, for instance, jurors are more skeptical of future wage earnings and whether a plaintiff's job still exists in a down economy.

Emotions and personal finances affect jurors' perceptions in a trial. The recession of 2008 affected jurors dramatically. A person pessimistic about the future may be more likely to award high damages to a plaintiff. By 2014, some jurors have become resilient, while others still feel the economic devastation. It is a good idea to *voir dire* about individual outlook on optimism/pessimism, as well as perceptions of the parties' goodwill in the community, damages, and greed.

In addition to considerations of the national economy, individuals relate to what is happening in their neighborhood and "what's in it for me." The state of the local economy affects jurors' pocketbooks. If the outcome of your trial will affect jobs in the local area, jurors take notice. Pay attention to the big picture and to the local ME factor. Will the company close its doors, or will jobs be eliminated when a corporation is being sued? Legally, it is irrelevant whether jobs will be added or lost following a verdict or damage award. Some jurors' decisions in insurance matters are biased in the same way. If jurors think their own insurance will cost more if there is a damage award, they may withhold damages.

How jurors feel about supporting their community, local businesses, and their school system is another part of the ME factor. Verdicts in lawsuits affect the local economy and job market. This impact is greater in a smaller community than in a large metropolitan area. To assess the ME factor in the community, ask whether jurors are business owners, friends with business owners, or involved in Chamber of Commerce activities in their town. Do they shop locally to support local businesses or shop online to avoid local and state taxes?

7. *Ask about the elephant in the room.* Some cases may involve issues about which many jurors will have already formed strong opinions. Take, for example, a case in which you represent a member of the financial services industry. Since the collapse of Lehman Brothers, the uncovering of Bernie Madoff's investment scams, and the subprime mortgage debacle, citizens who never thought twice about corporate America began blaming Wall Street and the government for financial problems. Jurors angered by the bailouts of the banks and General Motors will vary in how they see other cases. There are differences in perceptions of Wall Street institutions. A recent Harris poll reveals that 55 percent of U.S. adults believe that Wall Street benefits the country, while 42 percent believe it harms the country.[23] As in most attitudes, there is a continuum. For jury selection, it is important to know whether the economy factors into the case and, if so, where jurors fall on the continuum. For example, you may want to determine whether any jurors have had changes in occupational status or home ownership and any losses (e.g., bankruptcy) due to economic hardship.

Jurors in regions outside of New York may be harder on Wall Street and translate their beliefs about Wall Street to others. It is therefore difficult for financial institutions to get a fair shake at trial in a turbulent economic climate. The Harris Poll discussed above defined Wall Street to include "the nation's largest banks, investment banks,

---

23. Harris Interactive. *Large Majority of Americans Favor Tougher Regulation of Wall Street* (May 10, 2012), http://www.harrisinteractive.com/NewsRoom/HarrisPolls/tabid/447 /ctl/ReadCustom%20Default/mid/1508/ArticleId/1018/Default.aspx.

stock–brokers, and other financial institutions."[24] That poll revealed that most Americans see Wall Street as necessary, but believe the people who run it are dishonest and overpaid. Of note, 70 percent of respondents believe most people on Wall Street would be willing to break the law if they believed they could make a lot of money and get away with it; 68 percent of respondents do not believe that people on Wall Street are as honest and moral as other people.[25]

Wall Street institutions therefore have a problem in the public's eye. Large financial institutions have made the news on a scandalous list of accusations—laundering Iranian funds, laundering drug cartel money, manipulating LIBOR rates, bid rigging, fraud, and violating consumer protection statutes. Negative publicity and beliefs about an industry can undermine a case. If you represent a bank or other financial institution, you must *voir dire* on emotions toward banks and attempt to defuse any pervasive anger directed at your client. With your questions, humanize the bank and focus the jury on the relevant facts of the particular case and separate it from the negatives.

Adopt the same approach—dealing with the elephant in the room—in other types of cases as well. What if you are representing a wealthy individual in a case? Americans believe the rich are different than other people. A 2012 Pew Research Center poll revealed that most Americans view the rich as more intelligent, more hardworking, greedier, and less honest than "average" Americans. Americans value those who work hard.[26] While 6 percent believe that we should raise taxes on the middle class, 58 percent believe that the upper class should pay more taxes. The upper class is seen as not feeling the sting of tough times. Does this affect juries? Of course it does. We see the "Robin Hood effect" in jury research. Some jurors feel empowered to take money from the rich, or from corporate defendants, to give to the less fortunate. Jurors feel power in awarding damages and changing a plaintiff's life. Even when jurors find no liability, they feel that it is good public

24. *Id.*
25. *Id.*
26. Kim Parker, *Yes, the Rich Are Different*, Pew Research Social & Demographic Trends (Aug. 27, 2012), http://www.pewsocialtrends.org/2012/08/27/yes-the-rich-are-different.

relations for a corporation to award money to the plaintiffs. Thus, if you represent a wealthy individual, you will have to ask jurors about their views of the rich.[27]

Identifying Personal Qualities That Will Affect Deliberations

Myth: Jurors make up their minds at opening statements.

Reality: Opinions can change with the evidence. If the evidence is weighted evenly, jurors can change their minds throughout the trial and in deliberations. Some jurors gather more data than others and wait until they hear all the evidence before making decisions. Some jurors change their minds when they hear others in deliberation. Judgmental jurors cling to preconceived notions, regardless of the evidence.

In addition to examining venirepersons to uncover hidden biases, you will also want to *voir dire* on decision-making style and other juror attributes that may affect the social dynamics of jury deliberation.

There is no prescribed formula for deliberations. You can never replicate the dynamics of the real jury by doing a mock trial. What happens in the deliberation process for real jurors depends upon the evidence admitted, the jurors' perceptions of the case through their own glasses (whether they are rose-colored or dark), the jurors' social skills, and the collective intelligence of the group. Similarly, each jury deliberation has its own quirks, procedures, and sometimes misfits. Jurors entertain themselves and develop a human ecology in longer trials. You could walk into court one day to be surprised by the jurors' color coordination. (It is quite striking the first time you see it.) There can be different types of leaders within the group: a social leader, a content leader, and/or a procedural or rules leader. The social leader might be the one who encourages others to wear green on St. Patrick's Day. The content leader is the one pushing for a certain result. The rules leader is the one who enforces the judge's instructions. Sometimes the foreperson is a rules leader, and sometimes someone else takes that role. The point is that how a jury behaves will depend not just on the biases and preconceptions

---

27. You will want to consider what type of question is most likely to draw truthful answers. For example, jurors may be more honest on a questionnaire than they would be in open court. You could, therefore, ask on the questionnaire to have the jurors list some individuals they admire. See if any are successful businesspeople.

brought into the jury box, but also on the personalities assembled. You should focus on the personality traits as well during *voir dire*.

Look for Leaders During Jury Selection

You want to have someone on the jury champion your client's cause in the jury deliberations. Look for prior leadership experience. For example, you could ask, "Have you ever served on a board or been a president or an officer of any alumni, community, social, or professional association or club?" It is also important to look for social leaders who entertain or gather people. They can effectively recruit others jurors to a cause.

Find Out the Types of Intelligence on the Jury

"The jury didn't get it." "Jurors are stupid." "These jurors didn't know how to get out of jury duty?" Wrong! Stop there. If you lost a case, don't blame the jurors or attribute an undesirable verdict to intelligence lower than yours. That is just sour grapes. Jurors are in the driver's seat as decision makers on the facts. To win a jury trial, it is your responsibility to assess jurors' capabilities for comprehending the complexity of your case and how to teach and persuade them.

Intelligence comes in many packages—cognitive, social, and emotional. Cognitive or scholastic intelligence as measured through the school system is most familiar to us. We feel intelligent if we get good grades. Worldly people have a range of intelligence, including social and emotional intelligence. Educational degrees bring more opportunity for higher-paying jobs, but those who learn from family members, neighbors, or the streets have rich backgrounds in common sense or street smarts. We see social intelligence in mock jurors from all levels of education. Think about selecting jurors with social sense to get the panel to work together in deliberations. Look for jurors with high emotional intelligence that can convey your argument during these deliberations.

Place Jurors on the Continuum of Responsibility Versus Blame

Admitting responsibility or making an apology to a plaintiff goes a long way in resolving disputes or diminishing damages. Humanistic psychology is premised on "responsibility versus blame" theories. Carl Rogers and

Abraham Maslow published the first research papers on the existential approach in the 1950s and 1960s. Rogers and Maslow posited that there is a continuum of people who take responsibility for their own actions and those who do not. Those on one end admit that their behaviors have consequences. Those on the other end of the continuum blame others and look for others to take responsibility. Determine in *voir dire* where in the responsibility versus blame continuum the jurors reside. Develop the theme of choice by asking who takes responsibility and who does not. "Our auto insurance carriers teach us not to admit responsibility in an auto accident. What do you think about taking responsibility?" Be aware, however, that some jurors give socially desirable answers and are not truthful.

Examine for Decision-Making Style

Are individual jurors data gatherers or judgment makers? Jurors are asked, for good reason, to withhold their judgment until all the evidence is in. Some people are judgmental, however, and make decisions before hearing the full story. Occupational training also contributes to decision-making style. Some professions are trained to observe and make quick judgments. For example, an emergency room doctor may need to make a quick judgment before every clinical test is administered; other specialists collect batteries of tests first. A warehouse or grocery stocker may be instructed task by task or may have decision-making steps in his method for handling inventory. To get into the mind of the jurors to determine how they make decisions, ask questions at *voir dire* about the kinds of decisions they make on the job, in the household, or in their studies.

As a group, are the jurors judgment makers or data gatherers? Do they take a quick vote before looking at the evidence? Jurors problem solve to get the job done quickly to get back to their lives. Having a content expert among them makes their reliance on that person efficient in their minds. With a strongly opinionated foreperson, the data gathering process in deliberation tends to be shorter.

Making Proper Use of Challenges

Challenges for Cause

Now that you have asked all your questions, the next step is to make challenges for cause. As noted above, most jurisdictions have specified by statute or court rule the minimum requirements for jurors. In such instances, the courts generally screen out individuals not eligible for service by the time the venire assembles in the courtroom. In some instances, however, such an individual will slip through the cracks and make it into the venire. In such an instance, a challenge for cause is appropriate.

In the majority of cases, however, challenges for cause are used to exclude jurors whose bias renders them unable to serve as an impartial juror. The standard for removal for cause is a high one. Simple biases or preconceptions do not suffice. Rather, the juror must have some experience or connection to the case that makes it impossible for the juror to decide the case objectively.[28]

In some cases, the existence of such bias will be apparent, such as when the juror is related to a party. In other cases, it will take a bit of digging to uncover whether the venireperson has had experiences that produce a disqualifying bias. Such cause challenges are more likely to be successful when the juror's experience is firsthand and directly relates to the epicenter of the case. For example, a doctor is not likely to serve as an impartial juror in a medical malpractice trial.

Developing Challenges for Cause

Sometimes a juror gives you a gift, offering gratuitous comments that seem ready-made for a cause challenge. Such jurors may willingly expose themselves as biased in an attempt to get out of jury duty.[29] Other times, you will have to develop the basis for a cause challenge through your questioning.[30]

---

28. Having said that, in my experience there is great variability in whether the judge will grant cause challenges. You should not, therefore, hesitate in making a challenge for cause in the appropriate circumstances.
29. If you are using jury questionnaires, you can usually identify such jurors by their written responses. This is another benefit of using jury questionnaires—they avoid the risk of having a juror's description of a negative experience pollute the entire venire.
30. If a judge simply asks jurors if they can set aside their own experiences and be fair, that is generally inadequate. Jurors often don't recognize their own bias, believe they can be fair, are fearful of the judge as an authority figure, or lie about being fair.

Listening to the jurors and eliciting a disqualifying bias in open court represents a crucial trial skill. In the example of the medical malpractice, what if the juror in question was not a doctor, but rather the daughter of a doctor? The plaintiff's counsel may then need to pursue a line of questioning similar to the following:

Q. Do you have any close relatives who are doctors?

A. Yes, my mother was a doctor. The first doctor in the family.

Q. Would you mind telling us how your mother came to be a doctor?

A. She told me it was something she had wanted to do ever since she was a little girl. She worked hard in school, put herself through college, and then got into med school. After that, she did her residency at the hospital. Now she is a heart surgeon.

Q. Did she have to overcome any special obstacles to become a surgeon?

A. Oh, yes. In those days, there was a lot of resistance to women in the profession. Even now, you still have patients calling her "nurse" and asking to see a male doctor.

Q. This case concerns the only female doctor at the XYZ Practice. Do you think that she may have faced some the same obstacles as did your mother?

A. Probably so.

Q. Because of your own experience with your mother, might you have some special insight into the career of another female doctor?

A. I am sure that I would.

Q. Would it be fair to say that you would be sympathetic to the challenges that women face in the medical profession today?

A. That is fair.

Q. Now, given your relationship with your mother, and knowing what she went through to get where she is today, would it make you feel uncomfortable to listen to testimony that a female doctor failed to follow the rules and guidelines for caring for patients?

A. I don't know. I think that I would have to hear more about it.

Q. Well, what about this: what do you believe another person would think about your reaction to that testimony?

A. Probably that I am on the doctor's side.

Q.   Given that, do you think it might be better for you to sit on another trial, one that does not involve issues so close to home?

A.   Yes, I think it would.

With such a line of questioning, you would have a decent shot at making a challenge for cause. But that does not end the exercise. You should be prepared for the opposition to attempt to rehabilitate the juror. For example:

Q.   You are understandably proud about what your mother has accomplished. But you also understand, don't you, that this case has nothing to do with her?

A.   Yes, I do.

Q.   If you are asked to sit on this case, would you do your best to listen to both sides, to evaluate the evidence fairly, and to follow the judge's instructions?

A.   Yes, I would do my best.

Q.   So you could put aside your understandable pride in your mother and her career and give these two parties here a fair trial based upon the evidence presented in this case?

A.   Yes, I believe so.

How a judge would rule on a challenge to this juror for cause is anybody's guess. In my experience, each judge views jurors' prior experience and bias differently when it comes to cause challenges.

Of course, you must exercise both tact and caution in developing challenges for cause. Drawing out jurors' incidents in open court can be detrimental. In one case, a juror whose family medical experience was extremely close to the plaintiff's had a pending medical malpractice suit. When the judge asked if she would like to talk about it privately, the juror said, "No, I can talk about it from here." She stood up at the back of the courtroom, relayed her story, and subsequently was excused for cause. Unfortunately, the judge did not silence her, and it tainted the jurors in the remaining pool. If this happens to you, you will need to take quick action: jump up, interrupt politely, and request a sidebar.

Whatever you do, be sure not to get too aggressive with your questioning. Consider your tone and the atmosphere of the courtroom when pressing a strike for cause. The juror may be biased, but he is still a member of the group. Using a hostile tone toward one juror will offend other jurors. Sometimes inexperienced trial lawyers can try too hard to remove a juror for cause, unaware that they are alienating the other jurors. For example, it is a bad idea to ferret out a juror by bullying or hostilely asking a Transportation Security Administration agent, "You discriminate against people like me, don't you?"

Presenting Challenges for Cause

Jurors do not recognize their own biases readily. If possible, ask to present challenges for cause in sidebars or in chambers rather than in open court. This minimizes the risk of offending the juror and alienating the jury by making your challenge for cause. If the judge does not allow you to do so and you have to make your challenge in open court, it is important to be both tactful and respectful. In presenting a challenge for cause, simply say, "Your Honor, we would like to challenge juror #1." If you have to argue the point in front of the jury, avoid any arguments that sound like you are calling the juror names or impugning his integrity. Rather, you should argue that the jurors' views or experiences make it impossible for him to decide the case objectively.

Peremptory Challenges

Making a peremptory challenge is easy: "Your Honor, the plaintiff (or defendant) would like to thank and excuse juror #1." The trickier question is how to choose whom to strike. You need a system to evaluate the jurors, a system that will allow your entire team to be on the same page. Simply rating jurors with numbers (1 to 5) can lose meaning. Use symbols such as +, ø, and – instead. Leaders get "+ +" or "– –" marks and need the most scrutiny. Look for leadership abilities revealed through work experience, activities, social clubs, or prior jury experience.

What jurors say in court or write in the jury questionnaire will provide you with obvious strikes. Look at your strike list and consider whom you believe the opponent will strike. It is a chess game. Use your peremptory challenges strategically. The other side may surprise you and strike someone you believed they would keep. When you have doubt about which way a juror might lean, the other side may have doubt too. Know when to pass and whether to hold onto a peremptory to let the other side use up a strike. Who is coming up behind the jurors currently in the box? Eliminating a juror who is neutral to get the next juror seated is a plausible move if you count your available strikes and your opponent's strikes. When you pass, you are accepting the jury as constituted. The other side, however, may continue to strike. You can then challenge anyone replaced in the seat just vacated by the opponent's strike. When both sides pass on strikes, you have a jury.

Introducing Your Trial Themes and Testing the Jurors' Reactions

In addition to giving you time to identify whom you want to challenge or strike, *voir dire* also offers you the opportunity to test the juror's reactions to aspects of the case, such as your case theme. In a trade secrets case, for example, plaintiffs' counsel might want to use the "duck test." She might ask jurors their beliefs on "if it looks like a duck, walks like a duck, and quacks like a duck, is it a duck?" The defense counsel, on the other hand, might look for jurors who can differentiate swans from ducks. Jurors will pick up themes from your questions. As much as lawyers think that a case can be won or lost at jury selection, there is an art to selling your case at this point. The art comes from framing questions to expose opposing counsel's themes as well. Plant themes while listening to jurors talk about concepts. Your goal is to listen to jurors' responses to opposing counsel's themes.

If you are certain a juror will be removed on a challenge, use that juror as the focal point to further develop your themes. When the other side challenges a juror strongly in your favor, this will signal to the jury that your opponents are afraid of your themes.

Developing Rapport and Credibility with the Jury

We all know that first impressions matter. *Voir dire* represents your opportunity to make a first impression with the jury that will decide your case. Here, you can talk directly with the panel and interact with them. In doing so, you should attempt to build your rapport with the panel and establish your credibility.

Rapport

The best way to develop rapport is to interact with each juror. Use their names (and do so correctly), listen carefully to their responses, make eye contact, self-disclose when appropriate, and genuinely respect them. Avoid lawyerisms, and take pains to humanize yourself.[31]

Welcoming expressions and demeanor invite jurors to reveal more than subjecting them to cross-examination does. Being tough on a juror in open court will leave a lasting impression on the rest of the pool. Instead, practice your town hall voice with jurors. Use humor to develop a connection with the jurors only when it happens naturally and the humor is self-deprecating and not at the expense of a juror. A woman lawyer who literally fell flat on her face in trial when her shoe caught in her pantsuit's loose hem made a quick comeback. The next time she got up, she quipped, "I'll try not to trip this time." The jurors broke into laughter with her. Humor that embarrasses a juror is a big mistake. When a juror returned late from lunch during *voir dire*, the questioning attorney flippantly stated, "I thought FedEx was never late." The group laughed, but the juror singled out didn't appreciate the comment.

Credibility

Developing credibility with the jurors is a major goal. When you establish credibility, jurors are more likely to see you as more genuine, trust your arguments, and believe your case. Confidence, clarity, and expressiveness are the three factors that lead to credibility.[32] You demonstrate confidence via physically commanding the courtroom (or picking yourself up if you fall flat in front of the jurors). Clarity deals with graphics and verbal explanations. Expressiveness deals with tones of communication. Consider how you will use all three in *voir dire* to establish your credibility.

---

31. Judges vary as to whether they allow attorneys to self-disclose anything about themselves during *voir dire* (e.g., "My four daughters tell me I talk too fast, also.").
32. Cynthia R. Cohen, Demeanor, Deception and Credibility in Witnesses, ABA Section of Litigation Section Annual Conference materials, Chicago, IL (2013).

Ethics and Objectionable Conduct

Contact with Venire

The Rules of Professional Conduct prohibit an attorney from making direct or indirect contact with the jury panel.[33] Remind your client that the judge will admonish jurors against talking to any of the parties, and make sure that not only you but also your client remain beyond reproach.

One area in which this prohibition on communication with jurors can arise concerns stealth jurors. A stealth juror is someone who purposefully hides answers (or lies) in order to get onto a jury. Jurors with hidden agendas against corporations, hospitals, or insurance companies may seek to act on those agendas through the judicial process. Jurors seeking to change societal norms often believe they can make a difference or accomplish their goal by sending a message through high dollar awards.

An illustrative example is the character of Nicholas Easterly in John Grisham's *Runaway Jury*. (Unlike in *Runaway Jury*, trial consultants do not burn jurors' houses.) In jury selection, Grisham's Easterly acted as if he wanted off the jury. Similarly, a stealth juror does not appear eager to be on the jury. He hides true feelings and experiences. How then can we spot a stealth juror who resents a particular defendant or wants to punish a certain corporation? You may need to check up on the juror's social media history. Stealth jurors can be revealed when they claim in court that they know nothing about your client or case, yet express strong opinions on social media.

Googling a juror or searching Facebook or other social media during jury selection has become common in the last couple years. Judges now encourage lawyers to look up jurors before the trial concludes. Judges usually prefer that you catch a juror's lack of disclosure early in the process, rather than risk a mistrial. When judges tell jurors they will be scrutinized, it puts the jurors on notice about the sensitivity of a legal professional viewing their social media accounts.

For selection and protection purposes, have the judge ask jurors for the names of their blogs or their Twitter handles, if they have them. The judge

---

33. *See* MODEL RULES OF PROF'L CONDUCT R. 3.5(b).

may suggest to the jurors that the attorneys will be checking to make sure jurors are not violating this admonition. The judge's suggestion makes it easier for the investigator who checks on social media outlets. Premium LinkedIn accounts are notified when someone accesses their profile. (If the investigator's privacy controls are set to anonymous, the account holder simply sees that someone in the legal industry checked their page.) If you employ an investigator to monitor the social media use of jurors, you must admonish the investigator not to communicate or interact with jurors over any social media platform.[34]

Improper Questioning

Although it is proper in *voir dire* to explore juror background and to test out certain themes and issues, one may not go too far. Jury service is a form of public service. Judges recognize this and will protect jurors from unnecessarily embarrassing questions. You cannot pry too much into a juror's private life.[35]

Similarly, there are limits to what one can suggest in *voir dire*. Overly argumentative questions are objectionable, as are questions that refer to inadmissible evidence. Nor can a lawyer misstate the law or the facts in posing his questions. Any such questions would likely draw an objection.

Impermissible Use of Peremptory Challenges

Batson *Challenges*

Under *Batson v. Kentucky*[36] and *J.E.B. v. Alabama*,[37] it is unlawful to use peremptory challenges to remove jurors based on race or gender. *Batson* challenges are made during jury selection when one side believes the other

---

34. *Id.*
35. One way of handling this is by giving the jurors permission to refuse to answer a question. For example, at the beginning of *voir dire*, you can say: "The purpose of these questions in jury selection is to find out whether there are certain experiences or views you have that would make it hard for you to sit in this trial. There are no right or wrong answers; we just need to know what you think so that the parties can get a fair trial. I do not mean to get too personal with these questions. But if I make a mistake and ask you something that is too personal or makes you uncomfortable, don't answer it. Just tell me that you would rather not answer that question, and we will move on. OK? Just tell me."
36. 476 U.S. 79 (1986).
37. 511 U.S. 127 (1994) (extending *Batson* challenges to gender).

exhibits a pattern of eliminating jurors through peremptory challenges based on race or gender. The side challenged has to make the case as to what experience or other statements caused them to eliminate each juror of that race or that gender.

In the *State of Florida v. George Zimmerman* trial, the defense made a *Batson* challenge against the prosecution, stating that they were systematically removing women. Subsequently, two white women were reseated. This was an effective tactic for the defense, because their jury profile indicated that white women were more likely to favor their side of the case.[38]

Batson challenges increase attorney reliance on the organization of jurors' comments from questionnaires and during *voir dire*. It is not enough that the lawyer gives an additional reason for excusing the juror; it has to be a *unique* reason if a juror of another race has similar experiences and was not challenged. To be effective on the challenge, counsel must be ready to supply an answer based on the juror's attitudes or experiences. If the prosecution supplied reasons that were gender neutral (e.g., juror B37 in the Zimmerman trial had a concealed weapons permit), the juror should not have been reseated.

Focus on the juror's attitude, statements, or experience. Do not make the gross error of exercising peremptory strikes on the basis of racial or gender stereotypes.

Making Objections and Motions in Limine

If any of this objectionable conduct occurs, object and make your record. Try to do so outside the presence of the jury, or in a sidebar, in order to avoid polluting the jury pool.

Conclusions

Psychology is not linear. A multitude of theories about human behavior exists, and no one knows everything there is to know about jury psychology

---

38. Yamiche Alcindor, *Zimmerman Consultant Wanted All-Female Jury*, USA Today, July 17, 2013; http://www.usatoday.com/story/news/nation/2013/07/17/zimmerman-trayvon-martin-jury-consultant-killing-sanford/2530151.

or jury dynamics. No one knows what a jury will decide for certain. The more you know about what strangers think of your case, however, the better prepared you can be. Jury research can help you measure potential jurors' attitudes, experiences, and reactions to case issues. If your client has limited funds and cannot afford such profiling, you can nevertheless brainstorm themes with a tutor and get some critical feedback. From your themes, develop *voir dire* questions. Look for the epicenter of the case, and consider what experiences would lead jurors to react to it most strongly. All this will give you a road map for jury selection at your first jury trial.

Chapter 7

Opening Statement

Wayne Morse

The importance of the opening statement cannot be emphasized enough. An effective opening statement persuades the jury and lays the foundation for the trial. Remember the rule of primacy: people tend to believe what they have heard first. Studies show that 80 percent of jurors believe and make up their minds, to some degree, during opening statements. Do not waste time when delivering your opening statement. You must immediately impact the jury, hold their attention, and outline the evidence to be presented.

What Makes an Effective Opening Statement?

Opening statements must create a persuasive narrative, not preview or rebut every piece of evidence in the case. The "story" is the heart of the opening statement. Technically, the story consists of the facts, which are admissible evidence, used to prove your case. Usually it is best to explain what happened chronologically using key demonstrative exhibits the jury will surely remember. Reliable studies prove that 70 percent of the information we retain is presented to us visually. Structure your words and sentences so that the story is persuasive, identifying events, key witnesses, and players along with their testimony. Your theme is always a subtext. Disclose and explain flaws before your opponent does so.

An opening statement has several key points:

1. Tell the jury in a few sentences about the case by stressing the facts and establishing the theme that weaves through the presentation of the case and is the basis for your closing argument.
2. Introduce yourself and your team.
3. Describe your burden of proof and convey confidence you can meet the burden of proof.
4. Tell the jury how you expect to put on your case using a few points.
5. In common-sense terms, explain the elements of your case or what you have to prove to obtain a favorable verdict using the expected jury charges.
6. Persuasively tell the jury the facts you will prove with admissible evidence in an intriguing story.
7. Make the end of the opening statement concise, and lay the foundation for the requested verdict. Tell them what you want.

How do you prepare and deliver an effective opening statement for your case? This chapter walks you though each step of the process: preparation, selection of content, and delivery.

Preparation

The first step in preparing your first opening statement is to quit thinking and talking like a lawyer. You may have spent years and perhaps hundreds of thousands of dollars "learning to think like a lawyer." You will have performed well in your work if you are given the responsibility of delivering the opening. The jury, however, usually does not consist of only lawyers or professors but rather "real people," many of whom who work at manufacturing plants, construct buildings, and otherwise to keep the wheels of commerce moving. The courtroom is not their element. Almost without exception, the venires would prefer to be someplace else, at work or home. Their service comes with sacrifice. It is therefore important to get down to business.

Treat the jury with respect. First, jurors are intelligent. Individually and collectively, they have insight and wisdom. Second, your client's fate rests in their hands. Know your audience, and remember that most of them do not think or talk like lawyers.

Consider yourself in the role of a teacher instead of a lawyer as you draft and deliver the opening statement. Imagine the best professor you ever had, the one who had no condescension and believed passionately in the value of her subject. Remember also the words of Boston's Jerry Facher, one of last century's finest trial lawyers. Besides having a full calendar at Hale & Dorr, he taught trial advocacy at Harvard Law School. Jerry admonished that pride has no place in a courtroom: it has lost more cases than idiot witnesses and hanging judges combined. Think of a trial as a book with the opening statement as the first chapter. It is imperative to have a theme that weaves through each chapter, leading to the closing that harkens back to the opening.

Content

While you will find the outline of an opening works for you and the facts of your particular case, I find the following structure useful.

First, tell the jury in a few sentences about the case, stressing the facts. Example:

A person has the right to work without harassment and to fulfill his potential. This case is about a young man who suffered sexual harassment at Miracle Laboratories. Dr. Bruce Jones made Dr. Paul Harris's life miserable for a year with sexually suggestive and demeaning comments. Dr. Jones caused Dr. Harris to suffer depression and demoted him, but still Dr. Harris did not give in.

Dr. Harris did not expect utopia at work. He merely wanted to work without receiving unwelcome sexual propositions and being berated and undermined. Dr. Harris reported Dr. Jones's harassing conduct to Miracle Laboratories' Human Resources Department on multiple occasions, but Dr. Jones's harassment continued. Miracle Laboratories and management did nothing.

Dr. Harris studied and worked hard for years to earn a doctorate. He has school loans. As a college student, he labored long hours in laboratories when other students were at football games or socializing. He sacrificed to obtain a job at Miracle Laboratories. Dr. Jones caused Dr. Harris to be depressed and anxious, so much so his doctor prescribed medication. He couldn't eat or exercise. He couldn't concentrate. His relationships with friends deteriorated. He lost his girlfriend.

We're here today to ask for several things. We're asking for Dr. Harris to get his job back. We're asking for Miracle Laboratories to stop allowing supervisors to harass employees. We're asking for substantial damages.

This is the time for just a quick introduction of the case. A chronological outline of what the evidence will show comes later. *See infra.*

Second, introduce yourself and your team. Do not skip or skimp on this step. Introduce everybody—the jurors will wonder who each person is, and it shows respect for them and your team members to cover everybody.

Third, describe your burden of proof. "We have the burden of proving what we say, and we accept that burden." Be straightforward, and no poor mouthing. Do not whine about your burden of proof, but rather proceed confidently that you can satisfy your burden. "This opening statement will outline the facts that we will prove."

When representing a plaintiff, stress your burden is a preponderance of the evidence—that is, that more likely than not the plaintiff has proven his claims. Remind the jury of the difference between civil and criminal cases. In the exemplar case, it is unnecessary for Dr. Harris to prove beyond a reasonable doubt that Dr. Jones harassed him to the extent that he was unable to work, to eat, to concentrate, or to maintain relationships.

As defense counsel, keep the plaintiff on the hook, and do not assume a burden you do not have. Tell the jury that the plaintiff must prove his case.

Dr. Jones does not have to prove he did not harass Dr. Harris. The burden is on Dr. Harris to prove his claims. Dr. Harris has to prove that Dr. Jones harassed him, not just put on some evidence. Dr. Jones must convince you because you are the judge of the evidence.

In the opening statement, the defense must ask the jury to keep an open mind until hearing both sides of the evidence. Some lawyers ask the jury to look at their palms and remind the jurors they do not know what their hands looks like until they see both sides. Alternatively, "one side sounds good until you hear the other side, so please stay open minded until you hear everything." Emphasize that a real trial, unlike a trial on a television show, is not completed within an hour. After the plaintiff presents evidence, the case is only half complete.

Fourth, tell the jury how you expect to put on your case using a few points.

First, I will talk to you about Dr. Paul Harris, who he is, his education and training to become a research scientist at Miracle Laboratories.

Second, I will tell you about his experience at Miracle Laboratories, how he was mistreated by Dr. Jones, and why this mistreatment is illegal.

Third, I'll tell you all how Dr. Paul Harris was harmed. As I said in *voir dire*, when we prove our case, it is necessary to figure the amount of money in damages that puts Dr. Paul Harris in the position he would be in had this horrible conduct not occurred. If you make the findings we say the evidence supports, then you'll need to determine the amount of punitive damages Miracle Laboratories must pay.

Fifth, explain the elements of your case in common-sense terms, or what you have to prove to obtain a favorable verdict. Although the judge will not have settled on the final jury instructions yet, you can base this discussion on the pre-trial order.

Dr. Harris is young, a man, and a research scientist with a brilliant future. He was subjected to unwelcome verbal and physical conduct by Dr. Jones. One of the reasons Dr. Jones acted the way he did is because Dr. Harris is a man. Dr. Jones's unwelcome conduct had the effect of interfering with Dr. Harris's ability to perform his job. Dr. Jones was intentional about interfering with Dr. Harris, about distracting and tormenting him. He knew what he was doing. Dr. Jones made Dr. Harris's work environment intimidating and hostile. Dr. Jones wanted Dr. Harris to fail.

The evidence at this trial will show you that Dr. Jones was frustrated by Dr. Harris's denial of Dr. Jones's sexual advances, so Dr. Jones decided to get even and to drive Dr. Harris away from Miracle Laboratories. Dr. Jones also had a second motivation for harassing and undermining Dr. Harris. Dr. Jones was threatened by Dr. Harris, a brilliant young scientist who was well liked at Miracle Laboratories. Dr. Jones thought he might be replaced by Dr. Harris, or thought his role would be diminished at Miracle Laboratories. Why? Because Dr. Harris was smarter, worked harder, and was well liked.

So you will see all of the elements for harassment based on sex. You will see how Dr. Harris was injured. We have Dr. Jones physically touching and verbally abusing Dr. Harris, which caused Dr. Harris to suffer depression. The depression affected his work performance, which in turn affected his stature in his profession and his posture at work. Dr. Harris was demoted. Dr. Harris had to suffer all of this harassment because he was a man who spurned Dr. Jones's advances and threatened Dr. Jones's standing at work.

Sixth, tell the jury the facts you will prove with admissible evidence. This part of the opening is what has become known as "telling the story." Introduce the key witnesses, do not become bogged down, and let the jury know any problems with the case. A lawyer cannot regain credibility after losing it. In opening, never make promises you cannot demonstrate with admissible evidence during the trial. If you do, you will hear about it in closing. In our hypothetical, for example, if Dr. Harris had a tendency to tell lewd jokes, drink with co-workers, had a consensual fling with a colleague, or used marijuana, handle the subject in opening. By disclosing the warts in your case, you control them to a greater degree, and the jury is more likely to be forgiving. Jurors may not forgive if your opponent exposes poor behavior of your client on the stand. Smart lawyers race to disclose in *voir dire* and then explain more in the opening statement. The point is simple: No one is perfect. In our example, Dr. Harris's relationship with a colleague and going to a tavern with friends now and again and being "over-served" has nothing to do with Dr. Jones's threats and lies. If you represent the defendant, the same principles apply.

Again, most of the information people retain comes in visually rather than through our ears, so demonstrative aids are critical. Every juror is a member of a generation accustomed to absorbing information through television, computers, tablets, and phones. Every television newscast communicates with graphs, charts, and photographs rather than merely a talking head. A challenge in every case is how to take the information you want the jury to remember and present it visually because the jury is more likely to remember it that way.

Be judicious in selecting demonstrative aids for opening because jurors have only the limited background learned during *voir dire*. Remember the exhibit must be admissible evidence. Ensure admissibility with a pre-trial order or show the exhibits to the judge before starting the opening statement. Being chided (or worse) during opening because you are using inadmissible evidence distracts the jury and causes a lawyer to lose credibility.

Detailed and costly charts or summaries are not always necessary. Sometimes a simple white board and a marker are useful. In one case, at least 14 related businesses and wealthy persons were suing an individual. Writing the name of the defendant individual on one large tablet and listing the fourteen plaintiffs on another sent the jury the "David v. Goliath" message.

Likewise, deposition video clips can be too much too soon. If, however, you have an admission or inflammatory testimony, project the enlarged deposition transcript for the jury to read. Seeing and reading the testimony on a screen so jurors can review and ponder it for a moment, more than once if they wish, is more impactful than a single hearing.

One must be especially selective using video clips. Make them short and, again, impactful. I used them once in a trial involving a hospital patient's legal capacity to write a check. One minute of the attending physician's video deposition was played. The testimony was that the patient had ingested Demerol during the 12 hours preceding when the check was written. Considering his mental health and metabolism, his physician said, the patient was "definitely unable to understand the significance of signing a check." By playing this clip, the dispositive issue was presented (and decided) during opening.

In preparing the opening, never forget your theme. A theme does not consist of belittling the opposition or its lawyers. Rather, the theme is a message that gives jurors a reason for holding in your client's favor. At their best, jurors are levelers, making their findings based on the facts and the judge's instructions. Studies confirm what seasoned trial lawyers know: jurors want a reason for their verdict. They want to do justice. Ideally, the theme comes through in every phase of the trial, from *voir dire* through closing argument. It must be emphasized in opening.

Finally, *seventh*, make the end of the opening statement concise, and lay the foundation for the requested verdict. Tell them what you want.

The evidence in this case more than justifies a substantial verdict against Miracle Laboratories and Dr. Jones. We will ask you to return a verdict in Dr. Harris's favor for $900,000 in damages. This verdict will compensate Dr. Harris for back pay and emotional distress. This verdict also represents punitive damages for Dr. Jones's intentional conduct and Miracle Laboratories' failure to remedy the situation, to prevent Dr. Jones's harassment.

Final Tips on Preparation

As in most of life's endeavors, it is important to practice and obtain feedback regarding your performance. Lawyers love their own words, but others rarely find them as articulate and incisive as the speaker. It is unnecessary to have an expensive mock trial in each case; instead, use an area of your law office or borrow a courtroom. After a few solo performances, ask the lawyers and staff at your office for an evaluation. Your initial feedback should not come from the jury. Identify any flaws in your presentation and as many ways as possible to improve it. These exercises are not for the sensitive, so if critiques bother you, find another line of work.

Delivery

Stand and thank the judge who has instructed you to start, and then address the jurors as "members of the jury." Notes may be necessary, but do not read from your notes or at a podium. Be well familiar with the facts, and your mastery must come across to the jury. If the judge permits it, stand before the box and move. As early as opening, it may be possible to determine who in the jury will have influence in deliberations. Make eye contact with the jury and especially with the jurors who will likely lead.

As you become more comfortable in trial, you may develop some transition comments. Examples include:

- "It's becoming late, and everyone's ready to go home, but I thank Judge Bittner for allowing me to make my opening. There are a few things I really want you to know before you go home."
- "We listened patiently to the State's opening statement. Both sides have waited a long time and done a lot of work to get to trial. We believed it was important for you to hear what the State had to say, so we did not object. We hope that the State provides our client the same courtesy."

Remember these goals for your opening:

- make an immediate impact;
- hold the jurors' attention;
- be brief; and
- sit down.

Do not risk losing the jury at the outset of trial by delivering a long-winded, boring, unfocused, and poorly planned opening statement. With that, I will take my own advice, wish you good luck, and stop.

Chapter 8

Presenting Your Case Through Direct Examination

Neal W. Dickert and Eli Rosenbluh

Each stage of a trial can be critical, but the legal significance of a failure to present sufficient evidence to support a client's claim or defense cannot be overstated. Regardless of your eloquence or advocacy skills, the lack of supporting evidence for a claim or defense will result in a losing effort, either at the trial or at the appellate level. It is therefore imperative that, before you begin preparing your witnesses, you lay out the elements of your case, or the essential facts necessary to support your defenses, in an outline. Put the name of the witness next to the facts to be proven so you know which witness or witnesses are critical to prove those necessary facts to support your claim or defense. Keep this outline at the front of your trial notebook.

It is important to remember that much of what happens at trial is beyond the lawyer's control. Despite the attorney's best efforts to persuade the judge of a particular position concerning various evidentiary or pre-trial issues, the judge controls the outcome. Thus, the evidence actually presented may or may not reflect the attorney's preferred strategy. With respect to the evidence presented, there is always the possibility of witnesses being uncooperative, unpredictable, and irrational. Finally, your opponent's presentation of her witnesses is generally beyond your control. However, an advocate usually has much more control over the direct examination of her witnesses than she has over most other aspects of the jury trial. Effective preparation of both the questions being asked and the responses offered by each witness is therefore critical.

This chapter addresses issues relating to the choice of the witnesses to use, meeting and preparing the witness, preparation and use of a trial notebook, organization of the direct examination of the witnesses, use of documentary evidence, and handling the difficult witness. Finally, the chapter concludes with a discussion of several rules or principles of direct examination.

Witness Selection

Except for hired experts, every case has a limited pool of available witnesses that is dictated by the facts or events. For example, if you are involved in the trial of a personal injury claim arising out of a collision where eyewitnesses were present, you cannot simply create other witnesses to refute the testimony of the people who happen to have been at the scene. If you are involved in a contract case where a representative of your client was involved in the negotiation, signing, and performance of the contract, you cannot bring in another person who is more attractive and articulate to present evidence more favorable to your client. Regardless of where your case is being tried, personal knowledge of matters about which the witness testifies is essential. Make sure your fact witnesses can speak from personal knowledge of the facts; otherwise, their testimony may prove inadmissible. There may be some individuals in cases whom you will be forced to call as witnesses. For instance, unless your personal injury plaintiff cannot speak, it is hard to imagine not putting your client on the stand. The same would likely occur in a contract case where you have one individual who was involved in all aspects of the contract. It may not matter how weak you think these witnesses are or how poorly you expect them to perform. The jury will expect to hear from these people and may think you have something to hide by not presenting these witnesses. Opposing counsel will most assuredly make that argument. The failure to offer these critically important witnesses will likely hurt your case more than their poor performance at the trial.

Frequently, however, you may have multiple witnesses with overlapping knowledge of the important facts. In such instances, you have the luxury of choice. How do you exercise such choice? As a general rule, less is more. Juries tend to become tired and bored by repetition. Let each witness cover the area or facts that you think that witness is best able to project and leave other areas to other witnesses.

While repetition can bore a jury in some circumstances, a little repetition can be important and helpful in other areas. If you are representing a plaintiff in a serious personal injury case, it is frequently helpful to have someone other than the plaintiff talk about the plaintiff's injuries. If liability is seriously contested in a case involving a collision and you have three witnesses to support your theory while your opponent has only one, use all three of your witnesses. But if you have multiple witnesses with similar information and each witness is rather inconsequential, there is no reason to belabor an unimportant point by presenting several witnesses testifying to essentially the same facts. If you are representing a party in a collection action and you offer one witness who is able to present the appropriate record to establish the amount of the debt, there is no reason to present another witness simply to reiterate the same information presented by the first witness. Unnecessary repetition and cumulative evidence may, under certain circumstances, be stricken. Even if allowed, it is likely to cause a jury to lose interest in the case.

If given a choice about witnesses, you want a witness who is articulate and smart and who will relate well to the jury. Juries do not like jerks. There are some people who are so arrogant, rude, and insensitive that they turn off people regardless of their knowledge, experience, intelligence or other redeeming characteristics. On occasion, you may have to deal with a corporate witness who was presented for a Rule 30(b)(6) deposition. You may have to address the question of whether the witness should be recalled at the trial considering the testimony given at the deposition. If the witness is a troubling witness and you are concerned about his performance on the stand, and the deposition went reasonably well, you may opt for presenting excerpts from the deposition as opposed to bringing the witness back to trial.[1]

Closely aligned to this issue of witness selection is the question of the designation of the appropriate corporate representative to sit with you in the event that you are representing a corporation. Most courts allow a designated representative to sit with counsel and participate during the trial of the case. It goes without saying that you want a person with a pleasing personal appearance. It is also important to have someone sit with you who can assist in the trial of the case. Consequently, you will need a person who has some knowledge of the facts. Generally, most witnesses are sequestered and do not hear the testimony of other witnesses. Your corporate representative, however, would have the ability to listen to the trial testimony and, if he knows about the critical issues in the case, could assist in preparing your examination and cross-examination of witnesses. You also have to give some consideration to the fact that the presence of that witness in the courtroom opens the opportunity for having that witness called by the opposite party for purposes of cross-examination. If you have a corporate representative who is vulnerable and whom you would not otherwise offer as a witness, do not give your opponent the opportunity to call that witness because she was in the courtroom. Former employees and retirees may be appropriate witnesses, but consideration needs to be given to the person's attitude toward the company. Obviously, a fired employee or person who has a grudge against the corporation might expose that grudge through examination. Even though this former employee may have favorable information, it may be presented in such a fashion that the jury realizes that the witness does not have good feelings about the corporation and may have been mistreated. That witness may turn out to give some damaging testimony, even though she may have full grasp of the facts and may have pertinent information that would otherwise be helpful to your case.

---

1. You must meet the criteria of the local rules with regard to the use of deposition testimony, however.

Meeting Your Witness (Non-Parties)

It is important to realize that most witnesses who are encountered in the litigation process have had little, if any, experience with our justice system. Many of them feel intimidated by attorneys and judges. As much as anything, they are simply afraid of the unknown. It is important that you, as the trial attorney, provide them with the necessary support and encouragement to overcome that fear. Even when trying your first case, you likely are more comfortable in a courtroom than are most witnesses. It is therefore essential to develop a relationship and establish a rapport with your witnesses so that you are comfortable with them and vice versa. You also need to understand their strengths and weaknesses in order to present them effectively on direct examination and properly prepare them for cross-examination.

We have all encountered witnesses who are reluctant to talk to lawyers; people are generally wary of becoming involved in litigation. If a witness is a friend or acquaintance of your client, have your client make the first call to advise the witness that he may be hearing from you or someone in your office. Many of us like to use paralegals, assistants, or investigators when interviewing witnesses, and there is certainly nothing wrong with having an investigator or paralegal make the initial contact with a witness as it can save both time and money. If you are going to try the case, however, you should not wait until the day before the trial to have your first face-to-face contact with the witness.

It is also essential that you treat witnesses with courtesy and respect. Be accommodating in scheduling appointments. Offer to meet them on their terms. Law offices can feel foreign and intimidating to the inexperienced layperson. Putting the witness at ease from the start will be beneficial in facilitating your preparation of the witness and hopefully garnering favorable results for your client.

Preparing the Witness

One cannot overstate the importance of preparing a witness. A witness must know what to expect from you, and you must know what to expect from the witness. Go over the witness's testimony several times. If at all possible, meet the witness in person. However, there may be witnesses who are out of town, making face-to-face meetings difficult or impossible. If this is the case, consider using Skype or other teleconferencing techniques.

If your witness has given a deposition or any statement, provide her with transcripts of all of these. Make sure that she has read the deposition and statements before your preparation session. If her version of the facts differs from that of another witness, advise your witness of that and what this other witness has said.[2] Your witness will most assuredly be confronted with this contrary version on cross-examination. If the case involves observations of an event, take the witness to the scene of the event and provide her with pictures or videos of the scene.

One very useful tool for witness preparation is the video camera. Since witnesses will rarely look as nervous on video as they feel, recording their testimony and playing it back for them can build their confidence. Exercise judgment, though, in deciding whether to videotape your witness. If your witness is particularly weak, the camera may highlight his weaknesses and make the witness even more nervous and self-conscious.

Play the devil's advocate and put the witness through a thorough and shifting cross-examination. Without a simulated cross-examination, your witness is not prepared to testify and may collapse on real cross-examination. When you go through rehearsal, try to approximate the trial setting as closely as possible. If possible, have a colleague who will not serve on the trial team play the role of opposing counsel. He will be able to get very aggressive with your witness without adversely impacting your relationship with your witness. There is a fine line, however, between treating your witness aggressively in order to prepare her to testify and being so aggressive as to completely destroy the witness's confidence. As always, exercise judgment and do not needlessly alienate your witness.

Try your best to simulate the courtroom experience. Prepare your witnesses without interruptions or distractions. If you have an opportunity, take them to the courtroom so that they will know where they will testify,

---

2. In preparing a witness to testify during trial, be mindful of any order issued by the court regarding the sequestration of fact witnesses.

where they will sit, and where they will wait; this helps to make the setting as comfortable and as familiar as possible.

Witness Notebooks

Witness notebooks can be invaluable in preparing a witness to testify. Depending on the complexity of the case and the volume of documents relating to the witness, try to select the most important documents and organize them chronologically or topically into an examination outline. But be mindful of the fact that the existence of such an outline and a description of its contents may be elicited on cross-examination of your witness.[3] To avoid the appearance of coaching the witness, it is good practice, therefore, to only provide the witness with the documents themselves, but not with any outline of the direct that you prepare for yourself—and certainly not with your narrative of the facts or theories of the case.

In selecting the documents for preparation of your witness, be sure to include both the best and worst documents relating to your witness. Review the best documents with your witness to ensure that your understanding of those documents is correct and aligned with that of your witness. Once you have established your witness's narrative, review the "bad" documents with him and try to anticipate all the holes and flaws in your witness's narrative that your opponent may seek to exploit. Whenever possible—and without coaching the witness—help him explain any inconsistencies in the narrative or evidence. Even if there is no way to explain away those documents, you can, at the very least, eliminate your opponent's element of surprise and any resulting tactical advantage. Counsel the witness to explain the document and answer the resulting line of questions as truthfully and neutrally as possible, without becoming defensive or otherwise damaging his credibility. Above all, do not allow your witness to try to cover up inconsistencies. Any such attempt is bound to be exposed by your opponent, who will use it to destroy your witness's credibility.

---

3. For example, any documents used to refresh a witness's recollection must be shown to opposing counsel, even if covered by the attorney-client privilege or work-product doctrine.

Examination Technique

Effective Use of Documentary Evidence

As we all know, the printed word lasts longer than the spoken word. Thus, documentary evidence can be very important. There are also possible pitfalls associated with the use of documentary evidence. First, be selective in the use of documents. Use only your most important and effective documents. If you have only two good photographs and you introduce fifty, the jury may never focus on the two good ones. Remember the weight of evidence is dependent not upon the number of exhibits, but rather on each exhibit's impact. Second, know your rules of evidence. Memorize the applicable business records statute or Federal Rule of Evidence 803(6) governing the records of a regularly conducted business or, at a minimum, have a copy at hand. Write out the basic foundational questions necessary to admit these records. There may be rigid rules relating to certain pieces of documentary evidence, such as photographs (e.g., does the photograph fairly and accurately represent the person or place depicted?) or computer reenactments. Do not trust your memory for these basic foundational questions and other key evidentiary provisions. Your best documents are worthless if you cannot introduce them into evidence.

Try to secure a stipulation from opposing counsel before the trial disposing of as many technical issues concerning documents as possible. Have all the documents marked and their admissibility either stipulated or ruled upon by the court before trial, if at all possible. Foundation questions on documents are often distracting and, most likely, boring to the jury. If you avoid this exercise through a stipulation, your case will have a better flow. If necessary, make a motion in limine to obtain an early ruling on the admissibility of documents.

When using documentary evidence, the use of a PowerPoint or Elmo system may be extremely helpful. Avoid passing documents through the jury box if you can present them through a PowerPoint. If you pass documents among the jurors, it is likely that by the time the document gets to a particular juror, the testimony will have moved to another subject. You want the jury to look at the document and hear the witness testify at the same time. An Elmo, PowerPoint, or even the old-fashioned overhead projector helps accomplish this goal. But by all means, make sure the technology works before attempting to use it in the courtroom. Many attorneys are not technically savvy enough to manipulate a PowerPoint presentation. If you have paralegals or assistants who are proficient, utilize their expertise. The last thing you want is to stand in front of the jury and not be able to navigate your PowerPoint or use the Elmo device.

Organize the presentation of your documents in a meaningful way. You always want to keep in mind that you are telling a story through your witnesses. Proceeding in chronological order is generally the best practice. For example, if you are presenting testimony and medical records of a personal injury, present the records in chronological order from the oldest to the newest. The jury can follow the plaintiff's progress, or lack thereof, from the time of the accident to the present.

Summaries of voluminous records can also be very effective. Such summaries are particularly helpful in construction or contract cases that may be very document intensive. Federal Rule 1006 provides for the use of summaries at trial, and many states have similar rules. It is generally accepted that the use of a summary requires that the back-up documents be made available to the opposing party. Consult state and local rules to ensure that your summary complies with them.

Direct Examination of Witnesses—Rules and Principles

Have a Plan and Be Organized

The most effective way to present your case is by telling a story. Begin by introducing the witness and helping the members of the jury identify with her. For example, if one of the members of the jury is a plumber, as is the witness, be sure to let the jury know her occupation. Always start the examination by allowing the witness to talk a little about herself, her background, family, education, and so on. People like to talk about themselves. This approach also helps the witness relax and establish a rapport with the jury.

If you are representing a corporation, try to humanize the client. Explain to the jury that a corporation is an entity managed by individual employees and owned by a group of individual shareholders or pension funds in which individuals' and families' life savings are invested. It may be hard to make a big-city corporate officer compatible with a rural venue, but if the representative has a family and children, that helps to bring a human element into the picture.

After you have introduced your witness, start off with your most important point. End with your next most important point. Individual jurors normally remember what they hear first and what they hear last. The same philosophy applies to the order of your witnesses. Lead off with your best witness and end with your next-best witness.

As with storytelling, it is important that your examination be organized in a way that makes it easily digestible by the jury. In many cases, the best way to organize your examination is chronologically. This is especially true where the sequence and timing of events are critical to your case or defense. Oftentimes, however, it is not the sequence of events that is important but the events themselves. In such cases, you may want to begin with the most important event and end with the least important one.

For example, in a breach of contract case involving multiple discrete breaches, your first inclination may be to tell the story chronologically and recount the breaches in the order in which they occurred, but that may actually weaken your case in the eyes of the jury. If the first breach was a technical or minor breach, then the jury may think your client's case has little merit and that assumption could color the way they view the rest of the case. In such a case, it may be preferable to begin with the strongest point or the most damaging breach first, so the jury will take your case and your witness's testimony more seriously.

In addition to the impact it may have on your jurors' view of the case, the organization of your examination can also affect their memory of the testimony. It is important that you start out strong and end strong as well. However, do not leave your most important points for last, as you may run out of time before you have an opportunity to elicit that testimony or may fail to do so for some other reason.

Be Simple and Direct

Juries, like all of us, have a limited attention span. A juror's ability to absorb and process information is limited by his ability to sit for extended periods. Therefore, be as concise as possible with your presentation.

Regardless of the complexity of the case, it can always be reduced to a basic theme.[4] Keep in mind that while you may have lived with this case for months or even years, the jury has not. While you want to extract from the witness all that he knows about the case, this is not possible, and even if it was, it would bore the jury. What may be a fascinating and interesting case to you is not going to be as fascinating and interesting to the jury. Stick to the basic facts. The biggest failing of many good trial lawyers is that they try to overcomplicate their cases by presenting too much evidence and spending too much time presenting unimportant evidence.

Use simple, plain language in your examination. Lawyers love words like "subsequent" and "prior." Drop those words from your examination, and use "before" and "after" instead. Do not talk about the "day in question" or the "incident at issue." Talk about the "day of the wreck." We work with words all day long, and many of us have developed extensive vocabularies. This is a commendable skill and may be impressive in some circles. However, you will not impress a jury by using high-priced words. You will only confuse them and risk appearing condescending.

Lawyers are also prone to using convoluted and long questions. Keep your questions short. Use open-ended questions whenever appropriate. For example, instead of asking "Did you have a clear view of both vehicles driving through the intersection?" ask the witness to describe her view of the intersection in general terms. If necessary, follow up with a more specific question later, but do not put words into the witness's mouth. In addition to it being objectionable as a leading question, the jury can and will recognize any attempt to coach the witness and will find your witness's testimony less credible as a result. Let your witness tell her story in her own words—she knows it better than you do.

Use present tense to set the scene. For example, begin with "So you're at the intersection . . . tell us what you see." Or "You hear the plaintiff crying for help; what do you do next?" This brings the story to life and renders your client's injury and the defendant's actions more real and immediate.

You generally do not want to repeat questions, but certain words and phrases have powerful connotations and can be used for emphasis. For

---

4. *See* Chapter 1.

example, if you ask a witness about an intersection collision and the witness testified that she saw the "defendant's vehicle crash into the plaintiff's vehicle," your next follow-up question might be, "In what direction was Mrs. Jones's vehicle traveling when the defendant crashed into her?" Other impact words such as "collision" and "explosion" can help to paint a memorable picture for the jury. In addition to repeating impact words and phrases, by incorporating the previous answer into the follow-up question, you reinforce your narrative through repetition. This is known as looping. For example, if the witness just testified that the defendant crashed into the plaintiff, follow up with "After the defendant crashed into the plaintiff, what happened next?" Looping also has the added benefit of enlivening your narrative and making your examination questions more interesting. Compare the above follow-up question with the neutral "What happened next?"

Engage the Witness in a Dialogue During Examination

The best direct examinations unfold as a dialogue between lawyer and witness. While you may want to write down the foundational questions necessary to admit documents, you should not read your questions from a script. Refer to notes sparingly. By all means, listen to the witness's testimony. This is important for two reasons. First, the witness may not say what you expect. If so, you need to be able to adjust your questions to bring out testimony the witness overlooked or may have misstated. Second, if you do not listen to the witness, you give the impression to the jury that you are not interested in what the witness has to say. Remember that eyes follow eyes. What you focus your gaze upon will draw the eyes of the jury as well. If the witness is testifying and looking at you, and you are busy looking at your notes to prepare for your next question, one or more members of the jury are bound to notice. When they do, the thought will occur: why should I pay attention to this witness when the lawyer obviously is not?

It is also important to not isolate the jury or put up barriers between the jury and the trial lawyer. Many lawyers prompt a witness's testimony by directing the witness to "tell the ladies and gentlemen of the jury (or the Court) what happened." It is far more comfortable and natural to simply say to the witness, "Tell us what happened." We are all in this together: witnesses, jurors, parties, and attorneys.

Maintain Credibility with the Jury

You are a champion for your cause and an advocate for your case, but you also have to be a realist. All cases have strengths and weaknesses. Do not hide important issues from the jury in the hope that a particularly troubling problem does not come forward. If you have a bad fact that impacts your witness's credibility, address it in the direct examination. Let the witness explain it. You may be able to minimize the impact of your witness's weaknesses (and possibly thwart an impeachment effort) by giving the witness a chance to explain a credibility problem or a flaw in his testimony. For example, if you have a plaintiff's case of solid liability and discover that your plaintiff had several drinks before the accident, it is better to meet that head-on in direct examination. Let the witness admit to having the drinks, but offer testimony to show he was not in an impaired state from the alcohol. Even if you are not sure your opponent knows about the alcohol issue, do not take a chance by omitting the problem. The same consideration would apply if your witness has a prior felony conviction. If the conviction meets your state's criteria as proper impeachment, there is no reason to try to hide that fact from the jury. Ask the witness directly if he has ever been to jail, and then give the witness a chance to explain. If your opponent brings it out on cross-examination for the first time, it will destroy your client's credibility and yours as well. The jury might wonder what other important issues you are trying to hide from them. If your witness gave a statement that you know will be inconsistent with his trial testimony, it is better to give the witness an opportunity to explain that statement rather than having the cross-examiner use that to his benefit by impeaching your witness. Ask the witness if he made the prior statement. Then ask why his testimony is different. Was it confusion, lapse of memory, or some other reason?

Use Leading Questions

Finally, use leading questions when necessary. Federal Rule of Evidence 611(c) provides the following: "When a party calls a hostile witness, an adverse party, or a witness identified with an adverse party, interrogation may be by leading questions." This rule enables an attorney to examine that witness in the presentation of her case, as opposed to waiting until the other side presents its case or defense. This can be an effective technique, particularly to elicit an admission of a party or the party's agent. Most states have an analogous rule by which an examiner may pose leading questions to an adverse or hostile witness. Some trial courts may even limit or restrict the ability of opposing counsel to question that witness during your examination. You may need to consider this rule when making a decision as to the identity of the parties to be brought into the case. For example, consider the case of a personal injury claim, in which the responsible party is an employee of a corporate defendant at the time of the collision. If that party leaves the employ of the defendant before trial, she may not be considered to be identified with the defendant, unless that employee is also named as a defendant.

Use of leading questions with a non-adverse witness may also be appropriate on background matters that are not reasonably subject to dispute, as a way to save time. But you should not use leading questions on the key points of a non-adverse witness's testimony. Even if your adversary lets you get away with it, such a technique risks undermining the witness's credibility with the jury.

Chapter 9

Cross-Examination

Aaron Krauss

Trial cross-examination happens just like it does in the movies. Really. It is—or at least should be—that scripted. You should know the answer to every question before you ask it, and the answer to all of the questions— in all areas of cross-examination—should always be "yes." To the extent the witness says anything other than "yes," you should be able to pull out a document (you don't have to pull it out of your inside jacket pocket, but that is a nice effect if the document is small enough to be folded neatly[1]) that says the answer is "yes," figuratively beat the witness over the head with it until the witness says "yes," and then move on to the next question (the answer to which should, of course, be "yes"). And, whatever you do, don't ask that dreaded one question too many.

A well-trained—and well-prepared—trial lawyer makes all of this look effortless, just like in the movies. What the judge and jury don't see is all of the work that went into this seemingly effortless examination. That work never makes it to the big screen (or even the small one). After all, who would watch ten hours of a lawyer poring over transcripts and

---

1. Although you generally have to disclose all of the exhibits you will use during your case-in-chief prior to trial, you do not have to disclose documents you will use "solely for impeachment." *See* FED. R. CIV. P. 26(a)(3). With that being said, if you "pull out" a previously undisclosed document during cross-examination, be prepared for a blizzard of authenticity and admissibility objections, especially if the document does not bear bates stamp numbers showing that it was produced during discovery. Indeed, if the document was not produced during discovery, you may face a sanctions motion for failing to disclose its existence.

exhibits to extract the nuggets of information that can be used to construct a great cross-examination? Then again, the hours of work drafting (and re-drafting) a movie script never get shown either. Nor do the 28 takes the actors and actresses went through to get that spontaneous eruption during cross-examination. And you have to get it right on the first take.[2]

Why Are You Cross-Examining This Witness?

Believe it or not, why you are cross-examining a specific witness is a very serious question. As tempting as it is to answer "Because it beats document review," or, better yet, "Because it beats doing all the work to prepare for a cross-examination and then handing the materials over to a more senior lawyer who will get to have all the fun at trial," you should know why you are cross-examining a witness before you get up to do it. As heretical as it may seem, you do not have to cross-examine every witness called to the stand. Sometimes "No questions, Your Honor" is the most devastating retort to a witness's testimony. Among other things, it suggests to the factfinder that the witness didn't matter.[3] If the factfinder believes that the other side is calling witnesses who don't matter, it is likely to believe that the other side is wasting the factfinder's time. Although such a belief won't necessarily make a factfinder decide in your client's favor, it certainly doesn't help a lawyer's case if the factfinder believes the lawyer is a time-waster.

Before you start cross-examining a witness, you should know what information you need to elicit from that witness and how that information will

---

2. There is a wonderful *New Yorker* cartoon of a witness on the stand with a lawyer yelling "Objection, Your Honor! That wasn't the answer we rehearsed." As humorous as this cartoon might be, such an objection is unlikely to be sustained, unless you are a very senior lawyer. As you have no doubt already noticed, some "deans of the bar" can get away with things that you (or I) cannot. I view this situation as additional incentive to become a dean of the bar someday.
3. If the witness did matter, forgoing cross-examination will get the witness off the stand faster, without giving the witness a chance to repeat damning testimony. This is not to say one should pass up the opportunity to cross-examine a witness who has hurt your case. It is, however, an acknowledgement that, sometimes, there is nothing you can do, and it is best to minimize any additional damage. As they say, you cannot dig yourself out of a hole. If you find that you are in a hole at trial, stop digging. Because a factfinder is likely to react negatively (from your perspective) if you cut short a cross-examination after getting burned badly by the witness, sometimes the wisest (and gutsiest) course is not to start a cross.

support your case. Keep that information in mind. Cross-examination is very dangerous. By definition, the witness you are cross-examining will be hostile to you and will do what she can to hurt you. This is not the time to "fish." Nor is it the time to gloat or to gild the lily. It is the time to know what you need to get, and to go in, get it, and get out quickly (and ideally) cleanly. Only make the points you have to make with this particular witness. If you can elicit the information from a friendly witness, don't try to drag the same information out of a hostile witness (unless, of course, it is important to your case to show that the other side's witness agreed with you on this particular point).

Similarly, resist the temptation to try to show every inconsistency in the witness's testimony during cross-examination or to make a mountain out of a molehill. An apocryphal story tells of a young lawyer cross-examining the victim of a robbery because the witness had testified in court that the criminal defendant was wearing black pants at the time of the robbery, in contrast to the police report that reflected the witness had said that the defendant was wearing dark blue pants. The witness retorted, "I guess I was paying more attention to the shotgun he was waving in my face than to his pants." (The jury convicted.) The moral of the story is that factfinders can easily tell when cross-examination descends into nit-picking, and they will react negatively to it. More importantly, if the factfinder thinks you are nit-picking, the factfinder is likely to overlook (or ignore) any substantive points you made during your cross-examination. As in so many other areas, the bad can (and usually will) drive out the good.

Unlike in the movies, the witness you are cross-examining is not going to break down and say "I did it."[4] Leaving aside the fact that a hostile witness is more likely to cut out his own tongue rather than give you such an answer, the only way you will be able to get a witness to give such an

---

4. At least I have never seen, or even heard of, this happening. Perhaps there is some Perry Mason out there somewhere who has made a witness break down on the stand. In reality, as discussed more fully below, a cross-examination consists of many small steps that lead the factfinder to a conclusion. The factfinder should, however, draw its own conclusions. If the factfinder draws the conclusion, the factfinder will (by definition) believe its conclusion. If you try and draw the conclusion for the factfinder, the factfinder will fight you because the conclusion will be yours, not the factfinder's. You do not want a factfinder to fight you. You will lose that fight.

answer is if you already have the answer in writing. And if you have the answer in writing, so does the other side. Would you put a witness on the stand who was subject to such a cross-examination? Of course not. Neither would your adversary.[5] As a result, do not expect the witness to break down.

Even if you could break down a witness, you may not wish to do so. If you are viewed as a bully, the factfinder will not view you or your case favorably. This is why it is so difficult to cross-examine the proverbial (or the literal) widow or orphan. Not only should you watch your tone with such a witness (as with every witness), you should also watch what you suggest. You don't need to convince the factfinder that the widow was lying. For example, you may only have to suggest that she may be mistaken. We all understand how that could happen. After all, she was doing the best she could, but she simply didn't have her glasses on. And, although she doesn't really need them, they are helpful, aren't they?

The bottom line is that an effective cross-examination does not need to make the witness recant or say things favorable to your case. Sometimes the most effective cross-examination neutralizes the direct testimony, either by showing that the witness didn't have a good factual foundation for (or wasn't sure of) the testimony, or by deflecting the witness's testimony in such a way as to make it not hurt your client. Again, know why you are cross-examining the witness. Know what you need the witness to say. Get the witness to say it. Then sit down.

What Are the Three Areas of Cross-Examination?

There are three different areas of cross-examination.

First, you can use cross to bring out information (including evidence of bias) that was omitted during direct examination. The classic example of this type of testimony is bringing out the fact that the witness is related to

---

5. A good rule of thumb is to assume that your adversary is at least as smart, as well trained, and as well prepared as you are. If this turns out not to be true, by all means capitalize. Luck favors the prepared. And it is always better to overestimate your adversary than to underestimate your adversary.

the party on whose behalf he is testifying.[6] Other examples of this type of testimony are bringing out either delays in reporting the events to which the witness testified, or, conversely, that the witness has made similar claims in the past. Depending on the situation, you can argue that the witness is either "crying wolf" or always thinks things of this sort are happening.

Ideally, you can bring out the fact that the witness agrees with at least one or two points you want to prove in your case. Doing so can allow you to argue in closing that "even the other side agrees that . . . ."

Second, you can use cross to suggest that either the witness is unsure of the testimony given on direct or the witness (although sure of his testimony) may have lacked the ability to accurately observe the events to which he testified. Some witnesses will admit either that they are not sure or that there could have been another explanation of the events they described.[7] Even if a witness will not admit to any uncertainty, it may be possible to bring out the fact that it is improbable that the witness actually made the observations that were the subject of his testimony. Again, the classic example is bringing out the fact that the witness was not wearing his or her glasses; other examples include that the sun was in his eyes, that he was distracted at the time, and so on. Alternatively, it may be possible to bring out the fact that the witness was not relying on his own observation but had instead internalized the observations of others. If this is the case, you should be pressing a hearsay objection.

Third, you can use cross to show that the witness changed his story in a material way. Depending on the magnitude of the change, these questions

---

6. It is unlikely that you will ever be able to point out that a witness "forgot" that she was related to your opposing party. If opposing counsel is worth his salt, he will have brought out that fact on direct and will not have left it to cross. You may, however, be able to bring out the fact that the witness has been friends with the opposing party for years or has some other reason (such as a financial interest) to testify in a particular way.

7. When I am preparing my own witnesses to withstand cross-examination, I always caution them to respond carefully to a question that begins "isn't it possible that . . . ." The best answer I ever heard to such a question was "Madam, anything is possible, but there is not one shred of evidence that anything even remotely like that actually happened in this case." Admittedly, that answer was given by an expert witness. It is, however, a textbook response to a common type of question.

can suggest that the witness is not really sure of his testimony, or that the witness is intentionally changing his testimony to benefit the other side.[8]

Depending on the facts, you may want to go into one or more of these areas. You should, however, make sure that your questioning is not at cross purposes. For example, if a witness previously gave some testimony that was favorable to your client, you may want to bring out that testimony. If, however, you then try to show that the witness did not actually observe the events to which the witness has testified, you will undercut the testimony favorable to your client. You should therefore make a choice as to which is more valuable, the factfinder hearing (and believing) testimony favorable to your client (along with the rest of the witness's testimony), or the factfinder not believing anything the witness said.

Why Should the Answer to Every Question Be Yes?

Embedded in the rule of having the answer to every question be "yes" is the rule that you should only ask leading questions on cross-examination.[9] Cross-examination is not the time to ask a witness "why." Doing so opens the door to a five-minute answer that you will not like. You will not like the answer for two reasons. First, it will not help your client. Second, it will allow the witness to "get away" and make a speech during what should be your cross-examination. You should therefore restrict yourself to asking closed-ended questions to which you already know the answer.

Especially when faced with closed ended-questions, a hostile witness's every instinct will be to fight with you and to disagree with you. Don't give the witness the chance. Ideally, you don't want to give the witness the chance to talk. Unlike on direct examination (where the witness should be the one telling the story), on cross-examination, you should be doing the talking. The witness should just be agreeing with you. And when the factfinder sees that even the other side's witness is agreeing with you, how could you be wrong?

---

8. In the unlikely event that the witness changed his story in a way that is favorable to your client, it is best not to bring the change in testimony to the factfinder's attention.
9. *See* United States v. Pierre, 486 Fed. App'x 59, 65 (11th Cir. 2012); FED. R. EVID. 611(c).

Many lawyers have a habit of using double negatives when cross-examining. How many times have you heard a question start either "Is it not true that . . ." or "It is true, is it not, that. . . ." Let me suggest that it is easier (for both you and the factfinder) to simply make a statement and end the sentence with "right?" or "true?" or "correct?" So, for example,

- You had been drinking with your friends on Saturday night, right?
- You started drinking at about 9, right?
- You started drinking at the Bent Elbow, right?
- The Bent Elbow is on Main Street, right?
- You aren't sure how many drinks you had at the Bent Elbow, right?
- You and your friends had left the Bent Elbow, right?
- You were heading towards O'Shey's, right?
- O'Shey's is on Main Street at Elm Street, right?
- You were walking down Main Street towards Elm Street, right?
- You were talking with your friends while you walked, right?
- You saw the accident while you were walking to O'Shey's, right?"

Having the answer to every question be "yes" also "trains" the witness. The witness will get into the habit of just saying "yes" to every question, even if he doesn't want to. This habit can be hard to break.[10]

One of the ways to make sure the answer to every question is "yes" is to have each question focus on a small, discrete fact. The cross-examination I outlined above suggests that the witness was, at a minimum, slightly impaired and distracted when the accident happened. The questions are, however, broken up into small steps with which the witness cannot disagree. A hostile witness is not going to admit that he was slightly drunk and wasn't really paying attention when the accident happened. You should

---

10. Experienced lawyers refer to this effect as getting a witness "into the tunnel." A witness who is "in the tunnel" cannot see where she is going and tends to be hypnotized by the single bright light at the end of the tunnel. When you get a witness into the tunnel, don't let her out. Ideally, you will sit down before the witness realizes exactly what has happened or figures out a way to get out of the tunnel. One way to prepare your witnesses to stay out of the tunnel is to remind them that they do not have to accept the cross-examiner's phrasing, or description of events. "That isn't how I would describe it" or "those aren't words I would use" or "that isn't quite right" are good phrases that keep a witness out of the tunnel.

not, therefore, jump to the ultimate question. A witness will (and will have to) admit what he was doing that night. You can therefore slowly walk the witness through the progression of events that took place before the accident, asking small questions to bring out the facts you want the factfinder to hear. The key is to focus only on the facts and to break each fact into a separate question with which the witness cannot disagree.[11]

Many lawyers make the mistake of having the answers to the lead-in questions be "yes," and then setting up the key question so the answer is "no." Try to resist this temptation. At the very least, it will break your (and the witness's) rhythm. It will also cause the witness to fight you in a new way. Make it easy for both of you and make sure that the answer to every question is yes.

How Do You Prepare an Effective Cross-Examination?

Cross-examination preparation begins with a review of the available exhibits and transcripts. The starting point is the witness's deposition. If the witness has answered a question under oath, the witness will have to give the same answer at trial. If the witness does not do so, you can pull out the transcript and (figuratively) beat the witness over the head with it until the witness gives consistent testimony—or at least admits that she testified differently at a point closer in time to the events that are the subject of the testimony.

What if the witness's deposition was videotaped?[12] It is possible, albeit very expensive and difficult, to cross-examine a witness by using a videotaped

---

11. Even if your adversary does not object to compound questions, a witness is much more likely to say something other than "yes" if a question includes multiple facts. At a minimum, if your question gets long and complicated, a witness is likely to "lose the question" and ask you to repeat it. That will break your rhythm and can make you look as if you are trying to confuse the witness. If, on the other hand, the witness claims to be confused by questions the factfinder can easily understand, the factfinder is likely to think that the witness is being evasive and is therefore not credible.

12. There are a number of reasons to videotape a witness's deposition. It acts as a safeguard against the witness not appearing at trial (if, for example, the witness is beyond the scope of a trial subpoena). It helps to control the witness and opposing counsel. Because a picture is worth a thousand words, it may be beneficial to videotape a witness who looks "shifty" (think of Bill Gates's infamous deposition in the Microsoft antitrust case during which his body language did significant damage to his credibility). A videotaped deposition may also reduce the

deposition. The expense is twofold. First, you must rent the appropriate projection equipment to show the video clips to the jury. Second (and this is where the real expense comes in), you must pay someone to edit and cue up each video clip. Usually, the video clips are linked to bar codes in your cross-examination outline so that you can, with a wave of an electronic wand, make the relevant clip appear on the screen.

So why wouldn't you do this? Leaving aside the expense, you can't adjust video cross-examination on the fly. If the video clip does not precisely match up with your question, the cross-examination will not be effective. If you are cross-examining using a transcript, you can adjust the lines you read to the jury on the fly. You can also get into areas that you didn't originally think would be necessary. And a savvy witness (or an aggressive opposing counsel) can interrupt the flow of a video cross-examination by demanding that the witness be shown the transcript and insisting that the question was taken out of context. If you cannot play additional video that the witness thinks is important, the factfinder may view your cross-examination as being unfair.

Believe it or not, it is possible to cross-examine a witness who has not been deposed. Doing so requires a close examination of the available documents. It is ideal if the witness authored or received the document in question, but one can cross-examine a witness based on a document the witness did not send or receive. As set forth below, although there is a risk that a witness will deny knowing anything about a document that the witness did not explicitly send or receive, such a denial might not be believable. For example, it is possible that a witness will deny knowing anything about a 1040 form she did not sign. A factfinder is, however, unlikely to believe a witness who claims that the income listed on a 1040 is too high.

The end result of your cross-examination preparation is a script (just like in the movies). All of the lines are written out. Although this may seem stilted, if you are asking the exact question that appears in the document and the witness says anything other than "yes," you will be able to impeach the witness effectively. If you ask the question differently than the way it

---

likelihood that opposing counsel will misbehave. At the same time, however, it also limits your ability to browbeat a witness. It reflects any stumbles or pauses in your questioning. Personally, I rarely think that videotaping a deposition is worth the additional cost.

was asked in the document, at best the witness will have an opportunity to explain why the answer was different. If the question you asked was very different than the way it was asked in the document, you will have a misfire where the factfinder will be unsure of why you are trying to impeach the witness. Impeachment is also much more effective if it is done quickly. That is why you want to write down the exact location (i.e., the page of the transcript, exhibit, or other document) of the material you will use for impeachment if impeachment is necessary. Not only will a jury look askance at you if you need five minutes to flip through a transcript to find what you want during cross-examination, but you will probably not like what a judge is likely to say to (or about) you if you do so.

The hardest part of constructing an effective cross-examination is paring down your questions. Cross-examination is definitely a situation where less is more. Leaving aside the potential for getting burned with every question, a factfinder can only absorb so much information. If your cross-examination goes on for hours, the factfinder is likely to forget your important points. The "golden nuggets" will get lost in the piles of slag. And you do not want to make the factfinder sift through a mountain of slag to find the gold in your cross-examination. On the contrary, you want to get the gold quickly and then sit down.

Although there is no hard-and-fast rule for how long a cross-examination should last, as a general matter it should not be longer than half the direct examination. There are, of course, exceptions to this rule. The foremost is if the opposing party has called one of your witnesses as on cross in their case-in-chief. If your adversary does so, you will have to decide whether to do your direct as part of your cross.[13] Assuming it is a strong witness who you can recall to the stand,[14] you probably want to take two bites at the apple and "merely" cross-examine the witness on the points brought

---

13. Sometimes a judge will make this decision for you by insisting that a witness, once called, will not be recalled to the stand. It is both unwise and ultimately futile to argue with a judge who has made such a ruling. Even if you do not expect such a ruling, you (and your witness) should be prepared for it. It is always better to be safe than sorry.

14. There are some witnesses, especially third parties and executives, who are difficult to keep in the courtroom for long periods of time. If you insist on recalling a witness such as this, you run the risk of the favorableness of her testimony decreasing in direct proportion to the inconvenience the witness believes you have imposed.

out on direct (that is to say, you want to stay within the scope of the direct examination). You can then put the witness back on the stand in your case and have the witness tell the story in the way (and in the order) you want. Doing so will reinforce the witness's testimony in the factfinder's mind. If, on the other hand, your witness is not so strong and may not withstand the additional cross-examination that would follow a return to the stand, you probably want to complete your entire examination of the witness at once.[15]

Cross-examination can be both positive and negative. This is to say, cross-examination can establish that a witness did something. Cross-examination can also establish that a witness did not do something. The following is an example of a cross-examination outline showing that a witness did something (that the witness's lawyer was unlikely to bring out on direct examination):

- You quit working for XYZ company on September 18, 2009. (Paul's dep. at 29) (EXHIBIT 16)
- You resigned as an officer. (Paul's dep. at 30)
- You would no longer be treasurer as of September 18, 2009. (Paul's dep. at 30)
- You resigned as a director. (Paul's dep. at 30)
- You resigned as an employee. (Paul's dep. at 31)
- While you were working for XYZ, XYZ had issued you a laptop computer. (Paul's dep. at 253)

---

15. Some lawyers believe there is an advantage to disrupting your adversary's case by making an extensive examination of your witness if called first by the adversary. While doing so can interrupt your adversary's presentation of evidence and can give the factfinder additional favorable evidence earlier in the case (when presumably the factfinder's mind is more open), it leaves you with less evidence to put on in your case-in-chief. You should therefore consider what other witnesses, and what other evidence, you will have to present before completing the direct of a witness who has been called as-on-cross. As a general matter, a jury is likely to wonder why you did not put on a defense or view a very short defense as insubstantial. This is not the case with a judge, who will understand why your case is so short. As an aside, in some jurisdictions, if a defendant goes beyond the scope of cross and introduces evidence during the plaintiff's case-in-chief, the defendant cannot move for a directed verdict. Some jurisdictions have either abrogated this rule or decided that going beyond the scope of direct is not truly the introduction of evidence. You should be aware of the rule in your jurisdiction before you decide whether to complete the witness's testimony or ask to recall the witness during your case-in-chief.

- When you quit, you knew you had to give your laptop back to XYZ. (Paul's dep. at 254)
- You gave your laptop back to XYZ through your counsel. (Paul's dep. at 254)
- Prior to returning your laptop computer, you sought legal advice related to the return of that computer. (Paul's dep. at 254)
- You sought that legal advice from Attorney Doe. (Paul's dep. at 254–55)
- You deleted documents off your laptop computer before giving the computer to Attorney Doe to return to XYZ. (Paul's dep. at 255–56)
- You specifically sought out a program that you thought would delete files irretrievably. (Paul's dep. at 257)
- It was called the XL Delete program. (Paul's dep. at 257)
- You used the XL Delete program. (Paul's dep. at 257)
- You don't remember what files you deleted. (Paul's dep. at 269)
- You agree that you deleted files related to your work for XYZ with the XL Delete program right before you gave your laptop back to Attorney Doe to pass on to XYZ. (Paul's dep. at 272)

Although you should "find your own voice" and prepare materials in the way best suited to your style,[16] let me point out that this outline works well because it proceeds in small steps and has at least one document reference (more than one document reference can be helpful) in case the witness says anything other than "yes." Although the bulk of the outline tracks deposition testimony, note that the cross-examination outline does not follow the same order as the deposition testimony. Instead, the "raw footage" of the deposition has been "re-cut" into a new order. Some of this results from the elimination of material that was either unhelpful or not significant enough to be included in the cross-examination. Some of this results from bringing together "good answers" that appeared in different parts of the deposition.

---

16. Personally, I tend to keep exhibits in folders with a marked-up copy for me and a clean copy to hand to the witness. Other lawyers with whom I have tried cases swear by trial notebooks in three-ring binders. Still others prefer velo-bound exhibit books. A younger lawyer with whom I recently tried a case kept everything on his iPad. Each of these methods has advantages (e.g., a folder can't crash, freeze up, or run out of power, and the witness can only see the exhibit you have handed up) and disadvantages (e.g., folders can get out of order or can get dropped on the floor). Find the method or combination of methods that works best for you.

An example of a cross-examination outline showing that a witness did not do something is as follows:

- You were in charge of tax matters for the XYZ company. (Paul's dep. at 25)
- Absent information provided by you, the accountants couldn't prepare XYZ's taxes. (Paul's dep. at 17)
- The accountants would send you XYZ's year-end financials. (Paul's dep. at 64) (EXHIBIT 7)
- You made whatever corrections you thought were necessary to the financials. (Paul's dep. at 65)
- You re-booked things if you thought that something had been charged to the wrong account. (Paul's dep. at 66–67)
- Those reclassifications happened. (Paul's dep. at 68)
- You were doing these reclassifications as recently as July 12, 2009. (Paul's dep. at 316–17) (EXHIBIT 13)
- At the end of the day, you and the accountants always agreed on the proper classifications for XYZ's expenses. (Paul's dep. at 68–69)
- Your complaint about defendant's expense reimbursement requests is that the bookkeeper couldn't charge them to the correct account. (Paul's dep. at 39)
- The accountants would only finalize the tax returns after you corrected and approved the financials. (Paul's dep. at 65)
- XYZ's tax returns were never filed without you having first approved the financial statements. (Paul's dep. at 82)
- You claim that you told the accountants that you would no longer sign XYZ's tax returns. (Paul's dep. at 32)
- You claim to have told the accountants this when they were at XYZ in August or September of 2008 for the year-end review. (Paul's dep. at 32 and 34)
- You claim to have told accountant 1, and perhaps accountant 2. (Paul's dep. at 33)
- You claim that you told accountant 1 and accountant 2 that you would no longer sign XYZ's tax returns because there were expenses being charged to XYZ that were not business related. (Paul's dep. at 32)

- You say you never put this in writing. (Paul's dep. at 32–33) (Paul's dep. at 99)
- You never put this in any of your e-mails to the accountants. (Paul's dep. at 35)
- EXHIBIT 11 is a September 5, 2008, e-mail you sent to the accountants. (Paul's dep. at 97–98)
- EXHIBIT 11 is the transmission to you of the financial statements that lead up to the tax return that is labeled EXHIBIT 60. (Paul's dep. at 98)
- You asked a tax question in EXHIBIT 11. (Paul's dep. at 99)
- You never told the accountants in your September 5, 2008, e-mail that you wouldn't sign the tax return. (EXHIBIT 11) (Paul's dep. at 99)
- You say that the accountants never put it in writing that you weren't going to sign XYZ's tax return. (Paul's dep. at 100–01)

Finally, cross-examination can make a witness take a position that the factfinder is likely to think is not credible. In many ways, it does not matter if the factfinder thinks the witness is testifying incorrectly or if the factfinder thinks the witness is out of touch with reality. In either event, the factfinder is unlikely to credit the witness's testimony. That is the goal of an effective cross-examination. An example of this type of cross-examination outline is as follows. In this example, the licensor licensed technology necessary for the XYZ Company to make 80 percent of its products.

- You weren't surprised to receive EXHIBIT 19 because the licensor had called you before he sent EXHIBIT 19 and complained that the royalty sheet you sent him didn't balance. (Paul's dep. at 185–86)
- You never told the president of XYZ company about this conversation when you forwarded EXHIBIT 19 to him. (Paul's dep. at 231)
- You didn't believe that the president of XYZ company would have been in a better position to make good decisions on behalf of XYZ if he had known the content of your conversation with the licensor. (Paul's dep. at 233)
- You believed you were acting in XYZ company's best interests when you had this conversation with the licensor. (Paul's dep. at 233 and 234)

• You also believed you were acting in XYZ company's best interests when you chose not to share the contents of the conversation you had with the licensor with the president of XYZ company. (Paul's dep. at 235)

One final note on preparing for cross-examination. Your cross-examination outline should include anything you think might be necessary during cross-examination. This will result in a (potential) cross-examination that is too long.[17] Before you begin cross-examining, pick up your red pen, go through your outline, and cross out what you will not use.[18] This is, by everyone's estimation, the hardest part of preparing for cross-examination. Not only must it be done on the fly, but you have to make the hard decisions about what you need to do. Again, focus on what you need the witness to say and why you need the witness to say it. And, having seen the witness testify, estimate how hard it is going to be to elicit the testimony you need. You then trim accordingly.

What Documents Can You Use to Beat the Witness Over the Head?

In addition to cross-examining a witness based on the deposition he gave in the case at bar, you can cross-examine a witness based on any other testimony the witness has given under oath.[19] If the witness has testified, it is not necessary for the party against whom the testimony is being offered to have been present at the deposition.[20] As a result, you can use tran-

---

17. Among other things, you may not be sure of the order in which witnesses will be cross-examined. If you have already made your point during the cross-examination of a prior witness, you may not wish to revisit the topic. In addition to potentially boring the fact-finder, if the current witness gives an answer that is less favorable than the one you previously obtained, you will not have helped your case.

18. The judge will usually give you a five-minute break to "get organized," especially if you say that you need five minutes to eliminate some material and streamline your examination. Judges are quick to give you five minutes if they believe doing so will save thirty.

19. *See* FED. R. EVID. 801(d)(1)(A).

20. *See* United States v. Morgan, 376 F.3d 1002, 1007 (9th Cir. 2004). This contrasts with FED. R. CIV. P. 32, which allows a party to use a deposition against a party who was present during the deposition. Rule 32 governs cases in which the witness does not testify at trial. *See*

scripts of a witness's testimony in related cases (such as testimony before an investigatory agency) or even completely unrelated cases. The ability to cross-examine based on testimony in unrelated cases can be particularly useful when cross-examining an expert witness. You can often locate transcripts of an expert's testimony in other cases, showing that an expert has taken contradictory positions in what would appear to be similar cases. This is a very effective way of convincing a factfinder that the expert is a hired gun who will say whatever he is asked to say in any given case.

Sworn statements (such as tax returns, governmental filings, and financial applications) can also be used effectively on cross-examination. Many of these documents contain fine print above the signature line stating that the signer makes the statement under penalty of perjury or that the signer represents and warrants that the statements are true and correct, to the best of the signer's knowledge, information, and belief.

Even if a written statement does not contain this type of fine print, any document authored by the witness can be fodder for cross-examination.[21] Although the witness may claim that the statement in the document is erroneous, a factfinder is unlikely to believe such a claim if there is no written evidence of a retraction. Similarly, if a witness has received a document, but did not respond promptly and claim that the statements in that document are inaccurate, the factfinder is likely to disbelieve a currently voiced claim that the statements in the document were wrong.[22]

Finally, you can cross-examine a witness based on a document authored by someone else in the witness's organization, especially if the author is senior to the witness. A witness is usually understandably reluctant to contradict his boss. And if the witness does so, the factfinder is left to wonder

---

Nationwide Life Ins. Co. v. Richards, 541 F.3d 903, 913–15 (9th Cir. 2008). FED. R. EVID. 801(d)(1)(a) governs cases in which the witness does testify at trial. *See* United States v. Demmitt, 706 F.2d 665, 670–74 (5th Cir. 2013).

21.   Many documents, such as notes and e-mails, are not "signed." Even so, they can be used effectively on cross-examination.

22.   It is for this reason that lawyers are loath to leave a letter or an e-mail "hanging out there" if the statements in the document are false. Although there are many instances in which a step-by-step refutation of the incorrect statements would not be productive, you can protect the record by sending a written response that says (in sum and substance) that although you disagree with the statements, you do not believe it would be productive to discuss your disagreement at this time. Such a response can serve as a placeholder without unduly provoking the other side.

who is incorrect, the witness or the boss. Either result would be favorable for your client.

A side note on the Fifth Amendment: unlike in criminal cases, in a civil case the factfinder *can* draw an adverse inference if a witness asserts her Fifth Amendment rights.[23] It is therefore highly desirable to make an adverse witness in a civil case "take the Fifth." You still, however, have to ask the questions in the same way you would ask them if the witness were giving substantive answers. Lay the foundation, and lead the factfinder up to the desired conclusion, just as you would if the answer to every question was "yes." As tempting as it may be when you have a witness "in the tunnel" mindlessly repeating "I take the Fifth," you cannot ask a question for which you do not have a good faith basis for believing that the answer would be "yes."[24] For example, you cannot throw in a question such as "And you were high on crack cocaine at the time, right?" (unless, of course, you have a good faith basis for believing that the witness really was high on crack).

An important (but seldom used) hint for the effective use of exhibits relates to the fact that most lawyers mark deposition exhibits on the fly. They arrive at a deposition with a pile of papers and then instruct the court reporter to mark the papers as exhibits as they are used. Each exhibit gets its own number, usually preceded by the name of the witness. Jones 1 is followed by Jones 2, which is followed by Jones 3, and so on. That, in and of itself, is not a problem. The problem arises at the next deposition when what was marked as "Jones 1" is now marked as "Smith 1" (or worse yet, "Smith 28"). By the time the case gets to trial, the same document (the contract, for example) may have been given several different exhibit numbers. To make matters worse, the document is often given a new trial exhibit number.

The problem comes into focus when you sit down to prepare your cross-examination. Jones may have made a helpful admission about the contract. That admission, however, will look something like this:

Q: I show you the contract marked as Jones 1. Did you sign Jones 1?
A: Yes.

---

23. *See* Louis Vuitton Malletier S.A. v. LY USA, Inc., 676 F.3d 83, 97–98 (2d Cir. 2012).
24. *See* ABA MODEL RULES OF PROF'L CONDUCT R. 3.4(e) (a lawyer may not "allude to any matter . . . that will not be supported by admissible evidence").

Q: When you signed Jones 1, did you realize that it required you to pay my client's attorney's fees?

A: Yes.

As helpful as this admission is, it will lose a great deal of force if, at trial, the contract is marked as anything other than Jones 1. If, for example, the factfinder has seen and heard the contract referred to as Plaintiff's Exhibit 3, it will be wondering why this cross-examination regarding Jones 1 is important. It gets even more confusing if you are using Jones's testimony to cross-examine Smith.

The solution is easy. Once you mark an exhibit, do not change the exhibit number. Ever. Nothing says that the witness's name has to precede the exhibit number. Similarly, nothing says that you have to use (or even mark) exhibits in numerical order. You can begin Jones's deposition by showing the witness Plaintiff's Exhibit 28.[25] You can also file a motion to which you attach Plaintiff's Exhibits 3, 28, and 92 and the Jones deposition. Nothing says exhibits to a motion have to be referred to as "Exhibit A," "Exhibit B," and "Exhibit C." Similarly, exhibits to a motion don't have to be referred to as "Exhibit 1," "Exhibit 2," and "Exhibit 3." And you don't have to give the Jones deposition an exhibit number. The judge really will be able to find the Jones deposition if you refer to it by name.[26]

There are two additional benefits to pre-marking your exhibits. First, it allows you to insert exhibit references into your deposition outlines. These reminders to ask questions about specific documents can be very helpful at a deposition. It also makes it easier to use your deposition outline as a starting point for your cross-examination outline. Second, it eliminates the need to bring spare copies of exhibits to future depositions. If you have already handed opposing counsel(s) a copy of Plaintiff's Exhibit 28 at the Jones deposition, you don't have to hand out an additional copy at the Smith

---

25.   If you do this, the court reporter or opposing counsel will often ask you if you mean "Jones 28" or even "Jones 1." Say no, you mean Plaintiff's Exhibit 28. If you have pre-marked your exhibits, the court reporter will be thrilled not to have to do so. And if you stick to your guns, there is nothing that opposing counsel can do. After all, it is your exhibit, and you can call it whatever you like.

26.   In jurisdictions where hard, as opposed to electronic, copies are the norm, it is easy enough to make a tab that says "Jones dep." and insert it before the transcript of the Jones deposition.

deposition.[27] While not having to hand out additional copies of exhibits at future depositions may cut down on your exercise,[28] it does make it easier to fit your exhibits under the seat in front of you when you have to travel.

How Do You Know When You Have Asked One Question Too Many?

The traditional answer to the question of how you know when you have asked one question too many is that when you ask the question, you wish you could—in true cartoon fashion—chase your words across the courtroom and tackle them before they get to the witness. More helpfully, there are two telltale signs that you may be asking one question too many. First, if your question begins with the words "summary" or "conclusion," or (heaven forbid) includes the words "explain" or "explanation," it is probably one question too many. Leaving aside the fact that an adverse witness will not agree with your conclusions, you want the factfinder to draw its own conclusions.

Second, if you feel insufferably smug when you are phrasing the question, you probably don't want to ask it. Not only is such a question likely to backfire, even if it does not, the factfinder may feel sorry for the witness. That is not the impression you want to leave. As a result, you should quit while you are ahead, and say the magic words, "No further questions, Your Honor."

---

27. It is courteous to remind opposing counsel that you will not bring additional copies of exhibits to future depositions, and that you will only bring a copy for the witness. I suggest that you take the witness's copy back at the end of the deposition and re-file it. That way you will be prepared for the next deposition.
28. Many lawyers forgo gym memberships in favor of lugging trial bags full of exhibits to and from various proceedings.

Chapter 10

Dealing with Expert Witnesses at Trial

Alana Bassin

The examination of expert witnesses represents a crucial part of most trials. Students of trial practice have long recognized the potential for jurors to assign great weight to expert opinion testimony—despite the fact that the expert witness was not present at the crucial event that forms the basis for trial and has no personal knowledge of the facts. Rather, the expert merely offers an opinion based on facts found from investigation or furnished by others—even inadmissible facts, where such facts are reasonably relied upon by experts in the relevant field in forming their opinions.[1] The rules of evidence, therefore, limit the circumstances in which expert opinion evidence may be admitted at trial.[2]

---

1. *See, e.g.*, FED. R. EVID. 703.
2. *See* MICHAEL E. TIGAR, EXAMINING WITNESSES 368–70 (2d ed. 2003). For example, Federal Rule of Evidence 702 provides:
   A witness who is qualified as an expert by knowledge, skill, experience, training, or education may testify in the form of an opinion or otherwise if:
      (a) the expert's scientific, technical, or other specialized knowledge will help the trier of fact to understand the evidence or to determine a fact in issue;
      (b) the testimony is based on sufficient facts or data;
      (c) the testimony is the product of reliable principles and methods; and
      (d) the expert has reliably applied the principles and methods to the facts of the case.

This chapter gives you the basic tools necessary for dealing with this particular type of evidence at trial. Because my practice consists primarily of defense of civil litigation, I typically confront the opposing expert through cross-examination before I get to direct my own experts. The structure of this chapter follows that same order.

Cross-Examination of the Opposing Expert

As a defense attorney, you have the opportunity to cross-examine the plaintiff's experts before you call your own experts to testify. You cannot count on winning by relying on the defense experts alone; you must also develop your case themes in your cross-examination of the plaintiff's experts and undermine the plaintiff's case before beginning the defendant's case-in-chief. Similarly, for plaintiff's counsel, your cross-examination of the defense experts provides an opportunity to replay themes or key pieces of evidence introduced in the your case. No matter what side you represent, the cross-examination of the opposing expert represents an important opportunity to tell your story during the opposition's case.

Preparation

In order to conduct an effective cross-examination, you need to first become an expert on the topic area. One of the most effective ways to prepare is to seek input from your own expert. Your own expert will typically be able to educate you on the topic and point out the opposing expert's vulnerabilities. Meet with your expert, read the literature, and learn the area so that you become wholly familiar with the topic. In addition to knowing the substance of the testimony, be as familiar with the experts themselves, including their curriculum vitae (CV), their prior testimony, and their public statements (whether in books, online, or wherever you can find them). This means spending time pulling background information on the expert. With access to the Internet, there is typically an abundance of information to gather. Although a CV provided by opposing counsel is always helpful, your search for impeachment material or helpful testimony should not end there. Many experts have web pages or social media posts where they have made representations or statements that may relate to the content of your case. You should also try to track down all of their prior publications. The ability to impeach the witness is important, and thus you need to gather deposition transcripts to arm yourself with prior sworn testimony that may be inconsistent with the expert's testimony in your case.

Publications can be very helpful, as sometimes the expert will give advice or opinions on certain matters on a topic that will be consistent with exactly what your client did. Likewise, reach out to colleagues in the industry who may have encountered this expert to see if they have deposed the expert. In this regard, it is helpful to talk to colleagues familiar with her so you have a general understanding of the expert's typical demeanor and to develop strategies for cross-examination.

Former testimony is often a gold mine. You may find out that the expert has been precluded from testimony based on her lack of expertise. You may find out that the expert has testified against every other company in the industry or has testified to something wholly inconsistent. It not only gives you a feel for what the expert can say, but it can also lead to a very clean cross-examination with great talking points. Either the expert will testify consistently and you can get great sound bites for the jury, or you can impeach her early in the examination. (Once an expert realizes that you are prepared to cross her on former testimony, she is often much more willing to concede an answer.) In short, before cross-examining any witnesses, you want to make sure you have and are familiar with their CV, former testimony, former appearances in court, representations that they have made online, whether on a formal work website, social media, or anywhere else.

Of course, once you know the witness, you need to determine what your goals are with the witness. Your goals should correspond with your big picture trial themes. You should determine the points you want to make with the expert that are consistent with your trial themes and try to get them to come out during cross-examination of the opponent's expert. Sometimes key issues or key questions must be stated in a very precise way. If that is the case, write them down in advance so that you obtain the appropriate admissions using the right language.

When developing your questions, remember that you can control the witness with leading questions. Avoid asking open-ended questions that give the expert the opportunity to explain his opinion. Those questions usually begin with words such as "who," "what," "when," "where," and "how." Follow the "golden rule" of cross-examination: never ask a question unless you know its answer. A skilled cross-examiner may, on occasion, stray from this hard-and-fast rule, but the inexperienced lawyer that does so invites a seasoned expert to emphasize the facts and opinions that are most dangerous to the lawyer's case.

Finally, it is imperative to remain vigilant about the court's rulings on motions in limine. Do not ask questions that open the door to harmful evidence that you have succeeded in excluding from evidence prior to the trial.

General Framework

There are certain areas that you will likely want to cover in a basic cross-examination. This includes exposing weaknesses in tangential areas related to the expert's background, potential biases, and foundation in forming his opinion. As to the merits of the expert's opinions, you should seek to obtain admissions in areas in which the opposing expert agrees with the defendant's position and expose areas where the expert's opinions are inconsistent or unreasonable. You should further be attentive as to whether the expert has made any mistakes in his analysis. If the mistake is significant, it may form the basis for testimony amounting to a home run for the defense. If the mistakes are less significant, expose them anyway—so long as they are helpful to your case. You can later make mountains out of those molehills in closing argument.

The Tangential Areas
Expose the Expert's Background
In relation to the expert's background, the examiner's goal is to expose the expert's lack of expertise, education, authorship, or testing in the relevant area. Areas where she is not an expert should be obvious to the jury at the end of the cross-examination. Although the expert may have an impressive resume, she may have never published or had any unique training or practical work experience in the particular area relevant to the trial. To the extent that the opponent's expert is lacking some qualification possessed by your expert, the opposing expert should be compelled to describe the

additional training or study that would be required for that expert to claim the same level of expertise as your expert. Make sure that the jury is aware of the relative qualifications of the opposing experts in order to claim the high ground in the battle of the experts.[3]

Demonstrate the Expert's Bias and Expose the "Professional Witness"

An expert witness faces a serious challenge to his credibility once he becomes viewed by a jury as a "hired gun" or a "professional witness" who has been paid to come into the courtroom to provide an untenable position to support a litigant's case. When the facts support it, counsel should highlight the percentage of time and amount of income that the expert has made as an expert witness to emphasize the fact that the witness is a professional witness for hire. Showing that the witness charges significantly more per hour for serving as a "forensic consultant" than is normally earned by that witness in his trade is a simple way to demonstrate the expert's motives for being involved in forensics as opposed to his day job. This is especially so when the expert charges a half-day or full-day minimum charge for any court appearance, regardless of the amount of time spent on the case. Laypeople on juries can be offended by the idea that an expert may charge eight hours at an inflated rate when the expert only spent a fraction of that time in the courtroom. Additionally, most "experts" fail to list their forensic consulting work on their CV, when many earn a substantial portion of their income from legal consulting work. When appropriate, examine the expert on why he omitted it from a CV. The jury may well wonder whether the witness is attempting to conceal the amount of legal consulting work in order to portray himself as an unbiased professional.

Targeted research to determine whether the expert markets her services to lawyers can provide a treasure trove of information that undermines the expert's credibility, especially when the expert professes expertise in many discrete and unrelated areas. The "jack of all trades—master of none"

---

3. If you have strong objections to an expert's qualifications, consider asking for *voir dire* and making your objection to the admissibility of the expert's testimony before the expert offers any expert opinions on direct testimony. Even if unsuccessful in excluding the opinion, *voir dire* can provide a "dry run" outside the presence of the jury on questions to which the examiner does not know how the expert will answer. Armed with the transcript from the *voir dire*, counsel may then repeat the favorable inquiry in the presence of the jury.

cross-examination is particularly effective when your own expert can truly claim expertise in the subject area.

For instance, an engineer may satisfy the threshold requirements of being an "expert" in the design of products, though he may have no particularized experience with the product at issue in your case. Likewise, Certified Safety Professionals may qualify to testify on a plethora of subjects despite having no practical experience with respect to the crucial liability issues in your case. The same expert may purport to be an expert in one case as to the Occupational Safety and Health Administration's requirements for fall protection on construction sites one day and also claim expertise in the safe design of machine safeguards or the slip-resistance of walking surfaces in another case on the next day. Always acting as *the* expert undermines an expert's qualifications and goes directly to the weight of the evidence that a jury will ascribe to the expert's testimony.

Demonstrating that the expert typically offers opinions exclusively on behalf of a certain party or on a particular side of an issue further leads to the perception of bias. Moreover, if the opposing expert has testified in multiple areas or against multiple products or companies, expose that fact. For example, if the expert has testified against every manufacturer in the automotive industry—including against dozens of vehicles that are on the market and that are possibly being driven by members of the jury—you want the jury to hear this. This will not only show bias, but it can also show that the expert's views are extreme and are inapplicable in the real world. Expert witnesses are theoretically present in the courtroom to provide scientific or technical knowledge to a jury to aid the jury in its determination of the facts. When an expert crosses the line and appears to be an advocate for one side, the jury may simply disregard the expert's testimony before the merits of the opinion are even examined.

When the plaintiff has proffered several experts, defense counsel may rightfully accuse each of being part of the litigation team assembled by plaintiff's counsel for the purposes of asking a jury for money—rather than real-life consultants who are trying to help the injured person. This is a particularly effective technique when cross-examining damages experts who are not involved in the care or treatment of the plaintiff's injuries. For instance, a doctor who testifies as a retained expert who has not treated the plaintiff, or a vocational consultant who provides an assessment of the plaintiff's limited work capacity who has not been involved in trying to find a job for the plaintiff, are both vulnerable to attack in this manner, as illustrated in this example dialogue:

Q. Doctor, you were hired by plaintiff's attorney to examine Johnny Jones, were you not?

A. Yes.

Q. We can agree that plaintiff's attorney agreed to pay your fees in accordance with your fee schedule for litigation?

A. Yes.

Q. Plaintiff's attorney asked you to prepare a disability rating for him to present to a jury?

A. I can't say what counsel intended to do with it.

Q. Well, we can agree that you were aware that Johnny Jones had a pending civil lawsuit?

A. Yes.

Q. And we can agree that you were contacted by Johnny Jones's lawyer to conduct the examination?

A. Yes.

Q. You were not asked by Johnny Jones's treating physician to consult concerning Johnny's medical treatment?

A. That's right.

Q. Indeed, when you examined Johnny Jones, you told him that there was no doctor-patient relationship?

A. I did.

Q. And you informed him that you were *not* going to participate in his medical care or treatment?

A. Yes.

Q. And you remained true to your words inasmuch as you have *not* been involved in Johnny's care since you examined him for the purposes of this litigation?

A. That's true.

Q. You have not informed Johnny's treating physicians of your findings?

A. True.

Q. You have not prescribed treatment or diagnostic testing for Johnny?

A. Correct.

Q. You did not prescribe medication to lessen the subjective complaints of pain voiced by Johnny?

A. Right. But I wasn't his doctor.

Q. You were the doctor that plaintiff's counsel paid to be part of the litigation team to ask this jury to award money damages?

A. I did an evaluation and a disability rating.

Q. You haven't seen or heard from Johnny since the day his lawyer paid you to meet him?

A. Correct.

This line of cross-examination demonstrates that the hired gun has no interest in helping the plaintiff to mitigate his damages, but is simply in court as part of the "big business" of litigation.

Attack the Expert's Foundation

In particularly specialized or technical areas, the safest area of cross-examination for the young lawyer is addressing the weaknesses in the expert's foundation in reaching her conclusions. For instance, attempting to cross-examine a neurosurgeon on neuroanatomy in front of a jury can be a painful (and counterproductive) exercise—no matter how diligently the lawyer prepares to become educated on the subject. In cases where the expert truly is a preeminent expert on the subject matter, it is unwise to focus the cross-examination on an area of strength for the expert. As Sun Tzu said, "If your enemy is of superior strength, evade him."[4]

Attacking the expert's foundation alone can make for a successful cross-examination and can cause the jury to discredit the expert's opinion. The same neurosurgeon who may be untouchable on the finer points of neuroanatomy may not have read certain medical records or imaging studies and may have failed to review deposition testimony from witnesses that observed the force of a traumatic injury. Even when the expert has purportedly reviewed all of the relevant information, the amount of time spent

---

4. SUN TZU, THE ART OF WAR.

reviewing the materials can be gleaned from the expert's billing records to demonstrate that the expert could not possibly have actually read the material thoroughly. This is especially so where the expert has been provided a recitation of facts from plaintiff's counsel.

What's Good for the Goose Is Good for the Gander

One caveat to this type of cross-examination is that you need to ensure that your experts are not susceptible to the same criticisms and cross-examination. Retain experts who do not expose themselves to these types of criticisms. Calling an expert who is susceptible to the same attacks is an obvious way for the defense lawyer to lose credibility with the jury and seriously undermine his ability to argue the merits of his case in closing argument. Once the defense establishes the moral high ground in the courtroom by demonstrating that the plaintiff's expert is an unprepared professional witness for hire, it should not be conceded by calling the defense bar's equivalent of the hired gun. Doing so will reduce the effective cross-examination to hypocritical gamesmanship in the eyes of the jury.

Make the Expert Your Expert Witness

The ultimate success on cross-examination is when the lawyer can turn the opposition's expert into a favorable expert for her case. While the expert will rarely, if ever, concede the opinion on the ultimate issue in the case, a sharp focus on areas where the opposing expert and your expert agree forces the expert to concede key points. In a medical malpractice case, for example, there will likely be numerous treatments provided that are consistent with the standard of care. In a product liability case, you may be able to get their expert to admit that the client performed appropriate testing, that competitors' practices are similar, that industry guidelines were met, and so on. If the accident could have happened without breaching the standard of care, get the expert to admit that. If there has not been a recall, get the expert to admit that. If other manufacturers do it the same way, get the expert to confirm that fact.

In gaining these concessions on the merits, there is also an important opportunity for further development of the theme that the professional witness is biased. When the expert concedes facts that are favorable to the defense, but those facts were omitted from the expert's disclosure or testimony, an effective line of questioning for the expert may include the accusation that the expert does not want the jury to know about a particular fact. This is more powerful when the expert did not mention the fact in his direct testimony. Here is an example:

Q. Sir, we can agree that you omitted X from your testimony, can we not?

A. Yes, we can.

Q. And we can agree that if you wanted to be fair in your analysis, you would have included X in your opinion?

A. X wasn't significant to me in forming my opinions.

Q. We can agree at the very least you didn't tell the jury about X in your direct testimony this morning?

A. I wasn't asked about it.

Q. Well, we can agree that it is fair to tell the jury ALL of the facts, can we not?

A. Of course.

[If she doesn't agree to this, you can suggest that the expert thinks it is fair for the jury to reach their conclusion without knowing all of the facts.]

Q. And we can agree that it is fair to tell the jury about the facts that are favorable to my client's position, correct?

A. Yes.

Q. And it would be fair to tell the jury about the facts that are favorable to my client's position that you actually agree with?

A. OK.

Q. And we can agree that you did not tell the jury about those facts?

A. Correct.

Q. If you wanted to be fair in explaining to the jury your opinions, you would have told the jury about ALL of the facts, including those that are favorable to my client?

A. [Answer irrelevant]

Importantly, the expert may not always give you the answer you want. But sometimes the question is more important than the answer. Even if you have a difficult witness, the jury will at least understand the point that you are trying to make by the questions you ask.

Expose the Expert's Inconsistent, Unreasonable, or Inaccurate Opinions
The next area for your cross-examination is the attack on the merits of the expert's conclusions. Restate or list for the jury each opinion that the expert holds that you think is subject to cross-examination. Be an accurate scribe so that the jury trusts that you tell the truth. Once you list the opinion, show the jury how this opinion lacks credibility. You can do this in various ways, such as demonstrating that it is unsupported in the literature, contradicted by their prior opinions, unsupported in the marketplace, or even unsupported by the expert's own practice.

For example, if the expert's opinions are inconsistent with how things are done by all of your client's competitors, expose this fact. If the expert asserts an extreme position on safety or health but has never conveyed those concerns to a government agency, force the expert to admit this fact. If the expert has worked for an employer that does things the same way as your client, highlight the fact that the expert comes to the courtroom to tell the defendant to "do as I say, not as I do." It is okay to telegraph what you are saying here. Ask the witness that if "X" and "Y" are true, would he agree that his opinion is wrong.

Thorough preparation may reveal that the expert has actually made a mistake in arriving at her opinions. Perhaps the expert made an inaccurate assumption or an error in math, or simply misunderstood a crucial fact. Exposing the error in cross does not just impact the witness's credibility; it also can support your trial themes. For example, if you are defending a negligence case, your theme may be that a mistake does not necessarily constitute a breach of the standard of the care. When an expert is caught in a mistake, the usual reaction is to minimize its significance by stating that it was inconsequential. An effective attack in this situation is to ask the expert to agree that in her opinion, when she makes a mistake it is just a mistake, but when the defendant makes a mistake it is actionable as negligence. Such hypocrisy again exposes the expert's bias and sets the stage for a closing argument that "perfection" is not the standard of care against which your client is to be judged.

Impeachment

One thing a new lawyer may be uncomfortable with, but needs to understand, is impeachment. Impeachment of expert witnesses is accomplished primarily by introducing the prior inconsistent statements by the witness. Exhaustive pre-trial preparation is absolutely critical to develop potential impeachment material. Search for and collect prior written reports, deposition testimony, and articles authored by the expert that can be used to impeach the witness when necessary. A convincing cross-examination requires counsel to have chapter and verse of the prior inconsistent statement at hand when the opportunity arises.

Counsel must also fully understand the critical distinction between impeachment with prior sworn testimony and impeachment by a prior inconsistent statement that was not made under oath. A prior inconsistent statement may not be introduced to prove the truth of the prior statement itself, as the prior statement constitutes hearsay. Accordingly, a prior statement by the opposing expert in a report or an article may only be considered by the jury in assessing whether the witness is telling the truth on the witness stand. Conversely, pursuant to Federal Rule of Evidence 801, a prior inconsistent statement given under oath at a deposition or trial may be used to establish the truth of the statement itself. Stated another way, defense counsel may establish a favorable fact (i.e., the applicability of a particular industry standard or protocol) that supports the defendant's case simply by demonstrating that the opposing expert testified to that opinion in a prior proceeding. Provided that the prior inconsistent statement was made under oath, counsel may then argue in closing that the point was established by the plaintiff's own expert.

Procedurally, impeachment by use of a prior inconsistent statement is simply accomplished by contrasting the expert's direct testimony with the prior statement. Counsel may ask the expert if he agrees with a certain proposition in order to allow the expert to deny its truth. The witness should be handed a copy of the prior statement and asked to confirm that he was the author or orator of the statement. After obtaining this concession, the statement may be read aloud to the witness—or counsel may choose to ask the witness to read his own words to the jury. When the prior inconsistent statement was made at a deposition or trial, the witness should be further asked to concede that the statement was given under the same oath he took when he took the stand in the case at bar.

The Intangibles

It is important to remember that the cross-examination of the opposing expert represents your chance to tell your story. Try to make yourself—not the witness—the center of attention. If the judge allows it, position yourself in the courtroom where you can be visible to the jury when asking the questions. Do not get so focused on the examination that you forget to seek some eye contact with the jury. Emphasize the key points by asking the question clearly at the beginning or restating the answer in proceeding to the next question.

Listen carefully to every answer. While you should have an outline, your follow-up questions should flow from the expert's answer. And when you get the answer you want, move on. Sometimes, the flow of the examination leads you to believe that you can get a great answer from an expert, and you become tempted to ask the ultimate question. You should do this only with great caution, as it most likely will produce nothing more than an opportunity for the expert to correct herself or to make a speech. For example, perhaps you were able to get the witness to concede that the company did X, Y, and Z correctly and a culmination of X, Y, and Z means the company had met the standard of care or did not commit fraud. You may be tempted to take the leap and seek the final stamp of approval by getting the expert to concede that the company is not liable. Fight the temptation. Remember, you will get your chance at closing statement to summarize and wrap up everything the expert said. You will get your chance then to walk the jury through the admissions of X, Y, and Z and what that means. Do not ask the ultimate question in cross-examination of an expert unless you absolutely need to do so.

You also want to be sure that you have the right demeanor. In general, you want to be polite but firm. It can be good to beat up on an expert, but you want to do it in a manner that earns you respect without making you seem like a bully. If you can instill humor, do it.

You may want to keep the jury's attention with something demonstrative. This may mean using some sort of demonstrative exhibit, or it may just mean transcribing helpful admissions on an easel, Elmo, or smart board.

If the witness is uncooperative with his answers, try different techniques. Perhaps ask the witness if he is done answering the question. Then, ask if his answer was a "yes" or a "no." Alternatively, ask the expert if he has finished his answer and follow up by asking him if he would now care to answer the question that was asked. Or, if the witness continues to give long-winded answers, consider breaking your question into parts so he cannot give long, troublesome answers. If the expert still will not answer the question, perhaps note that you still do not have an answer, or, if you think that you have a helpful judge, ask the judge for an instruction. Do not let the witness recast the question. If he answers the wrong question, note that fact for the jury.

Successful cross-examination demands that counsel master the rules of evidence. Pay particular attention to key rules such as Rules 403 (probative value substantially outweighed by the danger of unfair prejudice), 404, 607, 608 and 609 (credibility), 611 (leading questions allowed), 612 (refreshing recollection), 613 (prior statements), 803 (published treatises are not excluded as hearsay and can be read into evidence but not received as exhibits), and any others that you think may be an issue with the particular witness's testimony.

If the expert is hurting you, cut your losses. These experts have been hired because they are smart and they have the skills to parry many tough questions. If they simply refuse to give you any responses and you cannot get help from the judge, move on. Hopefully the jurors will recognize that the witness is being evasive.

Finally, remember that you get the last word on the expert in closing statement. You will get to remind the jury what she said and argue over its credibility. You will get to remind the jury about all of the admissions that the expert made or refused to make (such as perhaps refusing to concede the most basic point). While it is always a good feeling to want to declare victory when you sit down after cross-examination, you will get another chance to talk to the jury about the expert when all of the evidence is in the record.

Direct of Your Expert

Similar to cross-examining the other side's expert, you need to be equipped for your own expert's direct testimony. On direct examination, the overall goal is to position the expert so that he comes off as an experienced and trustworthy teacher. The best take-away from your expert is for him to be plain-spoken and engaging so that the jury not only can learn but wants to learn from him.

Preparation

The key to a successful direct examination is to prepare your expert for his testimony thoroughly, so that he can appear as a preeminent expert and teacher in his field. Preparing your expert is not a simple process. Counsel should ensure the witness knows the state of the evidence and the evidentiary rulings. You do not want him opening the door to evidence that you worked hard to exclude. Also, make sure your expert knows the key themes of the case and the key facts and opinions that have gone into evidence already. The expert needs to know what the jury has heard to ensure that he is consistent with other defense experts and also what has been said by the opposing experts in order to focus on the key points that need to be addressed and rebutted.

It is important to have a general outline—not a script—with the key points of what needs to be covered. You want to ensure that the expert understands the key themes in the event that you are thrown off the general outline and for the forthcoming cross-examination.

In developing themes, try to come up with analogies that will make sense with the jury. Also, as part of the outline, you want to consider what exhibits will help illustrate your point. Demonstrative exhibits obviously help to teach and emphasize your points. However, you want to ensure that you know what you are going to use not only to have exhibits ready in advance, but also to have them ready at trial so that they will flow with the testimony.

In relation to cross-examination, you should prepare your expert regarding the potential attacks outlined above. Do not underestimate the importance of this. Make sure the expert is thinking about former testimony, publications, or representations online, so as to avoid being painted into a corner. You should anticipate all of the potentially tough questions and make sure that your expert has sound and reasoned responses to the same. There should not be any surprise questions left for trial.

In order to be properly prepared, you probably want to make sure the witness comes in at least one day before his testimony to bring him up to speed and go over his testimony and the state of the evidence in general.

Framework for the Testimony

Once the expert is on the stand, you generally want to follow the outline or walk him through the key points.

First, you must lay the foundation for expert opinion testimony by qualifying the witness as an expert in a relevant field. Start with the expert's background and experience, highlighting as much as possible why he is a leading expert in his field. In doing so, you want to establish who he is, where he was educated, where he works, what he does, and why he is qualified. Consider personal questions such as why he got involved in the type of work he does, or what are some examples of what he does on a daily basis.

To the extent the expert has been paid on this case or other cases, bring it out on direct to limit the impact of cross-examination. Demonstrating that the expert's fees for trial are commensurate with his pay for his day job is a particularly effective technique to use as a preemptive strike against the forthcoming challenge as to that expert's monetary bias. To the extent his testimony is subject to being perceived as biased, get the expert to explain why it is objective.

Once you have covered his background, move onto what the expert did for the case. This means you want to ask the expert what questions he was asked to consider, what he reviewed, and what work he did to reach his opinions. Establish that the expert has a solid foundation (i.e., a reliable methodology) to offer the opinions he is offering.

Ultimately, you want to ask if the expert has reached an opinion to a reasonable degree of scientific certainty in his field. If so, ask the expert what is his opinion. The goal here is to give the jury a clear view of his overriding opinion, as well as a thumbnail sketch of his underlying supporting opinions.

Once you have given the general outline of the opinion(s), you want to dig into each opinion, explaining to the jury the specific opinion and the basis for the same. Here is where you want the expert to become a teacher. This likely means discussing the underlying opinion in conjunction with things such as the medical background of the patient, the care provided to the patient, the relevant background of the product or practice, the company or product's compliance, the product or company's historical performance, the industry or government's position, the literature, the testing, and/or anything else the expert did. In essence, you want to draw out all things that support the expert's opinion.

An effective direct examination will allow your expert to convince the jury that his opinion is the right opinion. It is not sufficient to simply have your expert recite his opinions and the facts that support it. While a jury may ultimately credit his opinion, it is far more effective to have the jury truly understand *why* your expert has reached the right opinion. To accomplish this, the jury should be sufficiently educated to make them advocates for your client's position in the jury room. They should understand that the opposing party's theory, while plausible, is fraught with other risks that are potentially more hazardous, or that would have unintended consequences that may not be immediately apparent.

Here is an example of direct examination:

Q. Do you have an opinion to a reasonable degree of certainty as to whether the care plan for Mrs. Jones while a resident of the XYZ Nursing Home was in compliance with the standard of care?

A. Yes.

Q. What is that opinion?

A. My opinion is that the care plan was appropriate.

Q. What is the basis of that opinion?

A. Mrs. Jones had a right of self-determination and the right to ambulate freely in the nursing home even though she was at risk for falling. The appropriate interventions and supervision were provided to reduce the risk of falling, which is precisely what is called for by the standard of care.

Have the expert next explain why alternative measures suggested by the opposing party will complete the jury's understanding of the case:

Q. Do you have an opinion to a reasonable degree of certainty as to whether Mrs. Jones's fatal fall could have been prevented by the use of a restraint as suggested by the plaintiff?

A. Yes.

Q. What is that opinion?

A. It could not have been prevented by restraining Mrs. Jones and still been in compliance with the applicable standard of nursing care.

Q. Would you explain the basis of that opinion?

A. Congress has mandated that restraints be utilized in nursing homes only as a measure of last resort, and only when ordered by the resident's physician. In this case, it would have been illegal to restrain Mrs. Jones.

Q. Is there some reason why restraints cannot be used even though they may prevent serious falls?

A. Yes. There are several. First, residents are entitled to a dignified existence. The freedom to walk or go to the bathroom is not taken from us because we are admitted to a nursing home. Second, restraints can lead to bedsores, psychological trauma, development of new onset incontinence, and other unintended consequences. Third, the literature demonstrates that while restraints may reduce the number of falls, they increase the severity and likelihood of death when residents escape from them.

Q. Are there any other considerations that support your conclusions?

A. Yes. Prior to the change in the law, nursing homes utilized restraints liberally to prevent falls. Watching those debilitated elderly people tortured by being restrained was heartbreaking. That is why we no longer restrain patients.

You should also seek to refute the opposing expert's opinions and explain why your expert disagrees with them. This part of the expert's opinions should correlate to key themes or areas that you exposed during cross-examination. To the extent you asked questions during your cross-examination that implied certain things—but didn't get the response you needed—you want to readdress those issues and get your expert to explain to the jury what the appropriate response was. Before the expert gets off the stand, you want to arm the jury with explanations as to why the opposition's assertions are inconsistent, unreliable, or unrealistic to industry standard and practice.

Finally, before you close, you want to get the expert to give a summary of his final opinions so that the jury is left with a clear impression of the crucial opinions.

Nuances of a Good Presentation

Make sure you and your witness understand the nuances of what makes a good presentation. Following the general outline and making sure that the key points are established on direct examination is important. However, other things you want your witness to do, related to demeanor and presentation, should also be clearly understood.

Most importantly, when your expert is on the stand, you want your expert to be the center of attention. Ideally, as noted earlier, your expert will be viewed by the jury as a teacher. Assist your expert in achieving this goal by getting him off the stand and using demonstrative exhibits.

This is particularly effective with respect to the presentation of medical expert testimony by utilizing models or radiological studies to educate the jury on the relevant anatomy. For instance, a radiologist may be asked to stand in front of the jury with a laser pointer to explain how he interprets an X-ray or magnetic resonance imaging that is projected on a screen or presented with a light box. Educated juries are fascinated by the unique opportunity to gain an understanding of how a doctor diagnoses a panoply of common injuries, such as a subdural hematoma, a stroke, degenerative changes in the spinal column, osteoporosis, or a simple fracture. The presentation of visual evidence in this manner also reduces the monotony of listening to an endless parade of talking heads and will almost always engage the jury to listen more carefully to your key expert.

Ask short and direct (not leading) questions to get clear answers. Although you want to be crisp in your questioning, you also want to make the direct examination conversational so it is interesting and easier to follow. Recognizing that the expert may sometimes give you long explanations, you want to make sure you break up long narratives. For example, do not be afraid to interrupt the expert to ask why something is important or to ask for explanation of a concept in layperson's terms.

It is imperative that the presentation of the direct examination be concise. Brevity is the soul of wit. Counsel should take caution not to lose the key points in the middle of a lengthy presentation that is difficult for a jury to follow. The general themes should be declared at the beginning of the expert's testimony and reiterated at the conclusion of the examination.

As noted, your expert has to be prepared for cross-examination, and you need to ensure that he approaches it with the appropriate demeanor. You want the expert to be confident but not come off as a zealot. You want the expert to sound like the smartest person in the room without coming across as condescending or argumentative. He must be substantively equipped to deal with the tough questions.

Redirect

Ideally, you will not have to redirect your expert witness. Certainly, you will not want to do so unless your opponent has damaged the witness on cross-examination. Your opponent will get the last word on recross and may do even better the second time around. It may be necessary, however, to give your expert an opportunity to provide an explanation, clarification, or response to a line of questioning on cross.[5]

A redirect should be brief and focused—particularly in a jury trial. If something is unclear, this is your opportunity to clarify it. If the expert's credibility has been damaged, this is the time to rehabilitate it. If an explanation or further context is needed for an answer given on cross, this is the opportunity for the expert to provide it. Because you will not have had an opportunity to go over the redirect before doing it, you will need to preface

---

5. Redirect is limited to the scope of the cross.

your questions with a topic sentence to make sure that you and the expert are on the same page. For example:

Q.   Defense counsel pointed out that you did not perform the XYZ test during your statistical analysis of the plant's operating data. Why didn't you do that test?

A.   Because it was completely irrelevant.

Q.   Why?

A.   [The expert should then provide the missing explanation.]

Your preparation of the expert for direct testimony should also include discussion of how a redirect would go. You should certainly plan to end the redirect with a positive, strong point. For example:

Q.   Plaintiffs' counsel suggested X and Y during her cross-examination. Does that change your opinion at all?

A.   No.

Q.   Why not?

A.   [The witness should re-establish the key grounds for her opinions and state why they are sufficient, ending on a strong note.]

You will have developed the theme of the testimony with the expert and prepared her thoroughly for testimony, so the expert should understand where you want her to go. Remember, your goal is for the expert to appear to the jury as credible, likeable, and easy to understand.

Summary

In conclusion, expert witnesses have the potential to present some of the most powerful evidence at trial. By following the guidelines and examples contained in this chapter, you will acquire the tools necessary for dealing with this type of testimony.

Chapter 11

Dispositive Motions During Trial

Sandra B. Wick Mulvany

As this book makes clear, a lawyer has numerous areas to plan and items to prepare before a trial. One important aspect that a lawyer should not overlook in this preparation is dispositive motions at trial. This is so for two reasons. First, depending on the issue that ultimately may be subject to appeal in the event of an adverse judgment, failure to file a dispositive motion at trial may waive a party's right to pursue that issue on appeal. Second, if the opposing party truly has failed to meet its evidentiary burden to support its claims, a successful motion for judgment as a matter of law submitted at the close of the opposing party's case (particularly when the defendant is bringing the motion after the plaintiff has rested) avoids the moving party from incurring the expense and inconvenience of having to present evidence to support its case at trial. Familiarity with the relevant procedure for dispositive motions at trial is therefore imperative. Because the useful tools discussed in this chapter are procedurally based and case law is continually evolving, relevant law in the applicable jurisdiction should be analyzed as part of any trial preparation process. Notably, there are variations and nuances pertaining to dispositive motions at trial among the various federal circuits, as well as under state law. This chapter discusses generally dispositive motions at trial under the Federal Rules of Civil Procedure.

Federal Rule of Civil Procedure 50 provides the parameters for dispositive motions made during trial. Rule 50(a) covers a motion for judgment as a matter of law, which is made prior to a case being submitted to the jury.[1] The analog to Rule 50(a) motions for bench trials is found in Rule 52(c). These dispositive motions are appropriate when the opposing party fails to establish evidence to support its claims at trial. This may be a failure to provide evidentiary support for a particular claim, or may be in total for the opposing party's case. In any event, if the opposing party fails to establish sufficient evidence to support a legal claim against your client, Rule 50(a) and 52(c) motions are available, and should be used, at trial.

As a practical matter, if summary judgment motions were brought and denied prior to trial, Rule 50 motions may be particularly relevant to your case. If, for example, your summary judgment motion was denied prior to trial on the ground that there was a genuine issue of material fact, the failure to pursue Rule 50 motions may constitute a waiver of any challenge on appeal to the sufficiency of the evidence with respect to the issue briefed on summary judgment.[2]

Accordingly, best practices suggest that counsel should pay close attention to pursuing Rule 50 motions when summary judgment has been denied prior to trial, particularly when there is a possibility that the denial of summary judgment is tied to a factual dispute. Likewise, counsel for the non-moving party should be prepared to defend against Rule 50 motions by the party to whom summary judgment was denied. In circumstances where it is not clear whether denial of summary judgment was based on factual concerns, purely legal considerations, or a mix of both, counsel should err on the side of caution in pursuing Rule 50 motions if the opposing party fails to submit evidence to support its claims that could be the basis for a sufficiency of the evidence challenge on appeal. Indeed, there is little harm to pursuing Rule 50 motions when summary judgment is denied prior to

---

1. FED. R. CIV. P. 50(a). Rule 50(b) outlines a renewed motion for judgment as a matter of law, made after entry of judgment. FED. R. CIV. P. 50(b).
2. *See* Ortiz v. Jordan, 131 S. Ct. 884 (2011) (failure to renew motion for judgment as a matter of law under Rule 50(b) on qualified immunity issue raised and denied on summary judgment motion prior to trial forfeited right to appeal based on sufficiency of evidence on same issue following adverse jury verdict). Following the Supreme Court's ruling in *Ortiz*, at least one circuit has subsequently held that purely legal issues denied on summary judgment may be reviewed on appeal even in the absence of Rule 50 motions. *See In re* Amtrust Financial Corp., 694 F.3d 741, 750–51 (6th Cir. 2012).

trial, and significant appellate risk in not doing so, assuming of course that such motions are appropriate based on the evidence presented at trial by your opponent.

Motion for Judgment as a Matter of Law—Rule 50(a)

A motion for judgment as a matter of law was formerly known as a motion for directed verdict. As a result, cases prior to the early 1990s tend to use that terminology.[3] A motion for judgment as a matter of law applies only to jury trials.[4] It should be used when, after a party has been fully heard on an issue, a court could find that a reasonable jury would not have a legally sufficient evidentiary basis to find for the party on that issue.[5] In other words, the rule "allows the trial court to remove cases or issues from the jury's consideration 'when the facts are sufficiently clear that the law requires a particular result.'"[6] The underlying basis for this type of motion is a legal question: has sufficient evidence been introduced to raise a question of fact for a jury to decide a particular issue?[7] Because there are tensions between a court's ability to issue judgment as a matter of law and the responsibility for factual determinations by a jury pursuant to the Seventh Amendment, some courts view judgments as a matter of law with disfavor.[8] Indeed, it is well settled that this type of relief should be granted "cautiously and sparingly."[9] Importantly, in addition to raising a motion for judgment as a matter of law on the sufficiency of the evidence, a party

---

3. Rule 50 was amended in 1991, which renamed a motion for a directed verdict to its current name.

4. 9B CHARLES ALAN WRIGHT & ARTHUR R. MILLER, FEDERAL PRACTICE AND PROCEDURE § 2523, at 229 (3d ed. 2008).

5. FED. R. CIV. P. 50(a).

6. Weisgram v. Marley Co., 528 U.S. 440, 448 (2000) (quoting 9A CHARLES ALAN WRIGHT & ARTHUR R. MILLER, FEDERAL PRACTICE AND PROCEDURE § 2521, at 240 (2d ed. 1995)).

7. 9B WRIGHT & MILLER, *supra* note 4, § 2524, at 232.

8. *See, e.g.*, Lloyd v. Ashcroft, 208 F. Supp. 2d 8, 10 (D.D.C. 2002) ("Because a judgment as a matter of law intrudes upon the rightful province of the jury, it is highly disfavored.") (internal quotations omitted); United States *ex rel.* Yesudian v. Howard Univ., 153 F.3d 731, 735 (D.C. Cir. 1998) (same).

9. 9 JAMES W.M. MOORE, MOORE'S FEDERAL PRACTICE § 50.05[6] (3d ed. 2012).

may seek judgment as a matter of law on a purely legal issue.[10] It therefore makes sense to consider filing a motion for judgment as a matter of law when the focus of the case (or issue) hinges on a legal question, rather than a factual one. This may be particularly compelling when, after presenting evidence, it becomes clear that there are no factual issues the finder of fact needs to resolve, only legal issues.

A motion for judgment as a matter of law may be made orally or in writing.[11] While written motions are the best practice, as a practical matter, the exigencies of trial may not permit filing a written motion. Whether submitted orally or in writing, it is critical that a motion for judgment as a matter of law specifically articulate the judgment sought and the facts and legal basis that entitle the moving party to that judgment.[12] The purpose behind this requirement is to allow the responding party an opportunity to cure any deficiency in the party's proof and to allow the court to assess whether such deficiencies can be cured before the case is submitted to the jury.[13] Failure to include this information in a motion may result in the moving party not properly preserving the issue for appeal.[14] Moreover, if a motion lacks the required specificity, the opposing party must raise at the trial court a proper objection to the motion on that basis; failure to do so waives the objection.[15]

As a practice pointer, for trial preparation and trial purposes, one suggested approach is to develop a spreadsheet or checklist of relevant claims and defenses, including the evidence required to support the legal theories, for use in assessing your opponent's presentation of evidence as well as your own. Preparing such a tool is useful for two reasons: (1) it will help to focus your trial preparation efforts on presenting evidence critical to support your client's case; and (2) it will provide a mechanism for you to assess during trial whether your opponent has presented evidence sufficient to support

---

10. *Id.* § 50.05[3].
11. *See* Fed. R. Civ. P. 50(a); *see also* 9 Moore, *supra* note 9, § 50.22.
12. Fed. R. Civ. P. 50(a)(2).
13. 9B Wright & Miller, *supra* note 4, § 2533, at 495–97; Waters v. Young, 100 F.3d 1437, 1441–42 (9th Cir. 1996).
14. 9B Wright & Miller, *supra* note 4, § 2533, at 509.
15. 9 Moore, *supra* note 9, § 50.21[3].

the claims or defenses asserted by the opposing party in the case. Such a checklist should include at least the following information:

- a listing of each element of the claims and defenses to be heard at trial;
- the expected witnesses to testify on each of the elements and areas of expected testimony; and
- the key documents pertinent to the claims and defenses anticipated to be offered as evidence during trial.

Pattern jury instructions, outlining the elements of proof for each claim and defense in your case, will help you prepare your checklist.

In assessing whether to grant a motion for judgment as a matter of law, a court should not weigh evidence or assess the credibility of witnesses.[16] Rather, a court should assess the sufficiency of the evidence by determining whether there is but one conclusion that reasonable persons could reach.[17] Note that the standard for granting judgment as a matter of law mirrors summary judgment, and the court should review all of the evidence in the record.[18] There is general agreement among courts that the appropriate test is the reasonable person test.[19] Courts have used, however, various formulations in describing the test.[20] For that reason, it is important to rely on the language commonly used in a particular jurisdiction to describe the test for a motion for judgment as a matter of law accurately.[21] In assessing the sufficiency of the evidence, a court should view the evidence in the light most favorable to the non-moving party and give that party the benefit of all reasonable inferences arising from the evidence presented at trial.[22]

A motion for judgment as a matter of law may be made at any time before the case is submitted to the jury.[23] Thus, at any point during trial, a party may move for judgment as a matter of law on a particular claim or

---

16. 9B WRIGHT & MILLER, *supra* note 4, § 2524, at 270–85.
17. *Id.* at 369–70 (citing Simblest v. Maynard, 427 F.2d 1, 4 (2d Cir. 1970)).
18. Reeves v. Sanderson Plumbing Products, Inc., 530 U.S. 133, 150–51 (2000).
19. *Id.* at 374.
20. *Id.* at 366–74; 9 MOORE, *supra* note 9, § 50.60[2].
21. *See id.*
22. 9B WRIGHT & MILLER, *supra* note 4, § 2524, at 298–338; Reeves, 530 U.S. at 150–51.
23. FED. R. CIV. P. 50(a)(2); *see also* 9 MOORE, *supra* note 9, § 50.202[2][a]–[d] (discussing submission of a motion for judgment as a matter of law after opponent's opening statement

aspect of a claim after the other side has presented evidence on that issue. If the court does not grant the motion, the moving party may still offer evidence without having to reserve the right to do so, and the case may still be submitted to the jury.[24] In order to ensure all rights are preserved for appeal, however, if the moving party makes the motion prior to the close of the evidence, the best practice to preserve all arguments is to resubmit the motion at the close of *all* of the evidence.[25]

As a practical matter, courts may reserve ruling on a motion for judgment as a matter of law until after a verdict (or until the jury fails to reach one). This means the court is deemed to have submitted the action to the jury pending a later determination on the legal issues asserted by the moving party.[26] This option allows the trial court to follow what has been said to be the "better and safer practice"—because if a court grants a post-verdict judgment as a matter of law that is later overturned on appeal, there is no need for a new trial and the jury's verdict may be reinstated.[27] Of course, if the trial court reserves ruling on a motion for judgment as a matter of law, in order to preserve the issue, the moving party is required to renew the motion after the jury's verdict. Renewed motions for judgment as a matter of law under Rule 50(b) are discussed in Chapter 12.

Motion for Judgment on Partial Findings—Rule 52(c)

For bench trials, a tool similar to Rule 50(a) exists in Federal Rule of Civil Procedure 52: a motion for judgment on partial findings.[28] Section (c) of Rule 52 was added in 1991 to replace part of Rule 41(b), which previously allowed the court to dismiss the plaintiff's case at the close of its evidence

---

if clear no question for jury, after presentation of evidence on discrete legal issue, after close of opponent's evidence, and after close of all evidence).

24. *See, e.g.*, Sampliner v. Motion Picture Patents Co., 254 U.S. 233, 236–39 (1920).

25. *See, e.g.*, Campbell v. Keystone Aerial Surveys, Inc., 138 F.3d 996 (5th Cir. 1998) (motion for judgment as matter of law made at close of opponent's case and not resubmitted to the trial court at the close of the evidence resulting in applying only plain error review on appeal).

26. FED. R. CIV. P. 50(b); *see also* 9 MOORE, *supra* note 9, § 50.33.

27. 9 MOORE, *supra* note 9, § 50.33.

28. FED. R. CIV. P. 52(c).

if the plaintiff failed to meet its burden of proof.[29] The rule provides that "if a party has been fully heard on an issue during a nonjury trial and the court finds against the party on that issue, the court may enter judgment against the party on a claim or defense that, under the controlling law, can be maintained or defeated only with a favorable finding on that issue."[30] Accordingly, a motion may be pursued under this rule by either party and for issues that may not entirely dispose of a claim or defense.[31] Under this rule, the court has discretion to issue a ruling and enter judgment during the trial or to wait until the close of all of the evidence.[32] Any judgment on partial findings issued by the court "must be supported by findings of facts and conclusions of law as required by Rule 52(a)."[33] In sharp contrast to the court's review of a motion for judgment as a matter of law, in assessing a motion for judgment on partial findings, a court should evaluate and weigh all of the evidence, make determinations regarding witness credibility, and resolve the issue on the basis of the preponderance of evidence.[34]

Briefing the Motion

Best practices for briefing the motions discussed in this chapter suggest the following guidelines. First, the structure of any motion under Rule 50 or Rule 52(c) should be consistent with any legal motion filed with a court. It should be concise, but sufficiently detailed, to provide the court with the basis to rule in your client's favor. Further, Rule 50 motions should be written with an eye toward preserving the issues raised in the motion for appeal.

Generally, Rule 50 motions should contain an introduction that outlines for the court the issue(s) being briefed, recites the relevant rules, outlines the specific claims or legal counts at issue along with the pertinent evidence presented at trial, and applies the evidence (or lack thereof) to the relevant standards, all of which logically support the ultimate conclusion being

---

29. FED. R. CIV. P. 52, Committee Note 1991.
30. FED. R. CIV. P. 52(c).
31. FED. R. CIV. P. 52, Committee Note 1993.
32. FED. R. CIV. P. 52(c).
33. Id.
34. 9 MOORE, *supra* note 9, § 52.51.

argued to the court. Although Rule 50 motions should contain enough specificity to clearly relay the judgment sought and the facts and legal basis to support that judgment as a matter of law is appropriate, this requirement should be not interpreted to mean that the longer the brief, the better. To the contrary, courts appreciate motions and briefs that are just that—brief. For all intents and purposes, therefore, brevity and concise legal writing, which of course meets the required standards under Rule 50 and applicable case law, are the two most fundamental attributes to a successful motion under Rule 50 or otherwise. Research prior Rule 50 motions submitted and orders issued either granting or denying those motions. This will help you assess the preferences and dislikes of the judge presiding over your trial with respect to general motions practice and Rule 50 motions in particular.

Responding to a Dispositive Motion

You have finished presentation of your side of the case at trial. Your opponent stands up and makes a motion under Rule 50(a) or Rule 52(c). The judge listens to the argument, then turns to you and asks for your response. How do you respond?

For a Rule 50(a) motion, you should begin by outlining for the court the reasons why the evidence presented is sufficient to support each of the elements of your claims. In doing so, you should demonstrate how the evidence presented does not lead to only one conclusion that reasonable persons could reach. Structure your argument to emphasize to the court the varying inferences that may be made from the evidence presented. Argue that a jury must decide how to weigh the evidence, and assess the credibility of the witnesses presented, in order to find the facts necessary to resolve the case. You must convince the judge that she should allow the case to go to a jury verdict, rather than grant judgment as a matter of law. You should also rely on the heavy burden a moving party bears under Rule 50(a). In deciding the motion, the court must view the evidence in the light most favorable to the non-moving party and give the non-moving party the benefit of all reasonable inferences.

In contrast, when defending against a Rule 52(c) motion, which is most commonly filed by a defendant at the close of the plaintiff's case, the primary focus of the argument should be to highlight for the court what the evidence shows when appropriately evaluated and weighed. You should also argue the credibility of the key witness testimony supporting your claims. The ultimate objective in defending against a motion for judgment on partial findings is, of course, to convince the court that you have met your burden of proof, and, at a minimum, that full consideration of the evidence presented is necessary for the court to issue a ruling on the merits. Further, you should be prepared to respond to a court's request for submission of findings of fact on claims at issue in the trial, which is not uncommon in conjunction with Rule 52 motions and bench trials generally.

Concluding Remarks

In sum, dispositive motions at trial are procedurally strict in the sense of the technical requirements and necessary steps to preserve appeal rights. As outlined above, they contain traps for the unwary. As with any other aspect of trial preparation, however, understanding the framework and being prepared based on applicable law in the relevant jurisdiction will ensure that you are not caught off guard and will allow you to plan to position your case to take advantage of these tools. From a "big picture" perspective, consider the tools discussed in this chapter in the context of overall trial planning, strategy, and approach, including assessing your opponent's case. Consider whether the other side has made their case to the jury or the judge. If not, use these tools to hold your opponent's feet to the fire and to achieve the positive outcome for your client that is inevitably the focus of trial preparation. Also consider how the case you are making will be perceived in this respect based on the evidence, witnesses, and legal positions you intend to, and actually do, present at trial, so that you will be ready to defend against, and defeat, an attack along these lines by your opponent.

Chapter 12

Closing Argument

Brian Antweil

One of my favorite movie scenes of all time is Alec Baldwin's speech to the salesmen in *Glengarry Glen Ross*. Baldwin plays Blake, a character who has made it big selling Florida swampland. In this scene, he is in the New York office of the real estate company he works for, speaking with great emotion and not very nicely to several salesmen (played by Jack Lemmon, Ed Harris, and Alan Arkin) who have not met with the same success.

Baldwin's message is simple: "A-B-C. Always. Be. Closing." A great analogy for trial practitioners. You should always be closing no matter what phase of the case you are in—*voir dire*, opening, direct or cross-examination, or closing. You should be closing when you are just sitting at counsel table saying nothing. Always!

The culmination of that persuasive effort is the closing argument. It is where you get to sum up the whole of your presentation to the jury with the goal, like Mr. Baldwin admonishes to the not-so-successful salesman, to get them to sign on the dotted line. The goal of this chapter is to help you get there.

My suggestions are based on an entire career trying civil lawsuits. I have no criminal trial experience. That said, the fundamentals are the same, and I am confident that the process for preparing and making a closing argument is the same for both civil and criminal cases.

What Works

Theme and Theory

If you get anything out of this book, know that theme and case theory are the backbone of your case. The jury needs to hear your theme in *voir dire*, in opening, and in closing. It should be the first words out of your mouth in each of those trial phases. The theme is how you complete the sentence that begins "This is a case about . . . . " The theme should be the nexus of your argument, that is, all evidentiary roads lead to your theme.

The theory is the roadmap—the story—you should have assembled at the beginning of the case from the available record. In its most simplistic terms, the theory tells "what happened."

The theme determines what specific evidence you will use to tell a story consistent with the theory. It will help you streamline the case down to the essentials. There will be mountains of relevant evidence, but not all should be presented to the jury. Doing so will only confuse them and make the story much more difficult to understand.

Primacy

A good story has a compelling beginning and end. The same holds true here. The first few minutes of your closing argument need to be captivating. There is no end to the creative ways to get the jury mesmerized like I was with Alec Baldwin's speech. It could be some unrelated but analogous story about your (or better yet, your client's) past. It could be a juxtaposition of your client's life to that of his opponent's.

I once tried a case that could best be described as a business divorce. Two partners had split up, and it did not go so well. The theme was "you can't have your cake and eat it too." In closing, I started by telling the story of my client's blue-collar and uneducated upbringing and how hard work got him where he is today. I juxtaposed that with the story of his former partner, who was well educated when he came into my client's business, was paid a salary as an employee, and as promised was given nearly half of the business. As a "thank you," the former partner decided there were greener pastures, left in the dead of night, and vowed to ruin my client's business by starting a competing business and stealing my client's customers. The amazing thing was that this partner also wanted to continue to be treated as a partner in the old business while undertaking to ruin it.

Now all of these pieces were in evidence, mind you, but came from a variety of sources—testimony, letters, and e-mails—introduced at different points of the trial. My job at closing was to piece it together into a compelling story. I could not just dive in, however. At the core, I knew that my client was a more likeable person than the partner and that the jury could be made to feel the same—to empathize with my client. It was important for the jury to have that foundation before I walked through the evidence that supported the conclusions I wanted the jury to reach in the special issues in the jury instructions. It worked.

Tell the Jury Where You Will Take Them

After setting the stage with the theme and story, take a minute to give the jury a roadmap that you intend to follow through the evidence and where you expect it to take them. I am not a believer in chronological arguments. Bringing evidence into the trial record that way is fine, but when you argue, topical headlines work much better. So, at the outset—right after the primacy discussion—lay out the topics you intend to cover.

This is as good a place as any to talk about choreography. A closing argument should be a choreographed presentation, blending all forms of communication into a seamless presentation. Just don't confuse "seamless" with "slick." Overly slick presentations are risky. Some jurors might be impressed by the production values of your argument, but it can backfire in the end. Rather, there are many ways, other than through your voice, to present information. In the case of the roadmap, for example, rather than just voice them, why not write it down? You can do that the old-fashioned way—on a white board or blackboard—or in a more technologically advanced way—through the use of a slide or two. The point is, utilizing non-verbal tools is essential and will keep the jury engaged.

Talking About the Evidence

As you cover the topics outlined, you will hopefully have a plethora of evidence to support each of them. This evidence will come in a variety of types—live testimony, deposition testimony, documents, and demonstratives.

Rather than only talk about them, use them. If there is a piece of testimony that comes from a videotaped deposition, show it. But keep it short. Give the jury the sound bite. If there are pieces of an exhibit that are important to your argument, put the exhibit in front of the jury and electronically highlight the important parts.

Most courthouses today are pretty well-equipped with the basic technology necessary for lawyers to plug and play what they want. In the business divorce case mentioned above, I had the luxury of a litigation support person to project the exhibits on a screen as I talked about them. It was a seamless, choreographed presentation. I would say something like "Remember what Mr. Smith said to Mr. Jones in Exhibit 23, an e-mail regarding the personal expenses." My mention of Exhibit 23 was the cue for my colleague to bring it up onto the screen. As I discussed the specifics of the e-mail, he highlighted it for the jury. I never had to ask him to do anything during the argument. Our preparation allowed the closing to flow and maximized its impact.

Demonstrative exhibits are great tools as well. You can use them for a variety of purposes, but the most useful is summing up your argument on a particular topic by recapping what you have just shown the jury, with the goal of getting them to the sign on the dotted line.

Make It the Jury's Original Idea to Vote with You

You cannot force jurors to agree with you. They need to get to that decision on their own. It is your job to help them believe that they are arriving at their own conclusions, not what you think their conclusions should be.

I have found that many conclusions are reached based on plain and simple common sense. I remind the jury not to leave common sense at the door. As you formulate your argument on each issue that the jury must answer, look for ways to bring common sense into the discussion. If you can show that your conclusion makes perfect sense and your opponent's is lacking, the jury will conclude that your client should win.

Confront Weaknesses Head-On

Every case has weaknesses. You cannot ignore them. If you do, then the jury only has your opponent's explanation of them. You have to confront the weaknesses and do your best to explain, through the evidence, why your explanation is the right one.

I once tried a case where I represented a national manufacturer of home improvement products against one if its regional distributors. A witness who testified by deposition said some things that, taken out of context, were not good for our case. I had to deal with it. In this case, I put the testimony up on the screen and explained, in context, what should have been the takeaway in the first place. Maybe this was a bit risky, but it worked. More importantly, it showed the jury that we were not afraid of the testimony. That can go a long way to diminishing the effect of something negative in your case.

Use the Jury Instructions to Get a Signature on the Dotted Line

Just like Alec Baldwin and the salesmen in *Glengarry Glen Ross*, you have to get these jurors to sign on the dotted line. In a trial, the blanks for answers to the special issues are the dotted lines.

Jury instructions are the legal roadmap. After you have topically covered the evidence and (hopefully) gotten the jury to agree with the conclusions in your case theory, you will want to use these instructions to show the legal effect of these conclusions. Put the jury instructions in front of them and, one by one, go through them and tell the jury what specifically to write in the blank.

In my case involving the home improvement client, there were statute of limitation questions on each cause of action. I told the jury the specific date to put in the blank to represent when the cause of action accrued. The plaintiff did not have a date. On every question regarding statute of limitations, the jury put in the date I suggested. The point is, tell them the answer that you want on every question.

Finish Big

Start big and finish big. After you have presented all of your topics and covered the jury instructions, make what you say count. They are the last words the jury will hear from you about your case. Maybe you go back to the story you told at the beginning. Maybe you tell another one, an analogy, or something from *Aesop's Fables*. Whatever it is, make a closing point from which your theme resonates. Then, say "Thank you for your service," and sit down.

A Few (but Not Too Many) "Don'ts"

The Legal Stuff

Other than the much more intimate one-on-one discussion you will have had with members of the jury panel during *voir dire*, closing argument is the time when you have the most freedom to say what you want to the jury—but not without limitations under the law. You may not

- misstate the evidence or the law,
- argue facts that are not in evidence,
- state your personal belief in the justice of your cause (the "golden rule"),
- personally vouch for the credibility of witnesses,
- urge irrelevant use of evidence, or
- appeal to passion or prejudice.

Easy enough in concept, right? But in the emotion of your argument, you may get close to the line on some of these and garner an objection. Depending on the extent to which you violate one of these rules, the results could range from judicial indifference all the way to a mistrial. In preparing and presenting a closing, do your best to stay away from these objectionable arguments.

The Non-Legal Things to Avoid

How you look and every move you make during the entirety of the trial is being watched and scrutinized by the jury. What you do well (and not so well) reflects on your client's case—whether you like it or not. It is not fair, but it is reality.

The jury is taking in every move you make and every word you say and digesting them along with the case itself. In the context of preparing and presenting your closing argument, you should avoid some things that will diminish your effectiveness.

- Do not write out your argument in a narrative with the idea of reading it to the jury. Nothing will lose a jury faster. Your passion for the case will not come out and will be lost if you read from the page. Rather, work from an outline.
- Do not attempt to memorize your entire argument—just your case theme. Again, your visceral passion will be lost on the jury, and unless you are very good, it is tough to hide the fact that you are just spouting off a memorized speech.
- Do not talk above the jury. Use plain English, not legalese. Think of it as a conversation around the dinner table with your kids, the only difference being you are doing all of the talking.
- Do not start out by thanking the jury; this is probably one of the most overdone things in a closing. Get to it. If I thank the jury, it is as I am sitting down, and I'll simply say "Thank you for your service," and that's it.
- Let's face it: we live in a sound bite world. People process an extraordinary amount of information every day—in small bites. Just go to a movie some time and watch the people around you. Notice how fast they pull out their phones to check or send text messages while watching the movie. People just do not have long attention spans. So, do not rely solely on your voice to present argument. You must intersperse it with good, relevant visual stimulation. Otherwise, the jury will just zone out.
- Finally, and most importantly, do not try to be someone other than you. I have found that jury members, even those with little or no education, are good judges of people. If you are trying to change your personality with the hopes of making a better argument, don't. It will not work. The jury will see right through it, and your credibility (and your case) will go right out the window.

How to Prepare What You Present

So what do you need in front of you to make this presentation? Some of that depends on how much you will handle as opposed to what help you might have with the demonstrative evidence to be shown. For example, if you plan to show the jury documents in evidence through some electronic means (which I highly recommend), will you be the presenter or will you have someone there to work the slideshow? Either way, at a minimum you will need two things: some form of outline and the jury charge. If you will be a "one-person show," then you will need some means to present the non-verbal evidence.

So what goes into the outline? I attended an online continuing legal education class recently on presentation techniques and learned a great way to create a presentation outline. Essentially, each major topic is centered in large font with sub-points underneath. Here is an example:

CLOSING ARGUMENT OUTLINE[1]

REMIND WHAT CASE IS ABOUT
Case about Mr. Smith wanting his cake and eating it too
Get benefits of being a partner
At same time competing with partnership with new business
Can't have it both ways
COMPARE MY CLIENT TO MR. SMITH
CLIENT
Blue-collar background
Started business in garage
Wife worked for free
Brought Mr. Smith into business
No investment
50 percent of business
When going got tough—hunker down
MR. SMITH
Highly educated
MBA
Worked for big business
Never an entrepreneur

---

1. Each of the bolded sections is a headline of what you will talk about. This is not a complete closing argument, but I have included a few sections here to give you an idea of how it works with use of exhibits, the jury charge, and so on.

Given half of business

When going got tough—play the blame game

<u>SMITH—A WALKING DEFINITION HOW NOT TO TREAT YOUR</u>
<u>PARTNERS</u>

SMITH'S FRIEND, JONES = GREENER PASTURES

Exhibit 23—e-mail from Jones starts the plan

Exhibit 33—Smith and Jones secretly plan to start a competing business

Exhibit 44—Smith blames my client for misappropriating partnership
property; made up

Exhibit 201—Smith sends partnership finance info to Jones/new business

<u>DAMAGES</u>

SHOW ON WHITE BOARD

Write categories and damage numbers on white board

<u>HOW TO ANSWER THE JURY CHARGE QUESTIONS</u>

When you discuss the jury questions, have them available to show to the
jury on the "big screen." If you can write on what you are presenting, write
the answer on the form being shown. This creates a tactile connection to the
jury. As you go through the questions, remind the jury what the evidence
supports. Do not repeat it, per se. For example, if the question was whether
Mr. Smith breached his fiduciary duty, you could say something like "When
Mr. Smith misappropriated private partnership financial information, used
it to start his new business, and then began secretly contacting its customers, he breached his fiduciary duty. Answer Question 5 'Yes.'"

Some "Closing" Suggestions

Do not try to do this in a vacuum. Try out your case theme and theory on
someone totally unfamiliar with the case but who you trust to be honest
with you about it. (My wife fills that role for me.)

Practice, first in front of the mirror and then in front of a small group of
people you trust will give you honest feedback. I might suggest that if you
have kids who are between the ages of 10 and 18, make your argument

to them as well. If they do not understand it, then you probably need to simplify your argument.

Dress the part. Look professional, but be mindful of not overdoing it. I once heard a story about a defendant who had been indicted for using state property (a public university's aircraft) for personal use. The case was tried in a rural Texas county. The defendant had a team of lawyers. They all walked into trial impeccably dressed in dark, expensive suits. Many of the jury members, in contrast, did not even have a checking account. Not surprisingly, the trial did not go well for the defense.

Finally, be sure you know if the court has special rules regarding all aspects of the case, including for closing arguments. Time limits, for example, can be a game changer. Know ahead of time what the time limits will be and make your closing fit within the limits.

Let's face it, trial presentation is a craft. You never master it, but over time you get better and better at it. Closing arguments are where you can really utilize your presentation skills to their fullest. Here's to you getting those jurors to sign on the dotted line.

Chapter 13

It's Not Over Until It's Over: *Post*-Trial Proceedings

Joice Bass and Doreen Spears Hartwell

Congratulations on earning your stripes as a trial lawyer! Hopefully you have had at least one evening to celebrate this momentous occasion with family and friends and have caught up on a fraction of the sleep you lost during trial—because the fight is not over yet. Get ready for post-trial motion practice, where the fight is governed by different and, in some instances, more stringent time limitations.[1]

Post-trial proceedings are the reason you rarely see experienced trial lawyers celebrating (or mourning) jury verdicts and bench rulings right away. Instead, you will often see them immediately head home or back to the office to refresh and regroup. They know that the *trial* is the only thing that is over. The fight itself will likely continue on, until every last potential opportunity to prevail in the dispute has been exhausted. In some situations, this can take years.

This chapter walks you through the various types of post-trial proceedings under the Federal Rules of Civil Procedure, from entry of judgment to filing a notice of appeal.[2]

---

1. *See* FED. R. CIV. P. 6(b)(2): "A court must not extend the time to act under Rules 50(b) and (d), 52(b), 59(b), (d), and (e), and 60(b)."
2. Appellate practice and procedures are beyond the scope of this book. This chapter discusses the filing of a notice of appeal only to the extent that the deadline for doing so is impacted by post-trial motion proceedings.

Judgment: Memorializing the Result

Now that the adrenaline rush of trial is over, it is time to make the outcome—whether a jury verdict or a judge's ruling—official with the entry of a final judgment in the court's docket. After all of the blood, sweat, and tears (not to mention your client's money) that have gone into this case so far, it goes without saying that this last step should be handled with great care.

Every judgment (or amended judgment) must be set out in a separate document. It should not include extraneous materials such as recitals of pleadings, a master's report, or a record of prior proceedings.[3] However, orders disposing of post-trial *motions*—for judgment as a matter of law under Rule 50(b); to amend or make additional findings under Rule 52(b); for attorney's fees under Rule 54; for a new trial, or to alter or amend the judgment, under Rule 59; or for relief from judgment under Rule 60—are *not* required to be in a separate document.[4] A judgment may grant the relief to which the parties are entitled, and it is not limited by what is expressly prayed for in the pleadings.[5]

Obviously, the judgment that is entered should be accurate, clear, and precise, so that it will be enforceable and/or appealable. Sometimes this is easier said than done—particularly for bench trials, where the court is required to concurrently issue sometimes-lengthy findings of facts and conclusions of law in support of the judgment.[6] Even with jury verdicts, very often the final judgment includes facts or amounts and even forms of relief (e.g., interest on damages, attorney's fees, costs, or equitable relief by the court) that are determined or awarded separate from or *after* the verdict is rendered.

---

3. FED. R. CIV. P. 58(a).
4. FED. R. CIV. P. 58(a)(1)–(5).
5. FED. R. CIV. P. 54(c).
6. FED. R. CIV. P. 52(a).

Judgment After Bench Trial, and Findings of Facts and Conclusions of Law Under Rule 52

Form 71 in the Appendix to the Federal Rules of Civil Procedure provides a simple template for a "Judgment by the Court without a Jury" that can be adapted to most cases:[7]

❋ ❋

(Caption—See Form 1.)

This action was tried by Judge _____ without a jury and the following decision was reached:

It is ordered that [the plaintiff _____ recover from the defendant _____ the amount of $_____, with prejudgment interest at the rate of ___%, postjudgment interest at the rate of ___%, along with costs.] [the plaintiff recover nothing, the action be dismissed on the merits, and the defendant _____ recover costs from the plaintiff _____.]

Date _____   _____

                                  Clerk of Court

❋ ❋

In addition to the judgment, the district court at the conclusion of a bench trial must make findings of facts and conclusions of law that support its trial ruling.[8] "The purpose of findings of fact and conclusions of law is to aid the trial court in making a correct factual decision and a reasoned application of the law to the facts; to define for purpose of *res judicata* and *estoppel by judgment* the issues then adjudicated; and to aid the appellate court."[9] For these reasons, it is very important to make sure the findings and conclusions are not only accurate but clear and complete as well.

---

7. Fed. R. Civ. P. 84 and Appendix to Federal Rules of Civil Procedure, Form 71.
8. Fed. R. Civ. P. 52(a).
9. Montgomery v. Goodyear Aircraft Corp., 392 F.2d 777, 779 n.3 (2d Cir. 1968) (quoting 5 Moore, Fed. Practice ¶ 52.03, p. 2632).

The findings of fact and conclusions of law can be stated on the record after the close of the evidence *or* set out in a memorandum or decision filed by the court.[10] If the latter, the prevailing party is usually asked by the court to submit proposed findings and conclusions.[11] In response, the other side can submit objections or competing proposed findings and conclusions.[12] Even if a party does not request, object, or move to amend findings, that party can still later question the sufficiency of the evidence supporting the findings (e.g., with a Rule 52(b) motion for amended or additional findings or on appeal).[13] There is no specific format mandated by the rules for findings of fact and conclusions of law. As a practical matter, however, and in light of the important purpose of findings and conclusions, it makes a lot of sense to provide citations to the evidence in the record—that is, witness testimony and trial exhibits—and to applicable law that support each finding of fact and each conclusion of law, particularly in more complex cases.[14]

Judgment After Jury Trial—Rule 58(b)

After a jury trial, if a general verdict is returned, the judgment is prepared, signed, and entered by the court clerk on the jury's verdict. The court clerk may not wait for the court's direction on this task, although the court has the power to order the clerk not to enter a judgment where appropriate.[15] If the jury returns a special verdict or a general verdict with answers to written questions, or other relief besides "costs or a sum certain" is granted, then the clerk must obtain the court's approval of the judgment before it is entered.[16] Form 70 in the Appendix to the rules provides the following sample of a "Judgment on a Jury Verdict:"[17]

---

10. FED. R. CIV. P. 52(a)(1).
11. *See, e.g., In re* Doe, 640 F.3d 869, 872 (8th Cir. 2011) (discussing the historic practice of a judge asking the prevailing party to prepare proposed findings of fact, conclusions of law, and even the order itself).
12. *Id.*
13. FED. R. CIV. P. 52(a)(5).
14. The preparation of proposed findings and conclusions will therefore require you to have access to the trial transcripts. Try to obtain the transcripts as quickly as you can following the conclusion of the trial. In negotiating the deadline for filing your proposed findings and conclusions, be sure to allow yourself enough time with the transcripts.
15. FED. R. CIV. P. 58(b)(1).
16. FED. R. CIV. P. 58(b)(2).
17. FED. R. CIV. P. 84 and Appendix to Federal Rules of Civil Procedure, Form 70.

✳ ✳

(Caption—See Form 1.)

This action was tried by a jury with Judge _____ presiding, and the jury has rendered a verdict.

It is ordered that:

[the plaintiff _____ recover from the defendant _____ the amount of $_____ with interest at the rate of ___%, along with costs.]

[the plaintiff recover nothing, the action be dismissed on the merits, and the defendant _____ recover costs from the plaintiff _____.]

Date _____

_____
Clerk of Court

✳ ✳

Motion to Amend Findings or for Additional Findings Under Rule 52(b)

If it is later determined that the findings need to be, or should be, corrected, a party can challenge the sufficiency of the evidence supporting the court's findings of facts with a Rule 52(b) motion. Such a motion may request that the findings be amended or that additional findings be made.[18] If the challenge is successful, the court may then also amend the judgment accordingly.[19]

A Rule 52(b) motion must be made no later than 28 days after entry of the judgment following the bench trial.[20] Computation of this time period is governed by Federal Rule of Civil Procedure 6 and excludes the date judgment is entered but includes intermediate weekend days and legal holidays.[21] The last day of the period is included, unless it is a weekend day or legal holiday, in which case the period continues to run until the next day that is not a weekend day or legal holiday.[22] As with other post-trial time limita-

---

18. Fed. R. Civ. P. 52(b).
19. *Id.*
20. *Id.*
21. Fed. R. Civ. P. 6(a).
22. *Id.*

tions that are triggered by entry of judgment, the usual three-day extension of time when service is by methods other than hand-delivery (Rule 6(d)), does not apply here.[23]

A Rule 52(b) motion corrects "findings of fact which are central to the ultimate decision; the Rule is not intended to serve as a vehicle for a rehearing."[24] The purpose of Rule 52(b) is "to permit the correction of any manifest errors of law or fact that are discovered, upon reconsideration, by the trial court. Under the rule, the trial court is the first recourse for the correction of errors" and as such may not only reconsider its findings and conclusions but reverse itself as well.[25] The relief afforded by Rule 52(b) is very similar to that available under Rule 59(e) (motion to alter or amend judgment), discussed below.[26]

Entry of Judgment Under Rule 58(c)

For purposes of the Federal Rules of Civil Procedure, a final judgment after trial is considered "entered" when (1) the judgment is recorded in the district court's civil docket (Rule 79(a)), *and* it is a separate document; or (2) if the final judgment is *not* a separate document, 150 days have passed since the judgment was entered in the civil docket.[27] Statutory interest on money judgments begins to run from the date of entry of the judgment.[28]

Ordinarily, the entry of judgment cannot be delayed so that the court can decide post-trial motions for attorney's fees or tax costs (Rule 58(e)), even though a post-trial award of attorney's fees or to tax costs is logically part of the judgment in the case.[29] Unlike a final judgment, the award of fees and costs does not have to be set out in a separate document and, therefore,

---

23. *See, e.g.*, Cavaliere v. Allstate Ins. Co., 996 F.2d 1111, 1113 (11th Cir. 1993) (extension for mail service does not apply to filing of Rule 59 motions).
24. Crane-McNab v. Cnty. of Merced, 773 F. Supp. 2d 861, 873 (E.D. Cal. 2011) (citing Davis v. Mathews, 450 F. Supp. 308, 318 (E.D. Cal. 1978)).
25. Nat'l Metal Finishing Co. v. Barclaysamerican/Commercial, Inc., 899 F.2d 119, 123–24 (1st Cir. 1990) (citing Am. Train Dispatchers Ass'n v. Norfolk & Western Ry. Co., 627 F. Supp. 941, 947 (N.D. Ind. 1985)) (district court reconsidered its finding that there had been an implied contract between the parties and reversed its judgment).
26. *Id.* at 123.
27. Fed. R. Civ. P. 58(a) and (c).
28. 28 U.S.C. § 1961.
29. Fed. R. Civ. P. 52(a) and 54(d).

can simply be entered into the court docket once the issue is decided.[30] A post-trial motion for fees can, however, toll the time to appeal in the same manner as other post-trial motions affecting the judgment. Upon the *timely* filing of a post-trial motion for attorney's fees (i.e., 14 days from entry of judgment), if an appeal has not yet occurred, the court can order that the motion tolls the deadline to appeal.[31] The post-trial motion for attorney's fees should, therefore, request that the court do so in addition to awarding fees.

Entry of judgment after an invigorating but exhausting trial, and after wrangling over the language in the document, can be a huge relief. But do not get too comfortable just yet. The final judgment can still be challenged with a number of post-trial motions. Clients should be apprised of this possibility early on—ideally from the beginning of the case—so that they are not overly disappointed and frustrated by a motion seeking to overturn or amend the judgment or a motion for judgment as a matter of law.

Judgment: Changing the Result

Renewed Motion for Judgment as a Matter of Law Under Rule 50—Notwithstanding the Verdict

As discussed in Chapter 10, if the court denies a Rule 50(a) motion prior to the matter being submitted to the jury, the court is considered to have submitted the action to the jury subject to the court's later deciding the legal questions raised by the motion.[32] The mechanism for reviving the issues raised in a Rule 50(a) motion for judgment as a matter of law post-trial is via a *renewed* motion for judgment as a matter of law under Rule 50(b) (formerly known as a judgment notwithstanding the verdict or JNOV).[33] Unlike the motions under Rule 50(a), the Rule 50(b) motion *must* be in

---

30. FED. R. CIV. P. 58.
31. FED. R. CIV. P. 54(d) and 58(e).
32. FED. R. CIV. P. 50(b).
33. *Id.* The 1991 amendment to Rule 50 changed the terminology accordingly. Cases pre-dating the early 1990s therefore use the terminology reflecting a motion for judgment notwithstanding the verdict, which cases apply equally to what is now called a renewed motion for judgment as a matter of law.

writing. The renewed motion must be filed within 28 days after entry of judgment (or discharge of the jury, for motions addressing a jury issue not decided by a verdict).[34]

Critically, a party may only file a Rule 50(b) renewed motion for judgment as a matter of law if, prior to the case being submitted to the jury, that party made a Rule 50(a) motion.[35] A renewed motion for judgment as a matter of law is limited to the grounds raised in the earlier Rule 50(a) motion. The court may not render judgment as a matter of law *post*-verdict based on arguments not previously raised in a Rule 50(a) motion.[36]

The consequences for failing to submit a timely and proper Rule 50(a) motion for judgment as a matter of law are harsh: precluding the filing of a Rule 50(b) renewed motion for judgment as a matter of law and thus waiving the right to challenge the sufficiency of the evidence on appeal.[37] In that instance, the party challenging the jury verdict may be limited to seeking a new trial on appeal, which imposes a different (and higher) standard.[38]

A Rule 50(b) motion should be specific and should demonstrate to the court with citations to the evidence in the record why no reasonable jury could find as they did, or why the law compels a result that is contrary to the verdict delivered. In ruling on a renewed motion for judgment as a matter of law, the court can (1) allow judgment on the verdict, (2) order a new trial, or (3) direct the entry of judgment as a matter of law.[39] If the court determines that the moving party is entitled to judgment as a matter of law, it has discretion in choosing whether to order a new trial or direct

---

34. *See id.*

35. 9 James W.M. Moore, Moore's Federal Practice § 50.43[3][a] (3d ed. 2012). The general weight of authority suggests that a trial court may not consider issues raised for the first time in a post-trial motion for judgment as a matter of law and therefore appellate review is waived, unless review is necessary to prevent manifest injustice. *Id.*

36. *See* Fed. R. Civ. P. 50, Committee Note, 1991; *see also* 9 Moore, *supra* note 35, § 50.05[5][b][i].

37. 9B Charles Alan Wright & Arthur R. Miller, Federal Practice and Procedure § 2537, at 617–18 (3d ed. 2008) (discussing Unitherm Food Sys., Inc. v. Swift-Eckrich, Inc., 546 U.S. 394 (2006)). *See also* Hammond v. T.J. Litle & Co., 82 F.3d 1166, 1172 (1st Cir. 1996).

38. 9 Moore, *supra* note 35, § 50.40[1]; *see also* Fuesting v. Zimmer, Inc., 448 F.3d 936 (7th Cir. 2006). Whereas an appeal from a Rule 50(b) motion would be reviewed "de novo," an appeal from a Rule 59 motion for new trial requires a showing that the trial court "abused its discretion" in denying the request for a new trial.

39. Fed. R. Civ. P. 50(b)(1)–(3).

entry of judgment as a matter of law.[40] Notably, even if the court grants the renewed motion for judgment as a matter of law, the case does not end there; after all, the losing party can still move for a new trial within 28 days of entry of the judgment.[41]

A renewed motion for judgment as a matter of law may include an alternative or joint request for a new trial pursuant to Rule 59.[42] As with a renewed motion for judgment as a matter of law, an alternative or joint motion for a new trial must be filed no later than 28 days after judgment is entered.[43] Different standards are applied to a motion for a new trial (discussed below) than to a renewed motion for judgment as a matter of law.[44] Rule 50(b) requires a showing that there was insufficient evidence to support the verdict. "If there is substantial evidence presented at trial to create an issue for the jury, a trial court may not grant a motion for a directed verdict [(50(a))] or for judgment notwithstanding the verdict [(50(b))]."[45] The party who prevailed at trial does not get, however, "'the benefit' of unreasonable inferences, or those at war with the undisputed facts."[46] "'A mere scintilla of evidence is inadequate to support a verdict,' and judgment as a matter of law is proper when the record contains no proof beyond speculation to support the verdict."[47] The fact a court has denied prior summary judgment motions does not control the outcome of a motion for judgment as a matter of law after a trial has concluded.[48] If the trial court grants a renewed motion for judgment as a matter of law, it must conditionally rule on the

---

40. 9B Wright & Miller, *supra* note 37, § 2538, at 639–41 (discussing Cone v. W. Va. Pulp & Paper Co., 330 U.S. 212 (1947)).
41. Fed. R. Civ. P. 50(d).
42. Fed. R. Civ. P. 50(b). For purposes of seeking an alternative motion for a new trial as part of a renewed motion for judgment as a matter of law, "[o]ne ground that should be included in almost every alternative motion for a new trial under Rule 50(b) is that the verdict is contrary to the clear weight of the evidence. If the losing party thinks that there is insufficient evidence as a matter of law to support the verdict, that party, in most situations, also will think that the verdict is against the weight of the evidence." 9B Wright & Miller, *supra* note 37, § 2539, at 644.
43. Fed. R. Civ. P. 50(b) and (e); *see also* Fed. R. Civ. P. 59.
44. 9 Moore, *supra* note 35, § 50.44.
45. Landes Constr. Co., Inc. v. Royal Bank of Canada, 833 F.2d 1365, 1371 (9th Cir. 1987).
46. Larson v. Miller, 76 F.3d 1446, 1452 (8th Cir. 1996) (citations omitted).
47. *Id.*
48. Children's Broadcasting Corp. v. The Walt Disney Co., 245 F.3d 1008 (8th Cir. 2001); *see also* St. Louis Convention & Visitors Comm'n v. National Football League, 154 F.3d 851, 860 (8th Cir. 1998).

motion for a new trial to determine whether a new trial should be granted if the judgment is later overturned on appeal.[49]

Motion for a New Trial or for Additur/Remittitur (to Increase/ Reduce a Damages Award) Under Rule 59(a)

Federal Rule of Civil Procedure 59(a) allows the district court to grant a new bench or jury trial "for any reason for which a new trial has heretofore been granted in an action at law in federal court."[50] While Rule 59 does not specify the grounds for granting new trials, the courts are "'bound by those grounds that have been historically recognized.'"[51] A new trial may be granted based on "(1) a verdict that is contrary to the weight of the evidence, (2) a verdict that is based on false or perjurious evidence, or (3) to prevent a miscarriage of justice."[52] Unlike a Rule 50(b) motion for judgment as a matter of law, however, the "judge can weigh the evidence and assess the credibility of witnesses, and need not view the evidence from the perspective most favorable to the prevailing party" when ruling on a motion for new trial.[53] As stated in *Helgeson v. American International Group, Inc.*,

"Though the underlying basis for a new trial is always to prevent injustice, there are a number of specific injustices which courts may find in support of granting a Rule 59 motion. These include a prejudicial error of law on the part of the court, a verdict which is against the weight of the evidence, [or] damages awarded which are either too large or too small."[54]

---

49. FED. R. CIV. P. 50(c)(1).
50. FED. R. CIV. P. 59(a)(1)(A).
51. Cotton *ex rel.* McClure, 860 F. Supp. 2d 999, 1008–09 (N.D. Cal. 2012) (quoting Zhang v. Am. Gem Seafoods, Inc., 339 F.3d 1020, 1035 (9th Cir. 2003)).
52. *Id.* (citing Molski v. M.J. Cable, Inc., 481 F.3d 724, 729 (9th Cir. 2007)).
53. *Landes Constr. Co., Inc.*, 833 F.2d at 1371; *see Bippes*, 180 F.R.D. at 388–89.
54. 44 F. Supp. 2d 1091, 1103 (S.D. Cal. 1999) (citation omitted); *see, e.g.*, Wharf v. Burlington N. R.R. Co., 60 F.3d 631, 635–38 (9th Cir. 1995) (improper argument); Glover v. BIC Corp., 6 F.3d 1318, 1325–29 (jury instructions and evidentiary rulings); Murphy v. Long Beach, 914 F.2d 183, 187 (9th Cir. 1990) (erroneous jury instructions and the failure to give adequate instructions); Peacock v. Board of Regents of Universities and State College of Arizona, 597 F.2d 163, 165 (9th Cir. 1979) (excessive damages award).

A Rule 59(a) motion must be filed no later than 28 days after the entry of the judgment.[55] If the motion for new trial is based on affidavits, they must be filed with the motion.[56] The opposing party has 14 days after being served to file opposing affidavits.[57] The court may permit reply affidavits as well.[58]

Depending on the grounds for seeking a new trial, the motion can also be filed *prior* to the close of evidence. For example, if a witness were to testify before a jury about evidence that had previously been excluded by the court on the basis that the risk of unfair prejudice outweighed its probative value, then the injured party may wish to move for a new trial immediately.[59]

A fairly common scenario for a Rule 59(a) motion is when the damages award is inconsistent with the evidence presented at trial.[60] While the Federal Rules of Civil Procedure do not expressly provide for remittitur—or additur, which is generally a more difficult proposition[61]—a defendant may move for a remittitur under Rule 59(a) to reduce the amount of the jury award.[62] As stated in *Oltz v. St. Peter's Community Hospital,*

> Once the district court, after viewing the evidence most favorably to the prevailing party, concludes that excessive damages were awarded, it has two alternatives: it may grant a motion for a new trial or condition denial of such a grant upon acceptance of remittitur by the

---

55. FED. R. CIV. P. 59(b).
56. FED. R. CIV. P. 59(c). Unlike Rule 50(b) motions for judgment as a matter of law, the grounds for Rule 59 motions for a new trial need not be asserted during trial in a Rule 50(a) motion.
57. *Id.*
58. *Id.*
59. *See, e.g.,* Brown v. Royalty, 535 F.2d 1024, 1028 (8th Cir. 1976) (repeated, deliberate reference to evidence excluded by district court is clear misconduct and grounds for new trial); Adams Laboratories, Inc. v. Jacobs Eng'g Co., 761 F.2d 1218, 1226 (7th Cir. 1985) (plaintiff's counsel's reference to excluded evidence in direct contravention of the district court's order held to constitute prejudicial error).
60. A defendant can also use a Rule 59 motion to lodge a constitutional challenge to an award of punitive damages.
61. Roman v. Western Mfg., Inc., 691 F.3d 686, 702 (5th Cir. 2012) ("[t]he constitutional rule against additur is not violated in a case where the jury ha[s] properly determined liability and there is no valid dispute as to the amount of damages. In such a case the court is in effect simply granting summary judgment on the question of damages.") (quoting Moreau v. Oppenheim, 663 F.2d 1300, 1311 (5th Cir. 1981)).
62. Strathmere v. Karavas, 100 F.R.D. 478, 479 (D.Ariz. 1984).

prevailing party. . . . The district court may order a new trial, even though substantial evidence supports the jury's verdict.[63]

According to *Snyder v. Freight, Construction, Local No. 287*,

Where an award of damages . . . gives rise to an inference that "passion and prejudice" tainted the jury's finding of liability, a new trial may be in order, . . .[but] . . . [w]here there is no evidence that passion and prejudice affected the liability finding, remittitur is an appropriate method of reducing an excessive verdict.[64]

In an Age Discrimination in Employment Act case, for example, "[a] remittitur is in order when a trial judge concludes that a jury verdict is 'clearly unsupported' by the evidence and exceeds the amount needed to make the plaintiff whole, *i.e.*, to remedy the effect of the employer's discrimination."[65]

If the district court grants the motion, it may affirm the verdict if the plaintiff agrees to remit part of a jury award or order a new trial on the damages issue if the plaintiff refuses to do so.[66] The plaintiff must choose between these alternatives,[67] and a remittitur cannot be appealed after it has been accepted, even if the acceptance was "under protest"[68]—for example, to avoid the burdensome alternative of having to undergo an entirely new trial.

Even when the losing party has not moved for a remittitur, the court may reduce a damages award *sua sponte*.[69] It should be noted, though, that

---

63.　Oltz v. St. Peter's Community Hospital, 861 F.2d 1440, 1452 (9th Cir. 1988); *accord Bippes*, 180 F.R.D. at 389. (Note that a motion for remittitur carries a different standard than a motion for new trial.)
64.　175 F.3d 680, 689 (9th Cir. 1999) (internal quotation marks and citation omitted).
65.　Starceski v. Westinghouse Elec. Corp., 54 F.3d 1089, 1110 (3d Cir. 1995) (citations omitted).
66.　Stoma v. Miller Marine Services, Inc., 271 F. Supp. 2d 429, 433 (E.D.N.Y. 2003) (citing Textile Deliveries Inc. v. Stagno, 52 F.3d 46, 49 (2d Cir.1995)).
67.　Foradori v. Harris, 523 F.3d 477, 503 (5th Cir. 2008).
68.　Donovan v. Penn Shipping Co., 429 U.S. 648, 649–50 (1977).
69.　*Stoma*, 271 F. Supp. 2d at 433 (citing Peterson v. Cnty. of Nassau, 995 F. Supp. 305, 312 (E.D.N.Y. 1998)).

some courts do not employ the additur/remittitur procedure at all, relying only on their power to grant a new trial.[70]

The following is a form for a Rule 50(b) motion for judgment as a matter of law with a joint or alternative Rule 59 request for a new trial or remittitur:

* *

(Caption—See Form 1.)

Pursuant to Fed. R. Civ. P. 50(b), [Movant] moves this Court for judgment as a matter of law or, in the alternative, for a new trial or order of remittitur, on all claims submitted to the jury in this case, on the grounds and for the reasons of fact and law set forth in the following Memorandum of Points and Authorities.

MEMORANDUM OF POINTS AND AUTHORITIES

I. FACTUAL BACKGROUND

[insert facts with citations to the trial transcript]

II. LEGAL STANDARD

A. Judgment as a Matter of Law

[insert Rule 50(b) and related case law]

B. New Trial

[insert Rule 59 and related case law]

III. LEGAL ARGUMENT

A. Rule 50 Arguments

B. New Trial Arguments

C. Remittitur Arguments

IV. CONCLUSION

For the foregoing reasons, the Court should set aside the jury verdict and enter judgment as a matter of law in favor of [Movant]. In the alternative, [Movant] requests that the Court order a new trial on all

---

70. Westbrook v. General Tire & Rubber Co., 754 F.2d 1233, 1241 (5th Cir. 1985) (ordering a new trial when the verdict was a result of "passion or prejudice").

issues or substantially remit, in whole or in part, the damages award against [Movant], as set forth above.

(Date and sign—See Form 2.)

* *

Motion to Amend or Alter Judgment Under Rule 59(e)

If only portions of the judgment require correcting, a Rule 59(e) motion to amend or alter the judgment may be appropriate. A Rule 59(e) motion seeks "'a substantive change of mind by the court'" and may not be used to correct clerical errors, which should be done by motion under Rule 60(a),[71] or to "relitigate old issues, to advance new legal theories, or to secure a rehearing on the merits."[72] A Rule 59(e) motion involves the reconsideration of matters properly encompassed in a decision on the merits.[73] A motion to alter or amend judgment must clearly and convincingly demonstrate why the court should reconsider its previous decision[74] and must be filed no later than 28 days after the entry of the judgment.[75]

Absent "highly unusual circumstances," the court may appropriately grant a Rule 59(e) motion "where (1) the court is presented with newly discovered evidence; (2) the court committed clear error or the initial decision was manifestly unjust; or (3) there is an intervening change in controlling law."[76]

---

71. Garamendi v. Henin, 683 F.3d 1069, 1077 (9th Cir. 2012) (quoting Miller v. Transamerican Press, Inc., 709 F.2d 524, 527 (9th Cir. 1983)).

72. Fontenot v. Mesa Petroleum Co., 791 F.2d 1207, 1219 (5th Cir. 1986).

73. Osterneck v. Ernst & Whinney, 489 U.S. 169, 174–77 (1989) (post-judgment motion for discretionary pre-judgment interest is a Rule 59(e) motion because it involves reconsideration of matters encompassed within merits of judgment and interest is element of plaintiff's complete compensation). Rule 59(e) "may properly be invoked to request a district court to reconsider, vacate, or even reverse its prior holding." *Nat'l Metal Finishing*, 899 F.2d at 123–24 (internal citations omitted).

74. *See* Wendy's Int'l, Inc. v. Nu-Cape Constr., Inc., 169 F.R.D. 680, 684 (M.D. Fla. 1996) (quoting Cover v. Wal-Mart Stores, Inc., 148 F.R.D. 294 (M.D. Fla. 1993)).

75. Fed. R. Civ. P. 59(e).

76. *Crane-McNab*, 773 F. Supp. 2d at 874 (quoting Sch. Dist. No. 1J, Multnomah Cnty. v. ACandS, Inc., 5 F.3d 1255, 1263 (9th Cir. 1993)); *see also* Parker v. Midland Credit Mgmt., Inc., 874 F. Supp. 2d 1353, 1359 (M.D. Fla. 2012), reconsideration denied (July 31, 2012) (stating the same three bases for a Rule 59(e) motion).

Courts have considerable discretion, however, in determining whether to grant or deny a motion to amend or alter the judgment.[77]

Motion for Relief from Judgment Under Rule 60

Even if the foregoing motions attacking the substance of the judgment— i.e., for judgment as a matter of law, for new trial, or to amend/alter the judgment—fail, there remains the possibility of a motion for relief from the judgment. Unlike the prior motions, a Rule 60 motion can generally be made up to a year after entry of the judgment, and sometimes even after that.

Clerical Mistakes [Rule 60(a)]

If a relatively simple error is discovered after the judgment has already been entered in the docket, Rule 60(a) permits a party to file a motion "to correct a clerical mistake or a mistake arising from oversight or omission whenever one is found in a judgment, order, or other part of the record."[78] The focus of Rule 60(a) "is fidelity to the intent behind the original judgment."[79] "A judge may invoke Rule 60(a) [only] to make a judgment reflect the actual intentions of the court, plus the necessary implications."[80]

The mistakes that Rule 60(a) may correct are "blunders in execution."[81] The basic distinction between correctable "blunders in execution" and mistakes that cannot be corrected under Rule 60(a) is that the latter consist of instances where the court is asked to change its mind, either because it made a legal or factual mistake in its original determination, or because it should have exercised its discretion in a manner different from the way it was exercised in the original determination.[82]

The court can also make Rule 60(a) corrections *sua sponte*.[83] Because the court can exercise its authority under Rule 60(a) at any time, it may

---

77. *See* Edward H. Bohlin Co. v. Banning Co., 6 F.3d 350, 355–56 (5th Cir. 1993) (court's broad discretion must be balanced against need for finality and justice based on all facts).
78. FED. R. CIV. P. 60(a).
79. *Garamendi*, 683 F.3d at 1078.
80. *Id.* (quoting Blanton v. Anzalone, 813 F.2d 1574, 1577 (9th Cir. 1987)).
81. *Blanton*, 813 F.2d at 1577.
82. *Blanton*, 813 F.2d at 1577 n.2 (quoting United States v. Griffin, 782 F.2d 1393, 1396–97 (7th Cir. 1986)).
83. FED. R. CIV. P. 60(a).

do so only to provide "a specific and very limited type of relief."[84] "To be correctable under Rule 60(a), 'the mistake must not be one of judgment or even of misidentification, but merely of recitation, of the sort that a clerk or amanuensis might commit, mechanical in nature.'"[85] "Clerical mistakes, inaccuracies of transcription, inadvertent omissions, and errors in mathematical calculation" are within the scope of Rule 60(a).[86]

There is no express deadline within which a Rule 60(a) motion must be filed. However, after an appeal has been docketed and is pending, "such a mistake may be corrected only with the appellate court's leave."[87] Moreover, a Rule 60 motion can toll the deadline to file a notice of appeal—normally 30 days from entry of judgment—only if it is filed within 28 days from entry of judgment.[88] As such, 28 days is a good rule of thumb insofar as calendaring a drop-dead date for a Rule 60(a) motion, even if the rule allows otherwise.

Other Bases for Relief From Judgment [Rule 60(b)]

If, on the other hand, the request for relief from judgment requires convincing the court that the *substance* of the judgment was incorrect, then the motion must be made pursuant to Rule 60(b). "On motion and just terms," the court may relieve a party from a final judgment, order, or proceeding for the following reasons:

1. mistake, inadvertence, surprise, or excusable neglect;
2. newly discovered evidence that, with reasonable diligence, could not have been discovered in time to move for a new trial under Rule 59(b);
3. fraud (whether previously called intrinsic or extrinsic), misrepresentation, or misconduct by an opposing party;

---

84. Rivera v. PNS Stores, Inc., 647 F.3d 188, 193 (5th Cir. 2011) (quoting *In re* Transtexas Gas Corp., 303 F.3d 571, 581 (5th Cir. 2002)).
85. *Id.* at 194 (quoting *In re* Galiardi, 745 F.2d 335, 337 (5th Cir. 1984) (per curiam)) (quoting Dura–Wood Treating Co., Div. of Roy O. Martin Lumber Co. v. Century Forest Indus., Inc., 694 F.2d 112, 114 (5th Cir. 1982)).
86. *Id.* at 194; *see also* Sherrod v. Am. Airlines, Inc., 132 F.3d 1112, 1117 (5th Cir. 1998) (holding that Rule 60(a) may be used to correct mindless mechanistic mistakes that require no additional legal reasoning).
87. Fed. R. Civ. P. 60(a).
88. Fed. R. App. P. 4(a)(4)(A).

4. the judgment is void;

5. the judgment has been satisfied, released, or discharged; it is based on an earlier judgment that has been reversed or vacated; or applying it prospectively is no longer equitable; or

6. any other reason that justifies relief.[89]

Rule 60(b) motions "must be made within a reasonable time" and, if based on reasons 1, 2, or 3 above, "no more than a year after the entry of the judgment or order or the date of the proceeding."[90] A Rule 60(b) motion will toll the time limits for filing a notice of appeal only if it is filed within 28 days of the entry of judgment.[91]

Rule 60(b) provides extraordinary relief and requires the moving party to "demonstrate[] exceptional circumstances."[92] A Rule 60(b)(1) motion may be appropriate when, for example, the moving party was unaware of the judgment because of lack of notice.[93] To grant a Rule 60(b)(2) motion (for new evidence), the court must find that

(1) the facts were in existence at the time of the dispositive proceeding; (2) the movant must have been justifiably ignorant of them despite due diligence; (3) the evidence must be admissible and of such importance that it probably would have changed the outcome; and (4) the evidence must not be merely cumulative or impeaching.[94]

Under Rule 60(b)(3) (fraud), the moving party must present "convincing evidence of material misrepresentation."[95] A Rule 60(b)(4) motion may be

---

89. Fed. R. Civ. P. 60(b).
90. Fed. R. Civ. P. 60(c).
91. Fed. R. App. P. 4(a)(4)(vi).
92. Breslow v. Schlesinger, 284 F.R.D. 78, 82 (E.D.N.Y. 2012) (quoting Motorola Credit Corp. v. Uzan, 561 F.3d 123, 126 (2d Cir. 2009)) (quoting Ruotolo v. City of New York, 514 F.3d 184, 191 (2d Cir. 2008)).
93. *See, e.g.,* Wallace v. McManus, 776 F.2d 915, 917 (10th Cir. 1985) (notice of entry of judgment sent to plaintiff's former attorney rather than to plaintiff) (superseded by statute on other grounds).
94. *Breslow,* 284 F.R.D. at 83 (citing United States v. Int'l Brotherhood of Teamsters, 247 F.3d 370, 392 (2d Cir. 2001)).
95. *Id.* (quoting United States v. Mason, 477 Fed. App'x 846, 2012 WL 1638124 (2d Cir. 2012) (citing Fleming v. N.Y. Univ., 865 F.2d 478, 484 (2d Cir. 1989)).

granted when the judgment is void, for example, because of a lack of subject matter or personal jurisdiction.[96] Rule 60(b)(5) applies "when a judgment has been satisfied, released or discharged."[97] Lastly, the court may grant a motion brought under Rule 60(b)(6) "for all reasons except the five particularly specified . . . whenever such action is appropriate to accomplish justice."[98] Courts generally qualify this by requiring the moving party "'to establish the existence of extraordinary circumstances which prevented or rendered him unable to prosecute an appeal.'"[99]

Moving for Attorney's Fees and Costs: Recouping Expenses for the Result

Litigation can be very expensive. By now, you and your client may know this all too well. Assuming your client prevailed at trial, what are the chances of recovering the attorney's fees and costs incurred? Quite frankly, they are not great.

Our American legal system requires each side to a lawsuit to bear its own attorney's fees and court costs regardless of the merits of the positions taken, unless a statute, court rule, or written agreement provides otherwise.[100] Even when there is such a statute, rule, or contract, however, the practical reality is that chances of recouping anything more than a fraction of the legal expenses incurred by a client are usually slim. Absent unusual facts or circumstances, such as egregious conduct by a party, there is simply a natural resistance on the part of judges to go against the status quo by shifting all of the litigation fees and costs onto one side or party only. Also, it is understandably difficult for a neutral third party such as a judge

---

96. *Id.* (citing City of New York v. Mickalis Pawn Shop, LLC, 645 F.3d 114, 138 (2d Cir. 2011) (quoting Grace v. Bank Leumi Trust Co. of NY, 443 F.3d 180, 193 (2d Cir. 2006)).
97. *Id.* at 83.
98. Klapprott v. United States, 335 U.S. 601, 615 (1949).
99. Mackey v. Hoffman, 682 F.3d 1247, 1251 (9th Cir. 2012) (quoting Martella v. Marine Cooks & Stewards Union, Seafarers Int'l Union of N. Am., AFL–CIO, 448 F.2d 729, 730 (9th Cir. 1971)).
100. Design Pallets, Inc. v. Gray Robinson, P.A., 583 F. Supp. 2d 1282, 1285 (under "American rule," prevailing party generally cannot recover attorney's fees) (citing Alyeska Pipeline Serv. Co. v. Wilderness Soc'y, 421 U.S. 240, 249–52 (1975)).

to fully appreciate after the fact the true amount of time and resources that go into litigating a case competently.

Finally, the costs that are recoverable pursuant to court rules and statute do not include many of the tools that trial lawyers believe are necessary to taking a case all the way to trial and prevailing such as trial and technology consultants or vendors.[101] Every trial lawyer should have a serious discussion with his client early on in the case in order to manage expectations. The odds of your client recouping all of the legal expenses incurred are low. It is just as important, if not more so, to have a frank discussion with your client about the fact that she could actually end up *opposing* the other side's request to recover significant legal expenses in some circumstances.

Motion for Attorney's Fees

Rule 54 governs post-trial motions for attorney's fees, whether the entitlement to recovery is based on statute, court rule (e.g., FRCP 11 [Sanctions]), or contract.[102] A motion for attorney's fees must "specify the judgment and the statute, rule, or other grounds entitling the movant to the award; state the amount sought or provide a fair estimate of it; and disclose, if the court so orders, the terms of any agreement about fees for the services for which the claim is made."[103] The motion must be filed within 14 days of entry of judgment,[104] although the court may extend this time period for good cause "if the party failed to act because of excusable neglect."[105]

Cases where a statutory basis exists for recovery of attorney's fees include, for example, employment discrimination, civil rights, and some intellectual property litigation. In the area of employment law, Title VII, the Equal Pay Act, and the ADEA, among other statutes, provide for an award of attorney's fees to the prevailing party. For certain civil rights cases, such as those brought under Title VI (discrimination in federally funded programs) or Section 1983 (deprivation of constitutional rights under color of law), Section 1988 similarly provides for an award of attorney's fees to the prevailing

---

101. *See* 28 U.S.C. § 1920.
102. *Design Pallets, Inc.*, 583 F. Supp 2d at 1285 (citing *Alyeska Pipeline Serv. Co.*, 421 U.S. at 249–52).
103. FED. R. CIV. P. 54(d)(2)(B)(ii)–(iv).
104. FED. R. CIV. P. 54(d)(2)(B)(i).
105. FED. R. CIV. P. 6(b).

party.[106] In the area of intellectual property law, 17 U.S.C. § 505 provides that reasonable attorney's fees may be awarded to a prevailing party in a copyright infringement case as part of that party's recoverable costs. In "exceptional" patent cases (as defined by case law), 35 U.S.C. § 285 allows the court to award the prevailing party its reasonable attorney's fees.

These fee-shifting statutes have been determined by the courts to apply to both plaintiffs and defendants.[107] However, the showing that must be made, as to whether a party truly "prevailed" and whether the court should exercise its discretion to make an award, is generally different for plaintiffs (lower) than for defendants (higher).[108] This is because the purpose of these fee-shifting statutes is generally to encourage plaintiffs to bring particular types of litigation that have been deemed beneficial to society as a whole.[109]

In some circumstances, state statutes can provide a basis for recovery of attorney's fees. For example, the Ninth Circuit has held that an award of attorney's fees under a state offer of judgment statute is proper in federal court when state law claims are also at issue.[110] Not to be confused with an offer of judgment pursuant to Rule 68, some offer of judgment statutes under state law permit the recovery of certain costs *and* reasonable attorney's fees when the offeree recovers less than the rejected offer of judgment. In contrast, Rule 68 provides only for the recovery of certain costs when an offer of judgment is made pursuant to it.[111] Thus, if state law claims are also at issue in the federal action, a party may make an offer of judgment pursuant to the applicable state law offer of judgment statute.

---

106. 42 U.S.C. § 1988(b).

107. *See, e.g.*, Christiansburg Garment Co. v. EEOC, 434 U.S. 412, 421 (1978) (district court may, in its discretion, award attorney's fees to a prevailing defendant in a Title VII case upon a finding that the plaintiff's action was frivolous, unreasonable, or without foundation, even though not brought in subjective bad faith); Ellis v. Cassidy, 625 F.2d 227, 230 (9th Cir. 1980) (extending the doctrine to other civil rights actions, including those brought under 28 U.S.C. §§ 1331, 1343, and 2201, as well as 42 U.S.C. §§ 1983, 1985, and 1988); EEOC v. Pierce Packing Co., 669 F.2d 605, 609 (9th Cir. 1981).

108. *Id.*

109. *Id.*

110. MRO Comm. Inc. v. AT&T, 197 F.3d 1276, 1281 (9th Cir. 1999) (upholding an award of attorney's fees that found the statutory basis required by Rule 54(d)(2) in Nevada Revised Statute 17.115, Nevada's offer of judgment law).

111. Note, however, that for purposes of Rule 68, "costs" can include attorney's fees in circumstances where the underlying substantive statute defines costs to include such fees. Marek v. Chesny, 473 U.S. 1 (1985).

The party seeking an award of attorney fees has the burden of "establishing entitlement to an award and documenting the appropriate hours expended and hourly rates."[112] In contingency fee cases, courts generally apply the "lodestar method" of fee computation in determining an award of attorney's fees.[113] The basic lodestar formula requires the court to determine the number of hours reasonably expended multiplied by a reasonable hourly rate.[114] Because it is essentially a judgment for money, an award of attorney's fees is entitled to accrue interest from the date of entry of judgment.[115]

Rule 54(d) specifically provides that local rules may set "special procedures to resolve fee-related issues without extensive evidentiary hearings" and refer the issue of value of services "to a special master under Rule 53" as well as refer this motion to a magistrate judge under FRCP 72(b) "as if it were a dispositive pretrial matter." Accordingly, it is important to check and comply with the district court rules for the district in which your case is pending.[116]

Following is a sample form motion for attorney's fees:

* *

(Caption—See Form 1.)

[Movant], the prevailing party in this action, moves for an award of reasonable attorney fees under [applicable statute(s)][the attorney's fee provision in the contract]. [Movant] concurrently moves for an award of reasonable attorney fees under [insert applicable state law offer of judgment statute] and for non-taxable costs under Rule 54. The documents supporting this request [redacted for privilege] are attached as Exhibit A.

---

112. Hensley v. Eckerhart, 461 U.S. 424, 437 (1983) (party seeking award of fees should submit evidence of costs expended for attorney's fees).
113. *See* City of Burlington v. Dague, 505 U.S. 557, 565 (1992) (Court's decisions indicate shift away from percentage method to lodestar method).
114. *See* Lindy Bros. Builders v. Am. Radiator & Standard Sanitary Corp., 487 F.2d 161, 167–68 (3d Cir. 1973) (first extensive formulation of lodestar method).
115. 28 U.S.C. § 1961.
116. *See, e.g.,* N.D. Cal. Local R. 54-5 and M.D. Fla. Local R. 4.18.

Alternatively, but not exclusively, [Movant] requests an award of [insert amount] for reasonable attorney's fees for work performed after [insert date], the date of movant's offer of judgment to [Opposing Party], through [insert date], the date on which judgment was entered by the Court in favor of [Movant] and against [Opposing Party]. The billing information regarding attorney and legal assistant work performed after the offer of judgment is attached as Exhibit B. Finally, the non-taxable costs pursuant to Rule 54 are attached as Exhibit C.

In summary, [Movant] requests that this Court order [Opposing Party] to pay [Movant] [insert total amount sought]. This motion is based on the pleadings and other papers on file, the following memorandum of points and authorities, and the attached supporting declaration of counsel and exhibits.

Memorandum of Points and Authorities

   I. FACTUAL BACKGROUND

   [Insert procedural history justifying work done, including a description of the case, an explanation of the complexity of issues, a description of discovery conducted, an explanation of motions filed or opposed and the outcomes, *etc.* . . .]

   II. APPLICABLE LAW

   A. Attorney's Fees Award for Prevailing Party

   [Insert applicable federal or state statute or contractual provision]

   B. Attorney's Fee Award Based On State Offer of Judgment Law

   [Insert applicable state offer of judgment statute]

   III. ARGUMENT

   A. As the Prevailing Party, Movant Is Entitled to an Award of Attorney's Fees.

   [Apply facts to law]

   B. Alternatively, Movant Is Entitled to an Award of Attorney's Fees Incurred From the Date the Offer of Judgment Was Rejected

   [Apply facts to law]

C. The Amount of Fees Requested Is Reasonable

[Must include the actual hourly rate (or flat fee) charged per attorney on the case and demonstrate—for example, by supporting declaration—that such rates are equal to or less than the prevailing rates charged by attorneys in the local community, and the rates are commensurate with the experience, reputation and ability of the respective attorneys].

IV. CONCLUSION

For the foregoing reasons, good cause exists entitling [Movant] to an award of its reasonable attorney's fees incurred in this matter in the amount of [insert amount].

(Date and sign—See Form 2.)

* *

Motion to Tax Costs

Rule 54 also governs motions to recover, or "tax," court costs. Rule 54(d) provides that costs "should be allowed to the prevailing party" and that the clerk "may tax costs on 14 days' notice."[117] The rule does not specify, however, how long after entry of judgment the request must be filed. Absent a local rule specifying a time limitation,[118] therefore, a motion for costs is not subject to any particular time limitation besides "reasonableness."[119] Since the motion to tax costs does not seek to alter or amend the judgment, it does not normally toll the time for appeal.[120]

Unlike other pleadings and papers filed with the court, the bill of costs must be verified (by declaration or affidavit) by the party, the party's attorney, or the party's authorized agent.[121] The bill must be filed with the court

---

117. FED. R. CIV. P. 54(d)(1).
118. *See, e.g.*, N.D. CAL. LOCAL R. 54, E.D.N.Y. LOCAL R. 54-1, M.D. FLA. LOCAL R. 7.5(o).
119. *See, e.g.*, White v. New Hampshire Dep't of Employment Security, 455 U.S. 445 (1982) (motion for attorney's fees recoverable as "costs" under statute is proper if filed within reasonable time).
120. FED. R. CIV. P. 58(e).
121. 28 U.S.C. § 1924.

and is included in the judgment,[122] which means that post-judgment interest should be awarded from the date of the original judgment on the merits.[123] Under Rule 54(d), a district court's discretion to award costs "is limited to awarding costs that are within the scope of 28 U.S.C. § 1920."[124] Some district court local rules further itemize the types of costs that are taxable.[125] The court may properly grant an award for costs but deny an award for attorney's fees.[126]

After the request for costs is filed, "[o]n motion served within the next 7 days, the court may review the clerk's action."[127] The court may extend this time period for good cause "if the party failed to act because of excusable neglect."[128]

Appeal and Motion for Stay

Even if the judgment survives post-trial motion practice, depending on a number of factors—such as the amount of the judgment, the financial resources of the judgment debtor, and the legal issues that were properly preserved—there is still the very real possibility of an appeal to consider (or to anticipate from the other side). Fortunately for you, there are such things as appellate lawyers now; you just need to know when to hand the file over to one, if it comes to that. You, my friend, are officially a trial lawyer. (Keep in mind, though, that you could very well be trying this exact same case a second or even third time several years from now. Believe it. It happens.)

---

122. 28 U.S.C. § 1920.
123. 28 U.S.C. § 1961; Georgia Ass'n of Retarded Citizens v. McDaniel, 855 F.2d 794, 795–800 (11th Cir. 1988) (holding that when costs are taxed against losing party, award of costs bears interest from date of original judgment).
124. Hynix Semiconductor Inc. v. Rambus Inc., 697 F. Supp. 2d 1139, 1142 (N.D. Cal. 2010) (citing Summit Tech., Inc. v. Nidek Co., Ltd., 435 F.3d 1371, 1374 (Fed. Cir. 2006)).
125. See, e.g., N.D. CAL. LOCAL R. 54 and E.D.NY LOCAL R. 54.
126. See Metso Minerals, Inc. v. Powerscreen Int'l Distribution Ltd., 833 F. Supp. 2d 333, 355 (E.D.N.Y. 2011) (denying fees to patent owner who prevailed because case not "exceptional" under statute).
127. FED. R. CIV. P. 54(d)(1).
128. FED. R. CIV. P. 6(b).

Appeal

The appeal process (which is beyond the scope of this chapter) starts with the filing of a notice of appeal.[129] Federal Rule of Appellate Procedure 4 requires that a notice of appeal in a civil case be filed with the district court clerk within 30 days after entry of the judgment.[130] If a party timely files a post-trial motion for judgment as a matter of law (Rule 50(b)), to amend or make additional factual findings (Rule 52(b)), for attorney's fees (Rule 54, *if* the court extends the time to appeal under Rule 58), to alter or amend the judgment (Rule 59), for a new trial (Rule 59), or for relief from judgment (Rule 60, *if* filed no later than 28 days after entry of judgment), then the 30 days starts to run from the entry of the order disposing of these motions.[131]

Motion for Stay of Judgment Pending Appeal

Execution and enforcement of a judgment may begin after 14 days from entry of the judgment, unless stayed by the court or unless the action is one for an injunction or a receivership or the judgment directs an accounting in a patent infringement action.[132] The court can stay execution and enforcement proceedings "[o]n appropriate terms for the opposing party's security" (e.g., the posting of a bond) while the following motions are pending:

- motion for judgment as a matter of law under Rule 50;
- to amend findings or for additional findings under Rule 52(b);
- for new trial or to alter or amend judgment under Rule 59; or
- for relief from a judgment or order under Rule 60.[133]

The court can also stay execution and enforcement of a judgment if an appeal is filed, upon appellant providing a bond.[134] The court may waive the

---

129. FED. R. APP. P. 3.
130. FED. R. APP. P. 4(a)(1)(A).
131. FED. R. APP. P. 4(a)(4)(A).
132. FED. R. APP. P. 62(a).
133. FED. R. CIV. P. 62(b). Some jurisdictions have different rules. For example, the Middle District of Florida has a local rule especially for actions in rem and quasi in rem. Under Local Rule 7.5(p)(2), within the 14 days under Rule 62(a), if a motion under Rule 62(b) or a notice of appeal is filed, a further stay cannot exceed 30 days from the entry of the judgment or order, unless the court otherwise orders. Consult the local rules applicable in your jurisdiction.
134. FED. R. CIV. P. 62(d).

posting of the bond when "(1) 'the defendant's ability to pay the judgment is so plain that the cost of the bond would be a waste of money'; and (2) 'the opposite case, . . . where the requirement would put the defendant's other creditors in undue jeopardy.'"[135] If an appeal is taken from a judgment granting, dissolving, or denying an injunction, the court can "suspend, modify, restore, or grant an injunction on terms for bond or other terms that secure the opposing party's rights" during the pendency of the appeal.[136]

Conclusion

Your first trial, like the practice of law in general, is a marathon—not a sprint. After you have said good-bye to the jurors, cleared your trial exhibits out of the courtroom, and thanked the court staff for their gracious hospitality, keep in mind that the work on the case will likely continue on for many months still, possibly even years. So, remember to pace yourself and to take the time to savor the victories as they come, instead of waiting for the day when the case will finally, really, definitely, and completely be over and done with. You may be waiting for a while.

---

135. Cotton *ex rel.* McClure, 860 F. Supp. 2d at 1028 (quoting Olympia Equip. Leasing Co. v. W. Union Tel. Co., 786 F.2d 794, 796 (7th Cir. 1986)).
136. Fed. R. Civ. P. 62(c).

Index